DR AMBEDKAR AND UNTOUCHABILITY

CHRISTOPHE JAFFRELOT

Dr Ambedkar and Untouchability

Analysing and Fighting Caste

HURST & COMPANY, LONDON

Published in 2000 as *Dr Ambedkar. Leader intouchable et père de la Constitution indienne*, Paris: Presses de Sciences Po

Revised edition first published in the United Kingdom by
C. Hurst & Co. (Publishers) Ltd,
38 King Street, London WC2E 8JZ

Printed in India

A catalogue record for this book is available from the British Library.

ISBN 1–85065–449–2

For Milan

Acknowledgements

Biography has become a field of the social sciences in itself. Some scholars, mostly historians, devote their whole research activities to this speciality. For me it was not at all a natural project, even though I paid a lot of attention to Hindu nationalist ideologues and low caste leaders in my previous works. I wrote this book for very specific reasons and in a rather different perspective from these of the serial biographers.

I began to study the life and thought of Dr Ambedkar in the 1990s thanks to Olivier Herrenschmidt, then Professor of Anthropology at Nanterre University (Paris X), who initiated me into his writings. I gradually discovered that he played a pioneering role in the sociology of India. At that time this fact was largely unknown since Dr Ambedkar remained one of modern India's most neglected public figures. I decided to write this book first of all to do justice to a then marginalised key personality of Indian history.

I was first interested in Dr Ambedkar's sociological thought and then in the strategies of emancipation he evolved in the course of time to fight caste oppression. The book deals with these issues: it does not narrate Dr Ambedkar's life and for this reason is not organised chronologically but strategy-wise.

In addition to Olivier Herrenschmidt I want to thank Eleanor Zelliot, the most respected expert on Dr Ambedkar, for her comments on an earlier draft of this book. I greatly benefited from her erudite knowledge of the man and was able to attend several 'Dalit workshops' in the United States and Europe thanks to her help. I am also very grateful to Owen Lynch who gave me such valuable insights about the Dalits of Northern India and Ambedkarism at large. In India Hemant Deosthali, Guy Poitevin and Emma Rairkar have been immensely supportive for understanding the relevance of Dr Ambedkar in today's India. Last but not least, my students in

Nanterre enabled me to clarify some of the points I wanted to make in this book: I want to thank them for their not so candid questions!

The book would have been impossible to complete without the patience and love of Tara and our new-born, Milan, to whom I dedicate this message of hope: Dr Ambedkar's life, even scrutinised dispassionately, generates emotions that he may share one day.

CHRISTOPHE JAFFRELOT

Contents

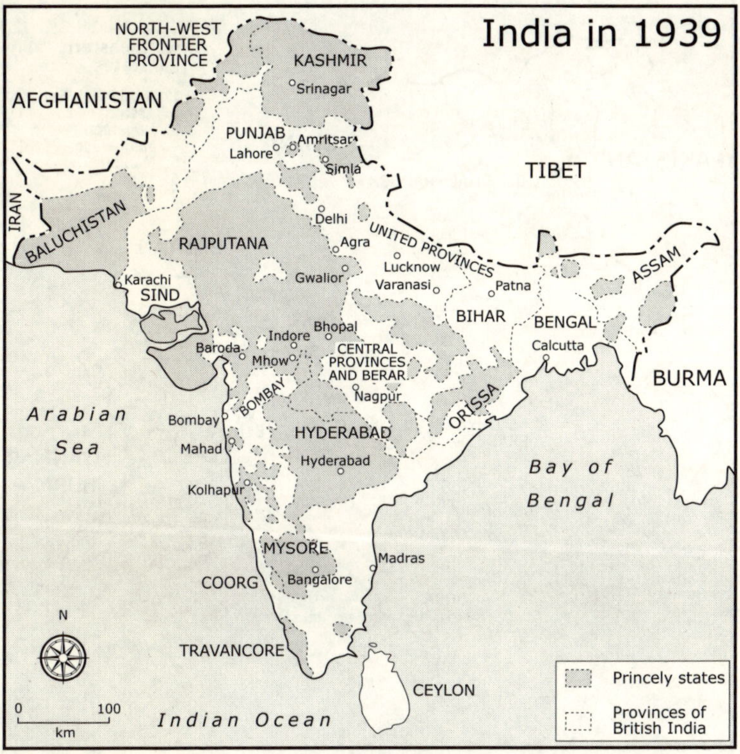
India in 1939
NORTH-WEST FRONTIER PROVINCE
KASHMIR
Srinagar
AFGHANISTAN
PUNJAB
Amritsar
Lahore
Simla
TIBET
IRAN
BALUCHISTAN
Delhi
RAJPUTANA
Agra
UNITED PROVINCES
Lucknow
Gwalior
Varanasi
Patna
ASSAM
Karachi
SIND
BIHAR
BENGAL
Bhopal
Indore
Baroda
CENTRAL PROVINCES AND BERAR
Mhow
Calcutta
BURMA
BOMBAY
Nagpur
ORISSA
Arabian Sea
Bombay
HYDERABAD
Mahad
Hyderabad
Bay of Bengal
Kolhapur
MYSORE
Madras
Bangalore
COORG
N
TRAVANCORE
CEYLON
Princely states
Provinces of British India
0
100
km
Indian Ocean

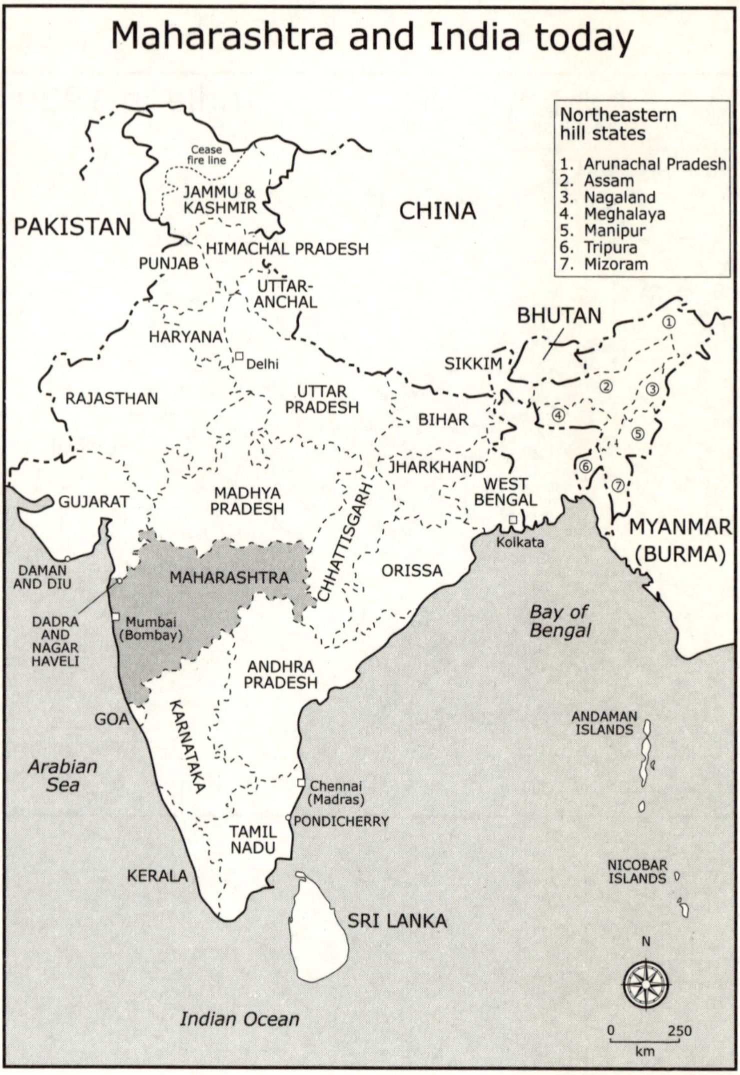

Maharashtra and India today

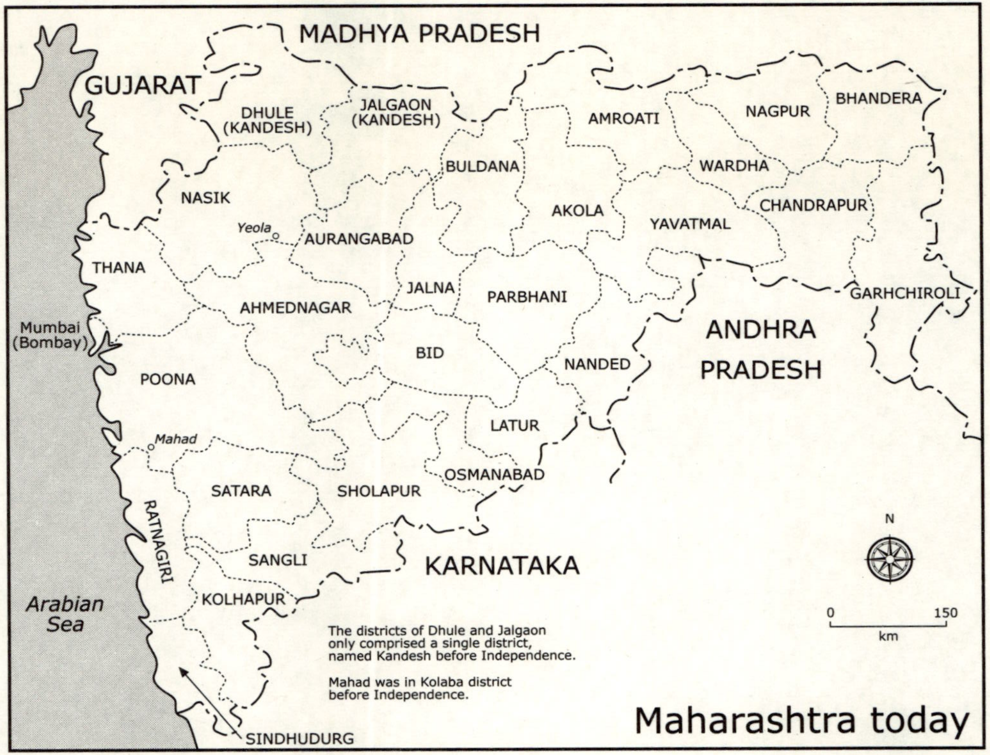

Maharashtra today

Introduction

The First Dalit Leader in India

'The last time that I saw Babasaheb [Ambedkar] was at his funeral procession. That morning I was heading to work as usual, when I read on the front page of the newspaper the news of his demise. I had the impression that the earth was shaking; I was as overwhelmed as if a member of my family had died. Leaning against the doorpost, I began to weep. Neither my mother nor my wife understood why I had begun crying on reading the newspaper. When I told them the news, the whole family burst into tears. On venturing out, I saw people huddled together in groups, discussing the news. Babasaheb had died in Delhi, and that evening an airplane was to bring his body back [to Bombay]. It was barely three months since I had started my job, and I went to the Veterinary School to ask for leave. My boss, furious on seeing why I had requested leave, said to me: 'Why have you said this? Ambedkar is a political leader and you are a civil servant. Give me a personal reason instead.' Though I am of a quiet temperament on that day, for sure, I did not want to change anything. On the contrary I told him: 'Sir, he was of our family. How could you know the abyss from which he rescued us?' I rushed to the governor's residence [Raj Bhavan] without caring about my job, and without waiting to hear if my request would be accepted. Huge crowds were moving towards Raj Bhavan [where the body of Ambedkar rested] in a continuous stream of humanity.' (Daya Pawar, *Ma vie d'intouchable*, Paris: La Découverte, 1990, p. 192)

This moving testimony of Daya Pawar, a Dalit writer from the Western Indian state of Maharashtra, does not convey the attachment of a close associate of Ambedkar: Pawar, even though he was involved in Ambedkar's political movement, did not know him personally. Nor does it reflect the feelings of the tiny Untouchable élite of Bombay, where Ambedkar spent most of his life.[1] Not only were Ambedkar's funeral rites followed by truly huge crowds—a vast sea of humanity, as Pawar suggests—but they gave rise to mass outpourings of grief and sympathy throughout India. Ambedkar's influence had indeed spread far beyond the borders of Maharashtra, as was born out by the electoral gains of the political parties that he founded in North India, and by the countless editions of his writings that have been published in languages other than Marathi. Ambedkar was unquestionably the first Untouchable[2] leader of India as a whole and none of his followers comes close to him in terms of prestige.

Why, in these circumstances, have there been so few studies of his life, his work and his thought? In 2000, Upendra Baxi could still write: 'Ambedkar remains a totally forgotten figure'.[3] Indeed nothing conveys better this neglect than the small number of books which had been devoted to him till the 1990s.[4] If many regional Congress leaders have been the subject of more than one biography—not to mention the countless books about 'Gandhi' and 'Nehru'—for a long time there were only a few books on Ambedkar of the same calibre in English.[5] Similarly, the publication of Ambedkar's collected works did not begin before the 1970s—in contrast to those of Gandhi, Nehru, Patel, and Pant.[6]

This anomaly is partly explained by the poverty of biographical writing in general in Indian social sciences,[7] partly by the disapproval—even fear—which Ambedkar still arouses within the Indian establishment and partly by the ostracism in which those who are accused of having collaborated with the British are readily held. The credit still goes predominantly to the leaders of the freedom movement. Ambedkar's struggle was different but vital nonetheless.

Ambedkar's life, on the face of it, appears to confirm the fairy tale of the self-made man. Bhim Rao Ambedkar was born on April 14, 1891 in Mhow, a garrison town close to Indore—the capital of a princely state of the same name which was to be incorporated into the province of Madhya Bharat (contemporary Madhya Pradesh) after independence. His family came from Maharashtra, like many of the inhabitants of the Indore princely state whose ruling dynasty was itself of low caste.[8] His native village, in Konkan, in the coastal region of Maratha country, was called Ambavade, and Ambedkar's real name, Ambavadekar comes from there (he changed it to Ambedkar in 1900, when his Brahmin schoolteacher, impressed by his intellect and personal qualities, decided to give him his own name).

Ambedkar was for many years protected from the discrimination afflicting Untouchables because of the particular circumstances of life in the cantonment where his father, a soldier in the British Indian army, was based.[9] Gradually, however, he was exposed to the vagaries of life as an Untouchable. As a child, he wondered why no barber would cut his hair.[10] Above all, he suffered a life-defining humiliation that he was never to forget. One day he set off by train with his brother and sister to meet his father at his place of work. On reaching their destination, the three children were questioned by the stationmaster who, learning their caste, 'took five steps back'.[11] As for the *tonga* (a horse-drawn cart) drivers, none of them would take them to their father's village. One of them agreed, provided that they drove the cart themselves. Later the *tongawala* stopped for a snack in a *dhaba* (travellers' inn), whereas the children had to stay outside and were reduced to drinking muddy water from a stream. Ambedkar's realisation of his own condition was all the more stark as he was a child blessed with a very sharp mind.

In 1907, these intellectual qualities enabled him to obtain his matriculation certificate at Elphinstone High School in Bombay, where his father had just settled. He then enrolled, thanks to a scholarship, at the prestigious Elphinstone College, from which he graduated in 1912 with a BA. Then he won another scholarship to pursue postgraduate studies in the United States, an opportunity which no one else from his background had had till then. He secured an MA from Columbia University in New York and then left in 1916 for London where he was admitted to Grays Inn to study law. Later he continued his studies at the London School of Economics, but soon after had to return to India—where he arrived in August 1917—because his scholarship had expired.

His academic achievements brought him to the attention of the British who saw in him a future representative of the Untouchables. Ambedkar was consulted in 1919 by the Southborough Committee that had been set up to revise the qualification criteria for voting rights and thus allow more Indians to vote during the elections to the assemblies established in the provinces and in Delhi. The stakes were very high as the 1919 reforms were intended to devolve greater power to the governments and to the provincial assemblies of British India. Henceforth Indian ministers (responsible to the Legislative Councils), were included in the government. Ambedkar, for his part, lobbied for the creation of a separate electorate and reserved seats for the Untouchables.

In 1920, he launched a new journal, *Mook Nayak* ('leader of the dumb', 'of those without a say') with the financial support of the Maharajah of Kolhapur, Shahu Maharaj, who was none other than the descendant of Shivaji. However he jumped at the chance to resume his studies when the prince offered him the funds to return to England. He obtained a Master of Science in 1921 and the following year he presented his thesis entitled 'The Problem of the Rupee'.

He then tried to settle down as a lawyer in Bombay but as an Untouchable found it hard to attract clients. Deeply hurt, he decided to devote his life to campaign against the caste system and in July 1924 set up the *Bahishkrit Hitakarini Sabha* (Association for the Welfare of the Ostracised) which he led till 1928. The previous year, he had been nominated by the British rulers to the Legislative Council of the Bombay Presidency. Here Ambedkar worked hard to secure for the Untouchables legal access to wells (it was to become the target of his first large mobilisation, at Mahad, on the Konkan coast, in 1927), and entry into temples. The agitation that Ambedkar led on the latter issue was to continue sporadically till 1935.

The 1930s marked Ambedkar's transition to party politics. He demanded from the British a separate electorate for the Untouchables, who, had this been granted, could have constituted themselves into a real political force. The British government partly concurred with his arguments in the arbitration (the Communal Award) which it announced on August 14, 1932. Gandhi, who feared that the measure would threaten Hindu unity, immediately went on a fast in Yeravda jail at Poona. This move forced Ambedkar to relinquish his demand for separate electorates and to sign the 'Poona Pact' on September 24, 1932. Ambedkar was immensely embittered by this development, even though Gandhi, in a more magnanimous mood, later recognised the right of the Untouchables to a substantial reserved quota of seats.

In 1936 Ambedkar created his first political party, the Independent Labour Party (ILP), in anticipation of the forthcoming 1937 elections, which took place within the framework of the Government of India Act (1935), a law giving to provincial governments and assemblies more power compared to the 1919 reforms. The ILP fielded candidates only in the Bombay Presidency and in the Central

Provinces, where it made some breakthrough, Ambedkar being elected together with nine other party cadres.

The Second World War accelerated the pace of change in Indian politics. Britain had involved India in the conflict without consulting the Congress, hence its representatives resigned from the eight provincial governments which they controlled. In an attempt to bind other Indians to the war effort, the British co-opted leaders of less important political parties, such as the Muslim League, the Hindu Mahasabha (a small Hindu nationalist group) and the ILP. This is how Ambedkar came to join the Defence Advisory Committee in 1941 before being appointed Minister of Labour in 1942.

Ambedkar combined this ministerial activity with a revival of his party-based strategy, and in 1942 he established a new organisation, the Scheduled Castes' Federation (SCF). The expression Scheduled Castes designates the Untouchable castes whose list had been established by the government so that they could benefit from employment quotas in the education system and the bureaucracy. After having tried to broaden his political base to all workers, Ambedkar henceforth concentrated his efforts only on Untouchables. Faced with an all-powerful Congress, the SCF met with crushing reverses in the provincial assemblies elections of March 1946, and Ambedkar himself was defeated.

But this did not thwart his political ascendancy as one of the most important representatives of the Untouchables. On August 3, 1947 Jawaharlal Nehru appointed him as Minister of Law and three weeks later, on August 29, he was made head of the committee charged with the drafting of the Constitution (the Drafting Committee). This was the focus of almost all his energy from 1947–50.

While the Constitution outlined a favourable framework for social reform, particularly by abolishing Untouchability and by prohibiting all discrimination based on caste, race and sex, Ambedkar was determined to attack the ills of Indian society in a more concrete fashion. This is why, in January 1950, he launched a campaign for the revision of the Hindu Code Bill, which regulated matrimonial relations (laws of marriage and divorce), inheritance, adoption, etc. According to him, it ought to be the instrument of a far-reaching reform of Hindu society. But Nehru, anxious not to alienate the more conservative elements of the Congress, distanced himself from his proposals and Ambedkar resigned from the government in September 1951. On returning to the opposition, he renewed his close links with the Socialists but this alliance suffered a severe setback in the elections of 1951–2.

He then turned to Buddhism, to which he dedicated his last work, *The Buddha and His Dhamma*, which was to be published posthumously in 1957. The year before he had chosen the day of the important Hindu festival of *Dasahara*, October 14, to convert to Buddhism during a big ceremony at Nagpur, where thousands of Untouchables followed his example. He returned to Delhi on November 30, where he died on December 6, 1956.

The object of the present work is not to recount Ambedkar's life, of which the salient points have just been briefly outlined, but to shed light on his contribution to the emancipation of the Untouchables and, more generally, to the social and political transformation of India.

How did Ambedkar analyse caste oppression and form his strategies of emancipation? Far from adopting a romanticised view of Ambedkar, I shall apply a strategy-oriented approach to respond to this question. His career lends itself to such a method of analysis. In the first issue of *Mook Nayak*, on January 31, 1920, when he had just entered the public sphere, he advocated the need for a forum 'to deliberate on the injustices let loose or likely to be imposed on us and other depressed people and to think of their future development and appropriate strategies towards it critically'.[12] Before turning to his strategies, however, I shall try to understand how Ambedkar *became* Ambedkar. To this end I shall begin by situating him in the context of Maharashtra and in his family as well as social environment. Then I shall analyse how, from early on, he thought about the caste system in order to better eradicate it. Ambedkar the statesman and man of action has often concealed Ambedkar the reflective thinker, which is unfortunate because his many publications are those of a true intellectual. But in contrast to other scholars, his own upbringing and situation were such that he exercised his talents as a sociologist in the service of a cause: he scrutinised the mechanisms of caste with the aim of annihilating this social system based on hierarchy and such an approach did not help him to be recognised as a true social scientist.

As a pioneer, Ambedkar moved cautiously from one objective to the next. At first he strove to reform the Untouchables, so as to enable them to advance within wider Hindu society (particularly via education), and later turned to politics in the 1930s. The parties that he founded emerged sometimes as Untouchable organisations and sometimes as the rallying-points of all the oppressed. However he did not limit his political action to party politics: he also collaborated with governments—whether they were British or Congress—in order to exert pressure from within on those in power. This approach permitted him, in his capacity as head of the Drafting Committee of the Indian Constitution, to advocate the Untouchable cause and to keep some of Gandhi's ideas at bay. But Ambedkar was not satisfied with this form of political activity, which eventually he regarded as useless. At regular intervals, he was tempted by a more radical strategy, an approach which was to find expression in conversion to another religion. This project ensued directly from his analysis of the caste system as being consubstantial with Hinduism, a view he expressed from the 1920s but abstained from implementing till the year he died.

Ambedkar therefore oscillated between the promotion of the Untouchables in Hindu society or in the Indian nation as a whole; and the strategy of a break that could take the form of a separate electorate, or of a separate Dalit party and/or of conversion outside Hinduism. He searched for solutions, explored strategies and, in doing so, set the Dalits on the path of an arduous emancipation.

1. Maharashtra between Social Reform and anti-Brahmin Mobilisation

Ambedkar was the first Untouchable leader of India. In this capacity, he is almost an enigma: how did he drag himself away from his social background to acquire this standing and become a genuine statesman? We cannot, here, content ourselves with a psychological explanation by emphasising the exceptional features of his personality. Certainly, he had the advantage of an extraordinary mind and an iron will: he could channel all his energy in the service of a wider project and his determination never failed him. But such an idiosyncrasy alone does not account for his career. As usual in such cases, an element of chance must be factored in too, but it does not explain everything either. And even certain facts which seem to reflect it, such as the support of Maratha Maharajahs, are in fact a part of the context—the regional circumstances in this case—in which Ambedkar's career was shaped. To understand this outstanding personality we have to look at the geographical, historical and social context from which it emerged. Ambedkar was the heir to a regional tradition; his struggle harked back to the anti-Brahmin movements which emerged in western Maharashtra from the mid-nineteenth century onwards, a precocity that only the Dravidian South—the other key area of anti-Brahmin mobilisation—could match[1].

Maharashtra and its socio-political system

Maharashtra is defined in the first place by its language, its borders corresponding to the area where Marathi is spoken. This fact was given an institutional framework with the creation of Maharashtra (see maps 1 and 3, pp. viii and x) in 1960. But during the British Raj, the districts composing this linguistic area were distributed among four entities (see map 2, p. ix): the coastal strip (the Konkan) and the *ghats* (the mountainous chain that descends to the sea) were part of the Bombay Presidency; the interior of the province *(Desh)* was shared between another British administrative region (the Central Provinces and Berar) and the Hyderabad princely state; and finally the much smaller princely states remained in the western part of the province (for example, Kolhapur).

If the princely states, whichever they were, had practically no political activity before the end of the Raj, the provinces under British administration developed arenas for political competition after the Local Self Government Act of 1882 established town councils, and the constitutional reform of 1909 introduced legislative councils in all provinces under British rule. Their importance was further increased by the reforms of 1919 and 1935, when the provincial governments became partly accountable before these assemblies and as the franchise was widened.

What did the society playing within this institutional framework look like? According to the 1931 census, the last one that took caste into consideration in a comprehensive manner, the districts which were to constitute Maharashtra some thirty years later accounted for, as regards upper castes, 3.9 per cent of Brahmins, 1.69 per cent of Vaishyas and 1 per cent of Kshatriyas. The Shudra category was dominated by the Maratha-Kunbis, a group of allied castes which together totalled 31.19 per cent of the province's population. No other *jati* of this *Varna* reached up to 5 per cent of the population of Maharashtra. Finally, the Untouchables accounted for 16.47 per cent of the total. Among them, the most numerous *jati* was that of the Mahars—Ambedkar's caste—which accounted for 11 per cent of the regional population.[2] Beyond these statistical aggregates, the creation of collective identity among these castes and their interactions at the local level merit particular attention.

In Northern India, the relations—social as well as economic and ritualistic—that the various *jatis* traditionally maintained among themselves made up a system, often called, in a generic way, the '*jajmani*' system, named after the chief (the *jajman*) around whom it hinged. It concerned an ancestral system of exchange of goods and services between castes, which organised themselves on an intra-village basis. The *jajman* was the 'chief', as he benefited from services provided by others and remunerated them a portion of the harvest on the threshing floor. The *jajman*, most of the time, was a landowner of the dominant caste, which was referred to thus because it was the majority caste and the one that possessed most land at the local level. In Maharashtra, the notion of *jajman* was not known; the village chief was the *patil*, the appointed leader of the village, not a *jajman*. His office was hereditary, but it could be lost in the case of migration to another village or to the city. It usually circulated among several families. The *patil*, in most instances, was a Maratha, even though Brahmins were significant in local agrarian relations because of their money-lending activities.[3] Brahmins mostly ranked second to the *patil* in the village hierarchy, as *kulkarni*, or village accountants.[4]

In Maharashtra, therefore, economic and social relations were organised at the village level according to the logic of a variant of the *jajmani* system, the *balutedari* system,[5] which was also known as the 'system of the *bara balutedar*' because there were twelve (*bara*) key castes in this arrangement.[6] The castes called the *balutedars* provided, in principle, precise hereditary services to the village—rather than to the *jajman*. The *balutedar* castes did not, however, provide the same type of services and it would be wrong to consider them as being on an equal footing. Among them the *patil* and the *kulkarni*, mentioned above, assumed naturally dominant roles. The other *balutedars*, with the exception of the astrologers (also Brahmins), came from the lower castes, such as the Sonas (silver-smiths), Lohars (ironsmiths), Sutars (carpenters), Khumhars (potters), Nahvis (barbers), Parits (washermen), Guraos (temple guards who officiated also as priests for the low castes), Mangs (Untouchable rope-makers), Chambhars (Untouchable shoemakers) and Mahars.[7]

The *balutedari* system formed the basic structure of the precolonial state as evident from the fact that the office of the *patil* and the *kulkarni* had equivalents at the regional level, the *deshmukh* and *deshpande* (the latter was systematically a Brahmin whereas the former could be a Maratha or a Brahmin). This administrative layout was consolidated in the course of time, so much so that it formed the framework of Shivaji's empire in the seventeenth century. The son of a notable of the Sultanate of Bijapur, Shivaji came from a Maratha lineage of *patils* before being recognised as a *deshmukh* and then, eventually, as a *kshatriya* of the highest origins (due to the complacent attitude of self-interested Brahmins who rewrote his genealogy).

This political structure was questioned when the *peshwa*—a noun meaning 'head of government' but which became the name of the Chitpavan Brahmin dynasty that administered the Maratha Empire—usurped the throne after Shivaji's death. The domination of the *peshwas* was greatly resented by the Marathas in general and more especially by the descendants of Shivaji who continued to reign over the small principality of Kolhapur. Thus, the social and political history of Maharashtra reveals important but latent tensions between Brahmins and non-Brahmins, in particular Marathas.

The questioning of the social order during the nineteenth century

The caste system of Maharashtra was to some extent undermined by the impact of British colonialism from the nineteenth century onwards. Following military defeat and acts of betrayal from within their own ranks, the last *peshwa* relinquished power in 1818. Only a few princes whose power was attenuated, like the ruler of Kolhapur, retained some autonomy. In social terms colonial conquest had two contradictory effects: on the one hand Brahmins reasserted their domination by penetrating *en masse* the British colonial bureaucracy and the professions (lawyers, journalists, etc.) to which their traditions of learning predisposed them. On the other hand, the British introduced a radical critique of the caste system through their schools and religious missions. These two tendencies eventually nurtured the parallel emergence of socio-religious reform movements dominated by the upper castes *and* anti-Brahmin associations.

The Western impact. Traditions of learning gave Brahmins and Kayasths (scribes regarded as upper caste who were not integrated into any of the 'twice born' *varnas* and even likened to Shudras)[8] a head start in gaining entry to the educational system that the British established to train native administrators. Untouchables were nowhere to be seen in this regard. The British-run schools, which in theory at least were open to them, proved to be inaccessible because the parents of upper caste pupils opposed their admission. At best, Untouchables followed the classes from the school veranda.[9] And while the government established schools which were reserved for them, the numbers involved were pitiful: in 1882 there were sixteen such schools (accounting for 564 pupils) in the Bombay Presidency and four schools (for 111 pupils) in the Central Provinces.[10] Such efforts hardly allowed Untouchables to benefit in large numbers from a genuine education: in 1911, only 0.5 per cent—and 1 per cent of Mahars, which was above the national average[11]—could read and write, and this rose only to 1.5 per cent in 1921 and 2.9 per cent by 1931.

Table 1.1. PROGRESS OF LITERACY AMONG THE ADULTS OF BOMBAY PRESIDENCY, ACCORDING TO CASTES, 1911

	Proportion (%)	
	Literate	*in English*
Brahmins		
Chitpavans	63	19.3
Deshasthas	61.5	10.22
Saraswats	54	10.77
Intermediate castes		
Marathas	4.6	0.22
Kunbis	9.4	0.27
Lingayats	13.6	0.3
Untouchables		
Mahars	1	0.01

Source: *Census of India*, 1911, vol. VIII, p. 148.

In 1886–7, of the 424 employees of the uncovenanted service[12] in the Bombay Presidency, 328 were Hindus of whom 211 were Brahmins, 26 Kshatriyas, 37 Prabhus (Kayasths), 38 Vaishyas, 1 Shudra and 15 'others'.[13] Among the Brahmins, the Chitpavans were known for their remarkable dynamism through which they quickly compensated for the social decline that the deposition of the *peshwa* dynasty had precipitated. Being the most educated, they dominated occupations which required a command of English. Of the 104 subordinate judges that the Bombay Presidency accounted for in 1887, seventy were Brahmins, thirty-three of whom were Chitpavans.[14]

This Brahmin skill at penetrating modern education and, in turn, monopolising posts of administrative responsibility aroused jealousy and hostility from the lower castes, from the moment they started to raise themselves, under the influence of egalitarian ideas spread by the British, and, in particular, by Christian missions.

In 1813 the revision of the Charter of the East India Company allowed Christian missions to settle in India, the Scottish Free Church and the American Mission being among the first to begin work in Western India. At first Scottish missionaries concentrated on education, but after 1829 the arrival of John Wilson in Bombay led to a more aggressive proselytism; public debates were even organised with *pandits* to promote Christianity at the expense of Hinduism. After Bombay and Poona, Ahmednagar was the third city to become a focus for missionary activity, in 1831. The American Marathi Mission there was concerned above all with education and conversion of the Untouchables, in particular the Mahars.[15] Everywhere, the missionaries used printed material to spread their ideas through pamphlets, books or the press (*Dnyanodaya*, a Marathi newspaper, was launched in this perspective in 1842).[16] Missionary propaganda consisted first of all in a systematic denigration of Hinduism: the cult of images was stigmatised as an idolatrous polytheism, beliefs such as reincarnation were denounced as superstitions and, above all, the caste system was condemned as an insult to human dignity. In the face of this onslaught, some Brahmins started to reform themselves in order better to counter the impact of the missionaries.

Socio-religious reform and its limitations. The first reformist organisation was the Prarthana Samaj (Society of Prayer). Its founders wished to replace the cult of idols (or images of the gods) by an abstract monotheism which reflected Christian influences. The most distinguished member of the Prarthana Samaj was M. G. Ranade (a Chitpavan Brahmin who by the late 1860s was a subordinate judge). He aspired to invent a 'Hindu Protestantism' which could combine the religious tradition of Maharashtra—mainly the *bhakti* cult which had flourished in the seventeenth century—and the achievements of the Reformation. Just as the latter had abolished the intermediary role between man and God that Catholicism ascribed to the priests, so he wanted Hinduism to rid itself of Brahmins. For him, the latter were obscurantists interested in perpetuating a system of social domination, and it was to their pernicious influence that he attributed the decline of India.

At Elphinstone College in Bombay, Ranade had been trained in the thought of Adam Smith, Edmund Burke, Jeremy Bentham, James and John Stuart Mill, and more especially Herbert Spencer, whom he particularly admired. His reformism however remained rather shallow.[17] While he readily criticised the caste system, he did not break its rules,[18] and above all he had no desire to question its 'social cohesion': far from subscribing to the individualism of English liberals, he reserved their principles for the political sphere and, as regards the social order, was more inspired by Burke in respecting tradition.[19]

The caution of the reformers was to remain a permanent feature. It was also characteristic of the Sarvajanik Sabha (Association for Public Good), an organisation founded in 1870 that counted Ranade among its leaders. It acquired a wider base than the Prarthana Samaj because of its political scope (moderately but firmly it demanded wider access to administrative posts for Indians).[20] The Arya Samaj (Society of the Aryas), founded in 1875 in Bombay by Swami Dayananda Saraswati, turned out to be very ambivalent too. From the outset Dayananda subscribed to the main tenets of the western critique of idol worship and of caste, but he argued that these two defects were only the latter-day corruptions of the original Vedic model, in which ancient Indian society had shunned polytheism and *jati*, relying only on non-hereditary *varnas.* For Dayananda, *varnas* were based originally on individual merit since *gurus* classified children in various *varnas* according to their personal qualities.[21] Hence he did not seek the dismantling of the system; rather his objective was a very limited reform of it. Although he denounced the parasitism of the Brahmins, whom he blamed for the decline of Hinduism, he aspired to rehabilitate a Vedic golden age from which caste was not excluded. He merely wanted to substitute *jatis,* deemed illegitimate in the face of Western criticism, with merit-based *varnas,* which continued to be organised along hierarchical and exclusive lines. That Swami Dayananda had no wish to question the moral economy of the system was reconfirmed when he recommended his fellow-believers to observe endogamy within each *varna.*

The socio-religious reform movements of nineteenth-century India, while manifesting unmistakable Western influences, were thus anxious to shield Hinduism from very severe criticism. Their objective was more to restore a certain legitimacy to Hindu practices, and in particular to redeem the caste system. This approach was doubtless motivated as much by an élite's desire to remain at the summit of the Hindu hierarchy[22] as by an inability to conceive of a world organised via categories other than that of caste.

The individualistic and egalitarian values of the West was to arouse much greater support from among the lower castes, key figures of which established, from the mid-nineteenth century onwards, the basis of an anti-Brahmin movement.

The birth of the anti-Brahmin movement in Maharashtra. The emergence of the anti-Brahmin movement in Maharashtra is inextricably linked to the personality of Jotirao Phule (1827–90),[23] to whom Ambedkar—who was born within a year of his death—dedicated one of his books. Phule was a Mali, or member of the caste of gardeners. He had the rare privilege of studying at his village school and later at the Poona Scottish Mission, where he learnt English and discovered the philosophy of the American Founding Fathers. They galvanised him against the caste system in the name of Western values. He regarded notions of equality and freedom as having reached their zenith in the United States, and later drew a parallel between the condition of the lower castes and that of the Blacks—on whom American society had, according to Phule, bestowed emancipation. This comparison is central to his book *Slavery* (1873) which he dedicated 'to the good people of the United States as a token of admiration for their sublime and selfless dedication and their sense of sacrifice with regard to the cause of slavery of the Negroes; and with the fervent desire that my fellow countrymen follow the noble example in the emancipation of their Shudra brothers from the fetters of Brahminical slavery.'[24]

Phule was particularly influenced by the thought of Thomas Paine, whose criticism of the role of Catholic priests in *The Age of Reason* he later emulated and applied to Brahmins. Moreover he discovered in this book a spirituality free of sacred texts and the promotion of personal freedom as well as equality—in short, the values of *Human Rights* (the title of another of Paine's works).

The impact of the West on Phule also accounts for his fascination with Jesus Christ, who embodied equality and the brotherhood of man and even served as the standard-bearer for the poor and the oppressed.[25] Such a response to Christian values would remain very dear to the Mahars till the early twentieth century, some of them going as far as converting themselves to Christianity under missionary influence.[26]

Drawing his inspiration from the Orientalist canon, Phule presented the Aryan invasions as the destruction of a purer indigenous civilisation of which the lower castes were the heirs. For Phule, the invaders were Brahmins who subjugated the autochthons, reducing them to the rank of lower castes.[27] As a result, all the non-Brahmin castes—ranging from Marathas to Untouchables—represented a non-Aryan, older and superior culture epitomised by King Bali.[28]

Phule believed that the lower castes, in order to advance, had to be the beneficiaries of an education comparable to that provided by the missionaries—who took particular care to attract Untouchables to their schools. Hence in 1853 he established a school that was intended above all to educate Mahars and Mangs. Meanwhile Phule poured out a torrent of documents and pamphlets about education in which he relentlessly depicted Brahmins as the oppressor, whether as greedy money-lenders or priests keen to exploit the ignorance and superstition of the most deprived sections of society.[29]

Phule also played a pioneering role in organising the low castes. While he was at first attracted by the Arya Samaj,[30] he soon turned against it and then against the Sarvajanik Sabha. Phule mistrusted these upper castes' efforts to bring to a successful conclusion the emancipation of the lower *jatis*.[31] Their leaders were in his view hypocrites who professed to fight caste while in reality observing its rules.[32] Phule also distanced himself from the Indian National Congress which, founded in 1885 in Bombay, projected itself as the spearhead of the Indian nation. He regarded it as a Brahmin pressure group, and one greedy for power at that.[33] Instead he lobbied the colonial power to limit the influence of Brahmins in the administration.[34] The brand of nationalism to which the founders of Congress referred had hardly any meaning for him, given Indian society's internal divisions.

'There can not be a "Nation" worth the name until and unless all the people… such as Shudras, Ati-Shudras [Untouchables] Bhils [tribals] and fishermen etc., become truly educated, are able to think independently for themselves and are uniformly unified and emotionally integrated. If [a tiny proportion of the population such as] the upstart Aryan Brahmins alone were to found the "National Congress", who will take any notice of it?'[35]

This quote reveals a genuine sociological insight, which tallies with Marcel Mauss's definition of the nation:[36] no nation can exist without the erosion of intermediate bodies—such as castes—the development of individualism and hence a minimal level of equality. Phule thereby distanced himself both from the socio-religious reform movements and the Congress to create India's first low caste organisation.

He founded the Satyashodak Samaj (Society for the Search of Truth) in 1873 to unite the lower castes and Untouchables.[37] He referred to pseudo-historical episodes testifying to an ancient solidarity between Mahars and Shudras[38] and denounced stratagems devised by the Brahmins to divide the lower castes.[39]

Over time, the Satyashodak Samaj gradually became a more Maratha-dominated organisation. Certainly, Phule strove hard to establish Shivaji as an inspirational figure for all the lower castes, including Untouchables and argued that they were all descendants of the autochthons who populated Maharashtra before the Aryan invasions.[40] But this discourse and Phule's emphasis on the defence of the peasants (often Marathas) resulted first in the recruitment of growing numbers of Marathas. From a lower castes' organisation, the Satyashodak Samaj thus became an association of Marathas opposing Brahmins *per se* and no longer one directed against Brahminism as a social system. The logic of caste also revealed its deep roots through the persistence of mechanisms of *Sanskritisation*,[41] or the imitation of the upper castes, which was especially evident among Marathas who tried to win recognition as Kshatriyas.

In the 1930s the Satyashodak Samaj, which had till then maintained its distance from Congress, a largely Brahmin-dominated party, decided to merge with it in order better to defend its interests. The party was very attractive then since it seemed to be in a position to win a majority in the Legislative Council of the Bombay Presidency and the Central Provinces—and these expectations were born out in the elections of 1937.

The fate of the Satyashodak Samaj highlights a liability that the Untouchables were to face structurally. The unity of the lower castes—especially the political consolidation of Untouchables and Shudras—proved very difficult to achieve because some of the low castes were often not against but *in* the system and sought to rise within it, according to the logic of *Sanskritisation* or by other means.

When Ambedkar appeared on the public scene in Maharashtra, the ground had already been prepared for the emergence of a social and political consciousness among some of the lower castes, albeit without promoting equality on a permanent basis. The specificity of Maharashtra lay above all in the demographic balance of power, which placed the 'twice born' in an ultra-minority position, and in tensions between Brahmins and non-Brahmins (in particular Marathas) which were revived in the colonial context. The complete domination of new professions by Brahmins reinforced the hostility of the lower castes, not least because they had imbibed notions of equality and freedom in Western schools without Brahmin reformers having done much to defuse their revolt. This assimilation in Western schools of notions of equality and freedom, which was mostly absent elsewhere at the turn of the century—except, perhaps, in the Tamil-speaking South—was but one manifestation of the social ferment upon which Ambedkar was to build himself up as an Untouchable leader. Another factor that accounted for his career was the uniqueness of his social background.

2. Ambedkar: Son of a Mahar Soldier

'The people say, *Mahar sarva jaticha baha*, or "The Mahar is outside all castes". Having a bad name, they are also given unwarrantably a bad character; and *Mahar jatich* is a phrase used for a man with no moral or kindly feelings'. (R. V. Russell and Hira Lal, *The Tribes and Castes of the Central Provinces of India*, vol. 4, op. cit., p. 142)

'*Jethe gaon tethe Maharwada*' (Popular Marathi proverb: Wherever there is a village, there is a *maharvada*—meaning 'to every house its storeroom')

The Mahar caste to which Ambedkar belonged was ranked within the Untouchable hierarchy between Mangs (rope-makers) and Chambhars (leather-workers), whose role sometimes permitted them to develop commercial interests. Nevertheless, Mahars gradually took over the leadership of the Untouchables, partly on account of their numbers. In 1931, they represented 68.9 per cent of Untouchables in the Bombay Presidency (compared to 16.2 per cent of Chambhars and 14.9 per cent of Mangs). In the wider population they were not as numerous as Marathas (20.2 per cent) but far ahead of Brahmins (4.4 per cent). Their role within the division of labour inherent in the *balutedari* system was not one solely of disadvantage: some of their functions brought them into contact with upper castes and allowed them certain responsibilities. More importantly, Mahars capitalised on their former presence in the Peshwa's army to join that of the British, with cantonment towns serving in several cases as springboards to social mobility. In the absence of any proven craft speciality, Mahars were also among the first to leave the village and experience modernity in the cities.

Mahars were also very much influenced by the historical importance of the *bhakti* movements which in Maharashtra, reached their pinnacle in the seventeenth century under the great poet Tukaram. The *bhakti* tradition promoted the message of salvation by worshipping forms of the Divine independently of the observance of rites codified by Brahmins—and independently too of the respect generally due to these religious intermediaries. Devotees of *bhakti* have constantly striven to promote the equality of men before God and to challenge caste hierarchies, encouraging the development of devotional cults and therefore of sects applying, as a rule, an egalitarian ethos.[1]

In Maharashtra, many Mahars joined the Mahanubhava sect, founded in the thirteenth century and shunned by Hinduism because of its rejection of caste distinctions. Certainly, this sectarian affiliation permitted some Mahars to establish their own rites and beliefs.[2] But *bhakti*, far from instigating Mahars to rebel against the caste system, advised them to accept it by deprecating the social conditions of existence: what is this concern with Brahmin oppression, when the main point of existence is to acquire salvation in the life beyond this world? The poet Chokhamela, a Mahar, who lived in the thirteenth century, gave remarkable illustrations of this reasoning in his magnificent verses.[3] Ambedkar inherited all these legacies but was able to invent his own emancipatory message.

Mahars, first of the last

Mahars occupied a peculiar, even unique, position in Maharashtrian society. As mentioned above they held a *baluta*; and they even ranked among the most important *balutedars* in the village, as evident from the payments they received. At harvest time every cultivator kept *pendhi* (sheaves) in his field for the *balutedars* as payment for their service. These *pendhi* were organised in three rows—one for each *balutedar* according to their rank—and Mahars were always allowed to take them from the first row. Not only were Mahars given an important share of the harvest, but their right to a *vatan* (an area of land free of tax) was also recognised, like the *patils* and the *kulkarnis* but unlike most other *balutedars*.

The 'Mahar *vatan* or *hadola* often was of good quality' as Traude Pillai-Vetschera points out, but the Peshwas ruled that it could not be sold or alienated[4]. In contrast to their status as *vatandars*, Mahars performed mixed functions, some of which were particularly impure. Pillai-Vetschera gives a list which is significant above all for its heterogeneity: not only the Mahars were gate-keepers and watchmen, auxiliaries to the police—for instance when a theft occurred—travellers' porters, guides for people to the next village and boundary referees, but they were also in charge of levying taxes and summoning landholders to pay taxes, escorting the government treasury, sweeping roads, carrying death notices and messages to other villages, bringing fuel to the burning grounds and removing cattle carcasses.[5]

Of all these tasks the last one was naturally the most impure,[6] all the more so as it came with the Mahar tradition of consuming dead cattle.[7] The stigma of Untouchability from which Mahars suffered was such that, in extreme cases, they were obliged to wear earthenware around their necks so that their spit did not defile the ground on which Brahmins walked. They also had to sweep the earth behind them to erase their footsteps or at least maintain a good distance from Brahmins to avoid contaminating them with their shadow.[8] According to Pillai-Vetschera, these and other restrictions were imposed on Mahars during the Peshwa period.[9] Correlatively, Mahars lived outside the village, in the *maharvada*, a separate neighbourhood. If Mahars enjoyed a *vatan* (a hereditary right to a plot of land) and a *baluta* (remuneration in kind while attached as servants to a village) they had to beg for their wages. Baby Kamble underlines in her memoirs the humiliation of collecting *bhakri*, or leftovers, from meals:

> Payment for this daily work carried out by the entire family consisted of going to beg for *bhakri*. [The Mahar head of the family] had little spherical bells hanging on to a stick, so that villagers could move away as soon as they heard the Mahar coming to beg. The Mahar who went to beg puffed out his chest on leaving the *maharvada*, twirled his moustache and walked ostentiously, clearing his throat, like a man. He regarded his stick and its little bells as a sceptre, and took the black woollen blanket on his shoulders for a lawyer's gown. But once he entered the village, his posture shrank, he bent his spinal column in the manner of a hunchback and crawled like a snail. On reaching a dwelling, without opening his mouth, he rang the bells on his stick three times. Then some scraps of rancid and stale food was thrown into his blanket. The blanket was more than half full after he completed his rounds of the village. The Mahar loaded the *bhakri* on to his shoulders and returned home delighted. He and his family filled their stomachs to the brim.[10]

Certain traditional Mahar activities were deemed respectable because they brought them in contact with the upper castes. As village guards, they had to record the identity of guests and the reasons for their visit. But the function from which they derived most prestige was well described by Robertson, who spent the first three decades of the twentieth century as a missionary in Maharashtra:

> The Mahar takes pride in the duties required of him as Government messenger; for he is often entrusted with the transport of large sums of money remitted to the district treasury, and he has inherited from his fathers a tradition of faithfulness in the discharge of such duties. When the administration officers need accurate information regarding the boundaries of holdings within the village, the Mahar is called on to produce this information. He defines the boundaries of any holding by walking solemnly along them. It is a Mahar who is employed to summon farmers to attend the revenue officer for the payment of rent and taxes due.[11]

Hence one could be proud of being a Mahar while carrying out certain tasks, a fact that has been widely acknowledged: Pillai-Vetschera points out that 'the Mahar, in spite of his low caste, held a highly respected position'[12] while Jayashree Gokhale underlines also that their 'role in the fixing of village boundaries and the adjudication of disputes pertaining to boundaries between villages' endowed the Mahars with 'a stature which no other *jati* had'.[13]

Some Mahars also manifested a degree of self-confidence. Daya Pawar remembers that those which he 'knew did not have the impression that they begged. Their remuneration (*baluta*), they considered it as a right. They had been told since generations that their ancestors had been granted a charter of 52 rights. Everybody was proud of this tradition'[14] The fact that Mahars sometimes seem to have been the first of the last was due also to their role as farmers, bound up with their status as *vatandar*, which gave them the right to hold and till land.

Mahars also took advantage of their substantial numbers in the army. The British recruited many Mahars to the regular army because of their martial qualities and also employed them in the armaments industry (they were, for example, well represented in ammunition factories). At one time there were up to seventy non-commissioned Mahar officers in twenty regiments of the infantry and a Mahar naval regiment,[15] which was conducive to the formation of a small Mahar élite. Till the 1857 Mutiny they accounted for one-sixth of the regiments of the East India Company under the Bombay command.[16] For Eleanor Zelliot, 'military service as such an early date exposed them [Mahars] to British institutions much before the dissemination of western culture took place on a large scale. Such an exposure socialised them sufficiently early to the new political order so that when new opportunities and alternatives became available, they were found prepared to use them more effectively than those groups which did not have this opportunity'[17].

Mahars also made inroads into other professions, sometimes under duress. The modernisation of the state and its communications under the aegis of the British meant that Mahars were often the first to lose their jobs as messengers given the development of postal services, as guards of the village 'treasury' because of the setting up of a fiscal administration, as 'owners' of hides because of the development of tanneries which established direct contractual relations with cattle-breeders or as arbitrators of land boundaries because of the setting up of a land register.[18] In short, Mahars were more or less compelled to leave their villages in large numbers because they could rely on no specialised craft capable of resisting the economic and administrative changes introduced by colonialism. In 1921 only 13 per cent of working Mahars exercised one of their traditional professions, against 55 per cent of Chambhars and 33.2 per cent of Mangs. Many migrated to Bombay, where they often found a post in the police, in factories or in the coaling area of the docks.[19] In 1918 one tenth of Bombay's textile workers were Mahars.[20] According to the Census of 1921, 12 per cent of the population of Bombay and its factory workers were Untouchables (mostly Mahars) while they accounted for only 4 per cent of the population of Bombay in 1864 and 1 per cent of factory workers in 1872.[21] Many of them—such as the father of Daya Pawar—became dock workers in the 1920s and '30s.[22] Before this, the railroads afforded also another important source of work.[23] This mobility—which we should not exaggerate because most Mahars continued to live in villages—was a means of freeing them from the *vatan* system and improving their social and political space for manoeuvre, compared, for example, to the Mangs, who, in the villages, took over some of the tasks abandoned by Mahars.

This initial social advancement in urban settings was accompanied by a drive for education. With the help of 'patrons' such as the Maharajah of Kolhapur (who financed a Mahar boarding school in 1909), Mahars opened schools and hostels for their community at

Nagpur, Poona, Ahmednagar and Amraoti. They thus attained a literacy rate of 2.3 per cent in 1921 (against 0.01 per cent in 1901), which represented 5,000 men and 3,000 women in the Marathi-speaking districts of the Bombay Presidency. Among them, 288 knew English, but only one, Ambedkar, was a university graduate.[24] To quote Zelliot, within Mahars, 'a group which could understand Ambedkar's modern idiom waited to be gathered.'[25]

M. G. Bhagat, author of a Master's thesis written in 1935, entitled 'Untouchability in Maharashtra', provides a precise ethnographical snapshot of the position of the Mahars in the six districts of Kobala, Thana, Nasik, Satara, Ahmednagar and Khandesh East. Based on a detailed examination of 542 families, he shows in particular that Mahars, although generally more underprivileged than other Untouchables, were more socially mobile and had a larger élite. In terms of incomes, the Mahar families in Bhagat's sample earned an average of 138 rupees a year per family, a little more than the Mangs (133 rupees) but much less than the Chambhars and the Bhangis (respectively 234 and 338 rupees).[26] As a result, of the 233 families who had to marry off a daughter, 199, or 85 per cent, got into debt to pay the dowry. Bhagat reports that besides having 'found many cases where the borrowers themselves did not know the exact amount of their debt and in such cases they were naturally at the mercy of the money-lenders.'[27]

He blames the extreme poverty of Mahars on the low incomes they drew from the *baluta* and *vatan* systems: the remuneration they received for their work in the service of the village was paltry and, if they possessed a hereditary land-holding, 'it was divided and subdivided to the point that it did not bring back hardly anything'.[28]

Their destitution compelled Mahars to seek other employment in the area studied by Bhagat: only 6.5 per cent pursued their traditional roles, as against 54 per cent of Chambhars, 62 per cent of Dhors (tanners), 79 per cent of Mangs and 100 per cent of Bhangis. About one quarter of Mahars tilled the land whereas 58 per cent declared it an occasional activity, generally as day labourers. Except for harvest time, they could in fact count only about ten work days per month,[29] and this explains why so many Mahars and Mangs were employed building the railway line that passed through Nasik district.[30] It was a first step towards the rural depopulation that ultimately pushed so many Mahars to the docks of Bombay. But others took a more prestigious escape route. Indeed, of the seventeen Untouchable civil servants that Bhagat listed in 1935, fifteen were Mahars and only two Chambhars. This is indicative of the strong polarisation of Mahars, which comprised both an impoverished stratum and an élite more significant and influential than in other Untouchable castes.

This pattern was repeated in terms of education. According to the 1931 Census, fewer than 12 per cent of Mahars and Mangs of the Bombay Presidency were literate as against 16 per cent of Chambhars and 13 per cent of Dhors. But, in the six districts studied by Bhagat, Mahars accounted for 67 per cent of the Untouchables who knew English (51 out of 75) as against 16 per cent of Chambhars.[31] At Nasik this is explained by the number of Mahar railway employees, who could learn English and enrol their children in a railway school. At Ahmednagar, the education of Mahars—and Untouchables in general—owed more to the Christian missions schools. The government tried hard, from the late nineteenth century onwards, to establish separate schools for Untouchables to counter social discrimination. In the mean time, their situation improved in many places, mainly because of socio-economic change brought about by urbanisation and industrialisation. Of the 217 villages visited by Bhagat, 134 permitted Untouchable children to mingle with others, thirty-nine forbade it and forty-four had no primary schools.

Mahars who had advanced through education were keen to rid themselves of impurity by relinquishing the consumption of beef and other meat.[32] Beyond that, the increasing rejection of *baluta* and *vatan* systems reflected an increasingly acute political consciousness: Mahars looked at these systems as the underlying cause of their degraded status and tried hard to free themselves from them.[33] Bhagat also noticed stirrings of revolt among Mahars who refused to dispose of the carcasses of dead animals, but the upper castes retaliated by subjecting them to a social boycott.[34]

All in all, Bhagat's inquiry highlights strong socio-economic and educational disparities among the Untouchable castes of Maharashtra. These differences reinforced the divisions resulting from their variable status. Indeed, these castes reproduced a hierarchical logic based on status to the extent that 'a Mahar is unwilling to take milk from the Mang and the Chamar [Chambhar] never takes it from the

Bhangi.'[35] Bhagat narrates many incidents in Sholapur district that pitted Mangs against Mahars. For instance, the latter refused the former access to a well by invoking their 'caste inferiority'.[36] Ambedkar was to spend much time and energy thinking about this obsession with hierarchy, so as to challenge it more effectively.

The other major lesson of Bhagat's inquiry concerns the Mahars' polarisation. On the one hand theirs is the poorest Untouchable caste of Maharashtra; on the other it has—among Untouchables—the best educated élite and the most mobile population. This combination that explains its militancy. It was particularly underprivileged, but its leaders had a more finely tuned political consciousness than the average. We should be less surprised, therefore, that the first Untouchable leader of pan-Indian stature emerged from among the ranks of the Mahars.

The family environment: the army and Western education under princely patronage

Ambedkar benefited immeasurably from being born in the garrison town of Mhow (Military Headquarters of War), where his father—Ramji Sakpal—as his father before him, was in the pay of the army. Sakpal joined in 1866 and had been promoted to Subedar and later appointed headmaster of an army normal school. Ambedkar's mother came from a Mahar family with a spectacular military lineage: her father and her six uncles were subedar-majors.[37] Since education was compulsory for the children of the military, not only Ambedkar's father but also the women of his family were literate.

A friend and admirer of Jotirao Phule, Ramji Sakpal was a demanding individual. He took an active part, for instance, in the 1890s campaign on behalf of Mahars' in the army.[38] The British government had decided in 1892–3 no longer to employ Mahars largely because other less impure castes, in particular Marathas, were reluctant to mix with them in the barracks. Ambedkar's father thus belonged to the last generation of Mahars permanently employed by the British army.[39]

He was pious, reciting Hindu epics to his children and chanting songs of saints such as Tukaram every evening. He imbued his family with a spiritual message with a strong social content, not least because he was a devotee of Kabir, one of the *bhakti* saints who fiercely denounced caste hierarchy. Indeed, in the second half of the fifteenth century Kabir promoted egalitarianism, first because it was inherent in his calling as an ascetic, and second because he too had modest origins: he came from a caste of weavers.[40] But the decisive factor in the making of Ambedkar's career was education and the support he received in pursuing it from Maratha Maharajahs.

Ambedkar went to the cantonment primary school from the age of five and spent several years at high school in Satara. Later, his father having moved with the army to Bombay,[41] he enrolled, along with his brother, at Elphinstone High School and subsequently at Elphinstone College. He graduated with BA in English and in Persian but his caste barred him from studying Sanskrit, as he would have wished. He joined the army of the princely state of Baroda the following year, 1913, as a lieutenant, but a fortnight later his father died and he then decided to resume his studies with the financial support of the Maharajah of Baroda.

Krishna Arjun (*alias* Dada) Keluskar, one of the professors who was particularly struck by his abilities, sought the assistance of the Maharajah of Baroda to finance Ambedkar's studies at Elphinstone College. This scion of the Gaekwad dynasty, whose Maratha origins partly explain his benevolence *vis-à-vis* other non-Brahmins, had already established schools for Untouchables[42] and supported the studies of promising young low caste men,[43] a policy that produced a non-Brahmin intelligentsia for his state administration.[44] Keluskar presented Ambedkar to the Maharajah, who immediately granted him a scholarship of 50 rupees a month with the promise of more if he did well.[45] He also offered him a formal contract after graduation: he would pay for him to study in the United States (his own son had been to Harvard) provided he agreed to serve the princely state for ten years on his return. It was a unique opportunity that was presented to Ambedkar. It was due to his intelligence and capacity for hard work, but his good fortune owed much to the Maratha princely élite: non-Brahmin solidarity was to be a decisive factor in his career.

Ambedkar went to Columbia University in New York in 1913, obtaining a Master's in economics in 1915 for his thesis on trade in ancient India. In 1916 his first foray at analysing caste occurred when he presented a paper entitled *Castes in India, their Mechanism, Genesis and Development* to an anthropology seminar. In this piece of work, to which we shall return, Ambedkar for the first time applies concepts derived from Western social sciences to India. At Columbia he was especially influenced by two of his professors: John Dewey (the initiator of the pragmatic philosophy) and R. A. Seligman. He also drew inspiration from Booker T. Washington, the founder of the Tuskegee Institute, who promoted education as a means of African American emancipation. He therefore immersed himself in new categories of thought, above all, the egalitarian individualism of Thomas Paine, who had already influenced Phule.[46] Zelliot points out that Ambedkar acquired in the United States 'a strong, unwavering belief in the power of democratic institutions to bring about social equality'[47] and that these ideas were to a large extent passed on to him by Dewey.[48]

In 1916 Ambedkar left the United States for England to study at the LSE. However, the Maharajah of Baroda asked him to return to India in July 1917. Once again, the army was the channel of social mobility since Ambedkar joined the state administration as Military Secretary to the Maharajah.[49]

Even in Baroda Ambedkar could not find accommodation when using his real identity and had to pretend to be a Parsi to find a room in lodgings owned by someone from that community. Unfortunately he was found out and had to leave, an experience that had a decisive influence on him:

> Throughout the day I searched for a house to live in but miserably failed to get any place to hide my head. I approached my friends but all turned me down on some plea or the other, expressing their inability to accommodate me. I was utterly disappointed and exhausted. What to do next? I just could not decide. Frustrated and exhausted, I quietly sat down at one place, with tears flowing out of my eyes. Seeing no hope of getting a house, and no alternative but to quit, I tendered my resignation and left for Bombay by the night train.[50]

Thus did Ambedkar start out as a political fighter. He returned to England in October, 1920 to complete his studies—he finished his Master's degree in June, 1921—thanks to financial help from another Maratha notable, the Maharajah of Kolhapur.[51] The latter had been very anti-Brahmin in outlook since 1901, when the Brahmins of Kolhapur had refused to grant the Marathas Kshatriya status, thereby barring them from Vedic rites, even for family ceremonies.[52] From that point onwards, the Maharajah of Kolhapur, Shahu Maharaj, assumed the same paternalistic role towards Ambedkar as the Maharajah of Baroda had once done.[53] His benevolence found its most telling expression in the letter of recommendation which he drafted in his favour for the London School of Economics—which also reveals much about 'anti-Brahmin' solidarity:

> [Mr Ambedkar] will explain you the difference between the Backward Castes and the Brahmin bureaucracy. Also he will tell you what suffering one who tries to sympathise has to undergo at the hands of the bureaucrat Brahmins who claim to have democratic ideas, wish to raise the backward castes but who really crave nothing better than an oligarchy for themselves. He intends to lay before you, the enlightened public of England, the view point of non-Brahmin Hindus who are unanimous in the opinion that in asking for Home Rule, the real object of the Brahmins has been to regain and establish their long lost power.[54]

Ambedkar presented his thesis in economics at the LSE, entitled 'The Problem of the Rupee', in 1922. As he had not given it much attention, it was rejected, in March, 1923, but after making revisions he successfully defended it in November of the same year. In 1927, he was awarded a PhD by Columbia University for his thesis entitled "The Evolution of Provincial Finance in British India".[55] He thus became the first Untouchable to obtain a doctorate.

Ambedkar registered at the Bombay Bar in 1923 and began legal practice at the High Court the following year. His Untouchable status put off many potential clients and he was forced to supplement his income by teaching. While in Britain in 1918 he had taught political economy at Sydenham College of Commerce and Economics and in 1925 he was appointed as a part-time lecturer at Batliboi's Accountancy Training Institute. One consolation was that Ambedkar's legal training was to stand him in good stead when defending Untouchables in the courts, around the negotiating table or in the political arena.

Thus it was not by chance that Ambedkar became the first pan-Indian Untouchable leader. His personal qualities—his intelligence and his energy—played a key role, as did the familial, social and regional contexts which shaped his destiny, notably as the heir of the pioneering anti-Brahmin movement of Maharashtra and as the recipient of the support extended to him by Maratha Maharajahs. His socio-political awareness and militancy were directly attributable to the predicament of his caste and family. But the decisive factor in shaping his revolt against the caste system was his education overseas, which exposed him to egalitarian values and allowed him to interrogate the mechanisms of caste. On returning to India, he further refined his tools of sociological analysis the better to contest a social system of which Untouchables were the prime victims.

3. Analysing and Ethnicising Caste to Eradicate it more Effectively

'I thought for long that we could rid the Hindu society of its evils and get the Depressed Classes incorporated into it on terms of equality. That motive inspired the Mahad Chaudar Tank Satyagraha and the Nasik Temple Entry Satyagraha. With that object in mind we burned the Manu Smriti and performed mass thread ceremonies. Experience has taught me better. I stand today absolutely convinced that for the Depressed Classes there can be no equality among the Hindus because on inequality rest the foundations of Hinduism. We no longer want to be part of the Hindu society.' (speech by Ambedkar reported in *The Bombay Sentinel*, April 28, 1942 [*Source Material on Dr Babasaheb Ambedkar and the Movement of Untouchables*, vol. 1, Bombay, Government of Maharashtra, 1982, p. 250])

Ambedkar was a scholar as much as a man of action and he analysed Hindu society *before* embarking on his struggle against the caste system. His intellectual training, which reflected an intense personal thirst for knowledge that stayed with him throughout his life, naturally predisposed him for such a role. From his travels he brought back hundreds of books which he drew on as sources for the innumerable quotations which punctuate his writings. A prolific author, he always had several manuscripts in various stages of preparation, not to mention the hundreds of newspaper articles he penned.

Ambedkar began investigating the origins of the caste system more than a decade before Govind Sadashiv Ghurye—the first Indian anthropologist to do so, whose *Caste and Race in India* was published in 1932. Yet his contribution to Indian sociology was overlooked for many years, as Olivier Herrenschmidt emphasises as a prelude to his own efforts to redress this inbalance.[1] The founding fathers of Indian anthropology, such as M. N. Srinivas and Louis Dumont, and most of their heirs, have ignored Ambedkar, even though he anticipated many of their arguments.[2] This is all the more surprising given that with the exception of a few texts which remained unavailable till the Government of Maharashtra reprinted them in the late 1980s and early '90s as part of the publication of Ambedkar's complete works to celebrate his centenary,[3] most of his writings were published and republished in his lifetime, beginning with his first article *Castes in India, Their Mechanism, Genesis and Development* (1917) to the final one, *The Buddha and his Dhamma* (1957), which appeared posthumously, passing via undoubtedly the best known of all, but very rarely quoted, *Annihilation of Caste* (1936).

In these and other writings Ambedkar strove hard to demonstrate the mechanisms of the caste system and to identify the origins of Untouchability in order to advance his fight for equality.

Ambedkar the sociologist. At the age of twenty-five Ambedkar's career as a sociologist of caste began when he attended A. A. Goldenweiser's seminar at Columbia. In May 1916 he gave a lecture that was published the following year in *Indian Antiquary* as 'Castes in India: Their Mechanism, Genesis and Development', in which he claimed 'to advance a theory of caste'.[4] He was still searching for an overarching explanatory model, but his insights, although occasionally rudimentary, were perceptive, owing much to intuition. Ambedkar thus confronted head on Western authors whose explanation of caste rested on theories of racial difference, namely that an Aryan 'invasion' had subjugated the Dravidians, thus relegating them to the ranks of the lower castes. For Ambedkar, such Western writers opted for race as the root cause of the 'problem of caste' because they were 'themselves impregnated by colour prejudices.'[5] But they could not have been more wrong, he argued, for caste is a social phenomenon, not a racial one.

Endogamy was the main springboard of caste, and the caste system, according to Ambedkar, crystallised after the Brahmins turned inwards, henceforth refusing all matrimonial unions save those among their own community. This is why Ambedkar defined caste as a 'closed class'.[6] He extrapolated from this phenomenon that *sati* and bans on widow remarriage were both mechanisms designed 'to mop up' surplus women—who otherwise would have had to marry outside their caste—as was the marriage of pre-pubescent girls, since it allowed widowers to find a wife from among their own caste.

Such rather implausible reasoning went hand in hand with flashes of real genius. He argued, for instance, that the caste system was not imposed on society by Brahmins; instead it evolved because Brahmins were *imitated* by other social groups which, for example, also opted for endogamy. Here Ambedkar draw his inspiration from Gabriel Tarde who characterised social imitation by two principles: it is the subordinate who imitates the superior, never the opposite; and the greater the social distance between the two groups, the more intense the effort at imitation. For Ambedkar, notions of caste spread through society via these two precepts, which were all the more powerful as Brahmins enjoyed an almost sacred position. This emulation process also explains why other castes began to practise *sati*, child marriage or bans on widow-remarriage. In so doing, Ambedkar advanced the basis of one of the most heuristic of concepts in modern Indian studies—the 'Sanskritisation' process—that M. N. Srinivas was to introduce forty years later.[7] While the term was coined by Srinivas, the process itself had been described by colonial administrators such as E. T. Atkinson in his *Himalayan Gazetteer* and Alfred Lyall, in whose works Ambedkar might well have encountered it.[8]

Beyond this, Ambedkar blamed other Western authors—from Emile Senart to H. H. Risley and including J. C. Nesfield and Denzil Ibbetson—for having defined 'caste as a unit by itself and not as one within a System of Castes'.[9] Castes form a system, and that is why, in Ambedkar's theory, Brahmins are the object of imitation by other groups. He emphasised that India's remarkable homogeneity ('there is no country that can rival the Indian Peninsula with respect to the unity of its culture'[10]) derives from the caste system because Brahmins are present throughout the subcontinent. As mentioned above, Ambedkar recognised that Brahmins could not have *imposed* the caste system;[11] instead he contended that this type of social organisation came about by virtue of a belief in the superiority of the Brahmin and of the acquiescence by other castes of their inferiority.[12] This analysis anticipated not only that of Srinivas but also Louis Dumont's interpretation of the 'holistic' character of the caste system: castes do not exist independently of each other but form a system. The acid test, here, lies in the lower castes' internalisation of hierarchy, which is borne out by the fact that the Brahminical value system was universally recognised as superior. The concept of Sanskritisation partly proceeds from this idea.[13] Dumont perceived this arrangement in an almost organicist perspective, as exemplified by the following metaphor: 'The caste isolates itself by submission to the whole, just as an arm which would prefer not to marry its cells to those of the stomach'.[14] In his view the caste system is virtually harmonious, with its constituent parts fulfilling complementary functions. Dumont does not ignore hierarchy but apparently absolves it from the function of domination, even social oppression, that Ambedkar regarded with such a deep sense of revolt.

In the mature writings, and in particular in *Who were the Shudras?* (1947), Ambedkar conducted a detailed re-examination of the foundational beliefs of the caste system. He applied his mind systematically and logically to the Vedic texts, and in particular to the *Rig Veda*, where he finds a myth of origin explaining the genesis of caste, the *Purusha Shukta*. This myth presents the birth of human society as proceeding from the sacrificial dismemberment of the primordial man, the Virat Purusha. The key strophe of the *Purusha Shukta* says: 'His mouth became the Brahmin/the Warrior [Kshatriya] was the product of his arms/His thighs were the Artisan [Vaishya]/From his feet were born the Servant [Shudras]'[15].

Ambedkar emphasises that, in contrast with the Old Testament notion of 'Genesis', this cosmology puts not man but the group at the origin of society: 'It preaches a class-composed society as its ideal.'[16] Above all, he regards *varnas* as complementary and therefore a means of helping society to 'function'. Such a view of society as essentially conflict-free was naturally of Brahminical origin: the authors of this cosmogony, as of all Sanskrit literature codifying social relations, were Brahmins. The *varna* system owes to them its religious sanctions. And Ambedkar rebelled against this scheme which 'not only regards class composition as natural and ideal, but also regards it as sacred and divine.'[17] He also denounced the organicist logic which underlies the *Purusha Shukta*:

> The equation of the different classes to different parts of the body is not a matter of accident. It is deliberate. The idea behind this plan seems to be to discover a formula which will solve two problems, one of fixing the functions of the four classes and the other of fixing the gradation of the four classes after a preconceived plan. The formula of equating different classes to the different parts of the body of the Creator has this advantage. The part

fixes the gradation of the class and the gradation in its turn fixes the function of the class. The Brahmin is equated to the mouth of the Creator. Mouth being the noblest part of the anatomy, the Brahmin becomes the noblest of the four classes. As he is the noblest of the scale, he is given the noblest function, that of custodian of knowledge and learning. The Kshatriya is equated to the arms of the Creator. Among the limbs of a person, arms are next below the mouth. Consequently, the Kshatriya is given an order of precedence next below the Brahmins and is given a function which is second only to knowledge, namely, fighting. The Vaishya is equated to the thighs of the Creator. In the gradation of limbs, the thighs are next below the arms. Consequently, the Vaishya is given an order of precedence next below the Kshatriya and is assigned a function of industry and trade which in name and fame ranks or rather did rank in ancient times below that of a warrior. The Shudra is equated to the feet of the Creator. The feet form the lowest and the most ignoble part of the human frame. Accordingly, the Shudra is placed last in the social order and is given the filthiest function, namely to serve as a menial.[18]

For Ambedkar the *Purusha Shukta* establishes a completely unique social system because 'no society has an official gradation laid down, fixed and permanent, with an ascending scale of reverence and a descending scale of contempt'.[19] The specificity of the system is indeed held together by this 'graded inequality' to which Ambedkar was to return many times in his writings and speeches, as emphasised by Olivier Herrenschmidt. In his last book he mentions 'an ascending scale of hatred and a downward scale of contempt [which] indeed could well be a perpetual source of conflict.'[20] The replacement of the words 'reverence/contempt' by 'hatred/contempt' reveals a shift: one element of the holistic logic of the system—respect for superiors—is downplayed in favour of a more spontaneous feeling in the heart of Ambedkar: hatred of the oppressor.

The notion of 'graded inequality' was indeed Ambedkar's main sociological finding.[21] The President of the Indian Republic in 1997–2002, K. R. Narayanan, a Dalit member of the Congress party who has nonetheless read Ambedkar, implicitly acknowledged this fact when he recalled Ambedkar's adage regarding the caste system: 'A progressive order of reverence and a graded order of contempt.'[22] For Ambedkar, this order possesses a strong resilience to social change: if the lower castes are not in a position to overthrow their oppressors, it is not only because they have partially internalised hierarchy but also because of the very characteristics of 'graded inequality'.

'Graded inequality', the key element of the caste system. Ambedkar was an ardent activist of social equality of which he learnt the philosophical roots in the West where he appreciated its benefits in practical terms. For him, all the values of the Republic and the French Revolution ensue from it:

Fraternity and liberty are really derivative notions. The basic and fundamental conceptions are equality and respect for human personality. Fraternity and liberty take their roots in these two fundamental conceptions. Digging further down, it may be said that equality is the original notion and respect for human personality is a reflection of it. So that where equality is denied, everything else may be taken to be denied.[23]

His defence of French or American egalitarianism naturally goes hand in hand with an ardent individualism—which can be seen in his own personal itinerary. But it was also reflected in his criticism of a social institution—the caste system—which denies any individual identity to a human being, while considering only his birth group. However, Ambedkar does not content himself with contrasting individualistic societies with so called holistic societies and equality with inequality. He distinguishes traditional inequality from graded inequality which, according to him, is at least twice as dangerous.[24] The notion of inequality includes a social condition where influential groups confront each other; in industrial societies the working class can struggle against the bourgeoisie. In the *ancien régime*, the Third Estate was able to raise itself against the aristocracy and the King. Ambedkar explains that the type of inequality from which caste-ridden society suffers is of a different kind altogether because its logic also divides the dominated groups, preventing them from uniting to overthrow the oppressor:

In a system of graded inequality, the aggrieved parties are not on a common level. This can happen only when they are only high and low. In a system of graded inequality there are the highest (the Brahmins). Below the highest are the higher (the Kshatriyas). Below the higher are those who are high ([the] Vaishya[s]). Below the high are the low ([the] Shudra [s]) and below the low are those who are lower (the Untouchables). All have a grievance against the highest and would like to bring about their downfall. But they will not combine. The higher is anxious to get rid of the highest but does not wish to combine with the high, the low and the lower lest they should reach his level and be his equal. The high wants to over-throw the higher

> that is above him but does not want to join hands with the low and the lower, lest they should rise to his status and become equal to him in rank. The low is anxious to pull down the highest, the higher and the high but he would not make a common cause with the lower for fear of the lower gaining a higher status and becoming his equal. In the system of graded inequality there is no such class as completely unprivileged class except the one which is at the base of the social pyramid. The privileges of the rest are graded. Even the low is a privileged class as compared with the lower. Each class being privileged, every class is interested in maintaining the system.[25]

Ambedkar exposes here one of the most powerful mechanisms of the caste system but he does not take his argument to its logical conclusion because he considers only the *varnas*, as if they constituted social entities. If this were the case, the highest castes would have been easily marginalised by the Shudras who represent more than half of the Hindu population, as the British census showed. In fact the mechanisms which he describes here are reproduced at the level of *jatis* because every *varna* gets subdivided into multiple *jatis* whose hierarchy also rests on a gradation of status. A strictly vegetarian Brahmin caste could thereby rise above those who consume eggs or fish. This differentiation process may even operate *within jatis*. For instance a section of the barbers' caste whose wives renounced midwifery—a renowned polluting practice—would rise above those who continue to practise this vocation, thereby gradually creating a new endogamous caste according to the schismatic principle.[26] Indian society here manifests, according to Herrenschmidt, an 'obsession [with] small differences',[27] especially at the lowest levels of the social scale, where each individual feels the need, more than elsewhere, for someone lower in status than himself.

Ambedkar was the first to underline this reality and to deplore the divisions among the Untouchables who were, in his opinion, 'a disunited body […] infested with the caste system in which they believe as much as does the high caste Hindu. This caste system among the Untouchables has given rise to mutual rivalry and to jealousy and it has made common action impossible.'[28]

Giving evidence to the Simon Commission on October 23, 1928, he stated with some bitterness that 'the caste Hindus have spread their poison to the rest'.[29] He was especially disturbed by the fact that in Maharashtra Mahars and Mangs did not marry among themselves. Moreover, he failed to project himself as the representative of non-Mahar Dalits: neither Mangs nor Chambhars were to join his political party in large numbers, hence confirming Ambedkar's view of the caste system: that it incorporated and institutionalised its own mechanisms of self-preservation.

To sum up, Ambedkar advanced a theory of caste which anticipated many dimensions of current anthropology. Castes exist only by forming a system; Brahmin values over-determine what is right for the lower castes, and the overpowering proof of this 'holism' lies in the Sanskritisation process; and last but not least, the hierarchy of caste reflects a very specific logic of graded inequality which prevents those most discriminated against from forming social coalitions against elite groups. For Herrenschmidt, it was the main reason why 'this society was incapable not only of revolution but more simply of reform'.[30] Yet through his analysis of the origins and mechanisms of caste, Ambedkar wished above all to facilitate this revolution by endowing the lowest castes with a distinct and prestigious identity.

Inventing a golden age for the lower castes: the prestige of autochthony

It was not merely intellectual curiosity that led Ambedkar closely to analyse the mechanisms of the caste system: above all he wanted to understand it better to fight the oppression of millions of Shudras and Untouchables. His analysis was but the first stage of an ideological counter-offensive in which he sought to endow Untouchables with a glorious past and a prestigious identity through which they could regain their self-respect and overcome their divisions.

Shudras, heirs of the Kshatriyas or the deep roots of Sanskritisation. Ambedkar tried first to establish a Shudra genealogy, of which the most celebrated conclusions were published in 1947 in *Who were the Shudras?* In his familiar style he began by attacking western theories of an Aryan invasion,[31] maintaining, on the basis of English translations of the *Dharma Shastras*, that the Shudras were Aryans and therefore belonged to the three superior *varnas*. He finds some proof of this in a detailed analysis of the Laws of Manu by the Sanskritist Dr George Buhler, according to whom—in the Vedic era—a Shudra could become a Brahmin in the seventh generation if his ancestors had married only Brahmins.[32] Moreover these Shudras also participated in the coronation ceremonies of kings[33] and according to ancient texts were often wealthy in their own right.[34]

It then remained to be determined to which superior *varna* Shudras could have belonged. Ambedkar claims that they were Kshatriyas, and constituted a key sub-set of this *varna*, from which some of the most eminent and powerful kings of antiquity had supposedly emerged.[35] They allegedly belonged to the solar lineage (*suryavansh*).

Ambedkar based his theory on the hypothesis that there were, from the outset, only three *varnas* and consequently Shudras appeared on the scene only much later. He argued that this *varna* emerged after some Kshatriyas had been demoted to this rank by Brahmins, who simply achieved their objective by refusing them *Upanayana*, a rite marked by the bestowing of the sacred thread to the sons of the three superior *varnas* which consecrated their passage to the order of the 'twice born'.[36] Their aim was to take revenge for the violence and humiliation imposed upon them by some other Kshatriyas.

Obviously Ambedkar had in mind the Brahmins' refusal to recognise Shivaji as a Kshatriya.[37] His theory, which is based on scant historical evidence, doubtless echoed this episode in Maharashtra's history, whereas in fact Shivaji, a Maratha-Kunbi, was a Shudra. Nevertheless, he had won power and so expected the Brahmins to confirm his new status by writing for him an adequate genealogy. This process recalls that of Sanskritisation, but sociologists refer to such emulation of Kshatriyas by Shudras as 'Kshatriyaisation' and describe it as a variant of Sanskritisation. Unfortunately, it did not allow the Shudras to emancipate themselves from the caste system and its hierarchical structure. Hence although he tried to endow Shudras with a prestigious history, Ambedkar here implies that they should regard themselves as constituents of a hierarchical society and hence imitate their superiors in order to regain their lost status. They could not, in such circumstances, claim a separate identity in order to facilitate their revolt against the caste system. Interestingly, he was to choose a very different approach in his study of the Untouchables' identity and history.

The Untouchables as persecuted Buddhists. After the appearance of his book on the Shudras, the next year, 1948, Ambedkar published another one entitled *The Untouchables: Who were they and why they became Untouchables?* Once again he began by refuting the Western thesis linking caste to race;[38] he also rejected explanations based on professional specialisation because 'the filthy and unclean occupations which the Untouchables perform are common to all human societies [...]. Why were not such people not treated as Untouchables in other parts of the world?'.[39] Ambedkar's hypothesis is remarkably complex. He explains that all primitive societies have been conquered at one time or another by invaders who set themselves above the autochthonous peoples. In the process of social fragmentation that followed, peripheral groups, or what he calls 'Broken Men', split off from the centre: 'In a tribal war it often happened that a tribe, instead of being completely annihilated, was defeated and routed. In many cases, a defeated tribe became broken into bits. As a consequence of this, there always existed in Primitive times a floating population consisting of groups of Broken tribesmen roaming in all directions.'[40]

When the conquerors became sedentary, they turned to these 'Broken Men' to protect them from the attacks of nomadic tribes. Ambedkar applied this theory by portraying Untouchables as the descendants of the Broken Men (or *Dalit*, in Marathi), and thus as the original, pre-Aryan, inhabitants of India. He clearly drew his inspiration from the Orientalist vulgate as propagated by the British, according to whom Mahars were autochthons *par excellence*, whose caste name found its way into that of the province of Maharashtra.[41] The notion that Untouchables were the primordial inhabitants of India had already been propagated by Gopalnak Vitthalnak Walangkar, a former soldier influenced by Phule who in 1886 had founded the first Mahar association,[42] the principal aim of which was to widen recruitment of his caste into the British army (see below).

According to Ambedkar, whose first wife was related to Walangkar, these Broken Men were the most steadfast followers of the Buddha after he began preaching in the sixth century BC. And they remained Buddhists when the rest of society returned to the Hindu fold under Brahmin pressure. Ambedkar drew two conclusions from it:

> It explains why the Untouchables regard the Brahmins as inauspicious, do not employ them as their priests and do not even allow them to enter into their quarters. It also explains why the Broken Men came to be regarded as Untouchables. The Broken Men hated the Brahmins because the Brahmins

were the enemies of Buddhism and the Brahmins imposed untouchability upon the Broken Men because they would not leave Buddhism.[43]

For Ambedkar the association of Broken Men with Buddhism did not suffice as an explanation of why Brahmins had relegated the Untouchables. The supplementary reason that he put forward was related to their eating habits: the Broken Men refused to become vegetarian and continued to eat beef whereas 'Brahmins made the cow a sacred animal'.[44]

Ambedkar's interpretation regarding the origins of Untouchability differed from that which he advanced about Shudras. The latter had been described as erstwhile Kshatriyas and were bound to recover their past status within the framework of the *varna* system. The logic of Sanskritisation thus continued to prevail. In contrast, Untouchables were presented as descendants of Buddhists who regarded themselves as endowed with a separate identity, external to the caste system and hostile to its logic because of the egalitarian nature of Buddhism. The suggestion that Untouchables were once Buddhists offered the former tremendous scope for social mobilisation. It bestowed on them an appropriate, egalitarian ethnic identity which could enable them to transcend their divisions into sub-castes, as much as in terms of geographical fragmentation given that Dalits are found throughout India and belong to different regional traditions and cultures.

Thus Ambedkar did not content himself with elaborating a theory of caste which culminated in the idea of graded inequality; he also devised an Untouchable 'tradition' that was to prove helpful in remedying social disparity. If they recognised themselves as former Buddhists, Untouchables would be better positioned to surmount their divisions and stand together as an ethnic group *against* the system as a whole. Gail Omvedt rightly points out that in this respect Ambedkar's views converged with those of Phule and Periyar. Their thought 'represents the effort to construct an alternative identity of the people, based on non-north Indian and low caste perspectives, critical not only of the oppressiveness of the dominant Hindu caste society but also of its claims to antiquity and to being the major Indian tradition.'[45] The notion of autochthony played a key role in Ambedkar's theory. He argued that if Hindu India had been invaded by Muslims, Buddhist India had been subjugated by Brahmin outsiders much before that. Omvedt considers that there was 'a racial ethnic element in all of this, in which Ambedkar identifies his heroes to some extent with non-Aryans...'[46]

Even before Ambedkar tried to endow the Untouchables with a noble and separate identity as is evident in *The Untouchables*, politically speaking he began to contest Sanskritisation by other means as early as in the 1920s.

How to resist Sanskritisation?

When Ambedkar asserted himself in the public arena of the Bombay Presidency, the anti-Brahmin movement was dominated by the Satyashodak Samaj. At that time Untouchable organisations still complied with the logic of Sanskritisation. The oldest of these, the Anarya Dosh Pariharak Mandal (Association for Eliminating the Stigma of Untouchability), had been founded in 1886 by G. V. Walangkar who[47] two years later also established the first Untouchable newspaper in India, *Vitalwidhwansak*, 'the destroyer of [ritual] pollution)'. Walangkar wanted to destroy the caste system, but at the same time he claimed that Mahars were formerly Kshatriyas—like Phule,[48] a stand that reflected the resilience of Sanskritisation among the low caste ideologues of the period. Walangkar also sought to challenge Brahminism by emphasising the vitality of Maharashtra's *bhakti* tradition—what Philip Constable calls '*bhakti* egalitaranism'. Walangkar wished to endow Mahars and Chambhars—given the fact that he had followers from both *jatis*—with an 'individualised *bhakti* culture'.[49] Such an attempt at emancipating the Untouchables by resorting to sectarian solutions was self-defeating because Walangkar was hardly offering an alternative to Hindu culture—he simply operated within it. But the Arya Dosh Pariharak Mandal was certainly the first attempt at giving Mahars a separate identity, a move which paved the way for 'Ambedkarism'.

However, the appeal of Walangkar's movement remained limited compared to the Untouchable associations imbued with an even stronger ethos of Sanskritisation. The Mahar Sabha was one of these. Founded in Nagpur in 1906 it promoted education and tried to purify the Mahars' social practices in conformity with the principles of Sanskritisation.[50] Kisan Fagoji Bansode (1879–1946), another Mahar leader, adopted this approach but did not focus only on his caste. He was inspired by the values of the *bhakti* cult (as shown by his particular interest in the poet Chokhamela)[51] and remained faithful to the values of Hinduism. Bansode even adhered in 1910 to the Prarthana Samaj. He called upon Mahars to abjure meat and alcohol and to educate themselves in order to obtain more government posts.[52] His main partner, a Mahar from Amraoti, Ganesh Akkaji Gavai (1888–1974), who was also a member of the Prarthana Samaj,[53] was to become Ambedkar's main rival in the region. Bansode and Gavai organised in 1903 a meeting against Untouchability where Mahars, Mangs and Chambhars were encouraged to resist conversion to Christianity, to refrain from eating meat or drinking alcohol and to educate themselves. In 1919 their movement, the Antyaja Samaj (Society of the Last Born—the Untouchables), recommended in a similar vein:

> We should not eat meat, drink, or sell cows to butchers. We should not read books of other religions. We should appoint a Hindu teacher and educate our children. We should not raise pigs—caste Hindus hold us untouchable because of this. Our women should not go to *tamashas* [public rejoicing which might involve dances or trances free from the usual social conventions]. We should take part in religious observances.[54]

J. Gokhale has argued that we cannot analyse the action of Bansode or Gavai through the concept of Sanskritisation 'because there is little suggestion that Untouchables aspire to a higher ritual status. Rather, it is more within the tradition of Hindu reformers, who urged that caste cease to have any relevance for social relationships in Hindu society, but denied that caste was an integral part of Hinduism. Bansode, for example, retained close ties to caste-Hindus through the Prarthana Samaj, and throughout his life insisted that the destiny of the Untouchables was inextricably linked to that of Hinduism and Hindu society as a whole.'[55]

To my mind, however, to link in this way the fate of the Untouchables to that of Hinduism and Hindu society reflects Bansode's failure to think of Untouchables as a discrete group and to endow them with a new identity, because of his faith in Sanskritisation. He thought they should be kept in their place as a committed part of a social system ruled by upper caste values. By emphasising the need for Untouchables to cleanse themselves according to the criteria of the high castes, Bansode and Gavai in fact support Sanskritisation;

they adhered to Brahminical precepts rather than trying to emancipate themselves from its value system.[56]

Politically, Bansode and Gavai supported B. G. Tilak, the Congress leader from Poona who tended not to put into practice the social reforms he articulated.[57] However, they also joined hands with higher caste Hindus who advocated social reform, such as Vitthal Ramji Shinde and Narayanrao Chandavarkar. The first was a Maratha—who also belonged to the Prarthana Samaj and the Congress[58]—and the second, a Brahmin. In 1906 they founded the Depressed Classes' Mission whose programmes—including the building of schools and the promotion of inter-caste dining—recalled the paternalism of certain high caste reformers.[59]

As an historian, Shinde reflected at length upon the origins of Untouchability; he was one of the first non-Brahmin ideologues to argue that Untouchables had formerly been Buddhists reigning over Maharashtra before their subjugation by upper caste invaders.[60] At one time Ambedkar was inspired by him but he soon distanced himself from Shinde and rejected upper caste reformism.[61]

Bansode and Gavai differed from Ambedkar not only on account of their links with reformers like Shinde, but also because they tended to focus only on Mahars. Certainly they established the Depressed Classes' Association in 1915 (while maintaining links with Shinde), and then, in 1920, the Akhil Bharatiya Bahishkrit Parishad (All India Conference for the Victims of Social Ostracism) but in 1924 they organised a Mahar Conference which showed that they continued to pay more attention to this caste.[62]

Ambedkar took part in the Akhil Bharatiya Bahishkrit Parishad and used it vehemently to criticise Shinde's initiatives.[63] As underlined by Gail Omvedt, Bansode and Gavai represented a 'generation of leaders' strongly in favor of 'a model of Hinduistic *integration* which included Sanskritic reforms and an appeal to *bhakti* religious roots, and linked itself to support from nationalists and Hindu reformers, even conservatives [which is not a contradiction in terms, as we have seen above].' On the other hand, Ambedkar asserted 'dalit *autonomy*, with an ideology that expressed contradiction and rejected Brahmanic and *bhakti* religious traditions'[64].

On the whole, Omvedt's analysis is a convincing one but it ignores the early phase of Ambedkar's public career, at which point he appeared in many respects as an heir to movements inspired by the *bhakti*; more importantly, he subscribed openly for some time to certain aspects of Sanskritisation. It was during the 1920s that he evolved towards a radical rejection of the Hindu socio-religious system.

Ambedkar, from Sanskritisation to the rejection of the system. In 1924, soon after he returned from England for good, Ambedkar founded the Bahishkrit Hitakarini Sabha (Association for the Improvement of the Condition of the Victims of Social Ostracism),[65] also known as the 'Depressed Classes Institute'. Among its objectives was the legal abolition of the *baluta* system;[66] it also sought to help Mahars assert their rights as *vatandars*[67]. *Bahishkrit Bharat*, the newspaper founded by Ambedkar in 1927 to replace *Mook Nayak*, also later campaigned for the abolition of the *vatan*. D. D. Gholap, the first Untouchable to have been appointed, in 1920, to the Legislative Council of the Bombay Presidency had introduced a bill for this purpose a few years earlier.[68]

In spite of its interest in *vatan*—which concerned primarily Mahars—and although the latter were over-represented in its ranks,[69] the Bahishkrit Hitakarini Sabha was not a caste association but, as the name implies, a body established to serve all Untouchables (Chambhars and Dhors were also represented in it).[70] Its motto was 'Educate, Mobilise, Organise'. The order of priorities here was not unimportant because it was revealing of an aspiration towards social reform via education. The education available to Untouchables remained of very poor quality, notwithstanding the efforts of Phule and the specialised schools established by the British, and this had prompted reformers to direct their efforts towards educating Untouchables. This was how Shinde had developed a network of schools in Bombay reserved for Untouchables which by 1916 accounted for 500 pupils.[71] Ambedkar shared his concerns about the lack of education of his caste brethren, and hence the Constitution of the Bahishkrit Hitakarini Sabha explicitly subordinated social reform to education, as testified by its formal objectives:

(1) to promote the spread of education among the Depressed Classes by opening hostels or by employing such other means as may seem necessary or desirable;
(2) to promote the spread of culture among the Depressed Classes by opening libraries, social centers and classes or study circles;

(3) to advance and to improve the economic condition of the Depressed Classes by starting Industrial and Agricultural Schools;
(4) to represent the grievances of the Depressed Classes.[72]

In addition to the quest for better education, the values of Sanskritisation remained deep-rooted in Ambedkar's psyche at that time. Moreover the cultural values that the association promoted were those of the upper castes. The Mahar Hockey Club, which was founded by the Depressed Classes' Institute, offered a telling illustration of this state of things, given that it was intended to divert the Untouchables from 'gambling, drinking and other vices, and unhealthy ways of recreations.'[73] It was as if the road to equality first passed via an attempt to persuade Untouchables to conform to Brahminical virtues of abstinence. The constitution of the Depressed Classes' Institute also opined that 'without the cooperation and sympathy of [the upper classes], it would not be possible for the Depressed Classes to work out their salvation.'[74] The organisation therefore focussed on two key demands to help integrate Untouchables into the Hindu world: entry into temples and access to wells, from which they were often excluded.[75]

The second issue was at the centre of the famous 1927 Mahad Conference, which was organised after the passing of the Bole Resolution in the Legislative Council of Bombay on August 4, 1923.[76] Introduced by S. K. Bole, a social reformer turned politician, it stipulated that Untouchables were authorised to use wells, *dharmashalas* (pilgrims' lodgings), schools, courts, administrative offices and public dispensaries.[77]

No tangible benefits followed in the wake of the resolution, so three years later, in August 1926, Bole proposed a new resolution, asking the government to withhold subsidies from municipalities and other local bodies which had refused to apply these measures. Many town councils then fell into line but their orders were rarely carried out in practice because of upper caste hostility. A notable case in point was the small Maharashtrian town of Mahad, in Kolaba district (today a part of Poona district), where Untouchables were denied access to certain wells.

A conference was held there in March 1927, organised by Ambedkar, and supported by non-Dalit leaders such as S. Tipnis, a Kayasth, and K. M. Jedhe, a Maratha then at the helm of the non-Brahmin movement in Poona and for whom Ambedkar had acted in a recent lawsuit. The keynote address which Ambedkar delivered at Mahad was in step with the principles of Sanskritisation:

'No lasting progress can be achieved unless we put ourselves through a three-fold process of purification. We must improve the general tone of our demeanour, re-tone our pronunciations and revitalise our thoughts. I, therefore, ask you now to take a vow from this moment to renounce eating carrion.'[78]

Soon afterwards Ambedkar led a procession, starting from the dais where he had spoken, to a water source—the Chowdar Tank—which, in theory, was open to Untouchables but to which access had been denied. In a symbolic and solemn manner, he drank some water from the tank—a gesture akin to that of Gandhi when he collected salt after the Dandi march.[79] This transgression was perceived as a provocation by local upper caste Hindus who attacked the demonstrators when they returned to the meeting place.

In the days and weeks that followed, Mahad's upper castes ostracised the Untouchables, sometimes even revoking their employment and tenancy rights. Above all, on August 4, 1927, the Mahad municipality revoked its 1924 decision granting Untouchables access to the Chowdar Tank. Ambedkar then organised a second meeting which marked the crystallisation of a new discourse. This second Mahad conference took place in December 1927. Ambedkar's speech called for a root and branch abolition of the caste system. The values he invoked were those of the French Revolution, and he even compared the Mahad conference to the *Etats Généraux de Versailles*, where, for the first time, the Third Estate had expressed its revolt in a collective and formal fashion.

'At the outset, let me tell those who oppose us that we did not perish because we would not drink water from this Chowdar Tank. We now want to go to the Tank only to prove that, like others, we are also human beings [...]. This Conference has been called to inaugurate an era of equality in this land. Removal of untouchability and inter-castes dinners alone will not put an end to our ills. All departments of services such as courts, military, police and commerce should be thrown open to us [...]. Hindu society should be reorganised on two main principles—equality and absence of casteism.'[80]

This speech was followed by a show of hands vote in favour of the statement of human rights and a resolution on the inalienable equality of men. Two other resolutions asked, first, for the eradication of internal divisions within Hindu society so that eventually it would consist of only one category of people, and, second, for the priestly profession to be opened to all. Finally, several speakers attacked the Laws of Manu, a copy of which was placed on a stake set up for the occasion in front of the stand, and solemnly burnt by a Dalit ascetic.

The next day, Ambedkar launched a *satyagraha*[81] to obtain free access to the Chowdar Tank and some 4,000 people volunteered to take part in it. The District Magistrate urged them to maintain the peace, arguing that the case had been taken to court by upper caste Hindus claiming that it was a matter of private property and that it was therefore advisable to wait for the judgement.

Ambedkar hence postponed the *satyagraha* and instead organised a procession around the water source. This approach reflected a tactic he was to follow in similar circumstances in the future: his inclination to leave matters to the courts generally overrode his determination to settle disputes in the streets. This stance reflected Ambedkar's legalism, even his constitutionalism, and in this particular case the courts would uphold his stand in a judgement given in 1937.

How to break with Hinduism? By the late 1920s, Ambedkar had firmly emancipated himself from the logic of Sanskritisation and embraced a complete rejection of the caste system. He went even further and also rejected the path offered by the *bhakti* tradition. *Mook Nayak*, the newspaper he launched in 1920, had in its masthead verses from the poet Tukaram about the contempt in which the 'simple' people, those without a voice, had been held. But Ambedkar acted fast against what he regarded as the debilitating impact of worshipping saints on his followers. During major festivals he went to places of pilgrimage and met Untouchables in order to persuade them from cooperating with Hindus. He even opposed his wife's wish to go to Pandharpur to pay homage to Chokhoba (another Dalit saint) at the Vithoba temple, since she would be refused access to the temple itself. He told her: 'We have to create another Pandharpur by a virtuous life, a selfless service and a sacrifice without any stains for the cause of the oppressed.'[82]

Gradually, Ambedkar increased his attacks on Untouchables who continued to go on pilgrimages. During the big festival of Khandoba he declared:

'How many generations of ours have worn themselves out by rubbing their foreheads on the steps of the god? But when did the god take pity on you? What big thing has he done for you? Generation after generation, you have been used to clean the village of its garbage and god gave you the dead animals to eat. In spite of all that, god did not show you any pity. It is not this god that you worship, it is your ignorance.'[83]

Thus Ambedkar consummated his break with Hinduism by rejecting all types of religious practice. Invited in January 1928 to chair a meeting of the Depressed Classes at Trymbak, near Nasik, where the construction of a temple dedicated to Chokhamela, the great fifteenth-century Dalit saint, was to be discussed, Ambedkar vigorously opposed the project. In his opinion, the saints and their spiritual legacy could promote equality between a Brahmin and a Shudra only from the viewpoint of their spiritual practice, but not between a Brahmin and a Shudra *per se*:

'…from the viewpoint of the annihilation of caste, […] the struggle of the saints did not have any effect on society. The value of man is axiomatic, self evident; it does not come to him as a result of the gliding of Bhakti. The saints did not struggle to establish this point. On the contrary, their struggle had a very unhealthy effect on the Depressed Classes. It provided the Brahmins with an excuse to silence them by telling that they would be respected if they also attained the status of Chokhamela.'[84]

Ambedkar thus outflanked the diversionary tactics on the path to equality as advocated by men of religion: he rejected an equality limited to the spiritual sphere; what he demanded was social equality. He followed the same logic regarding the problem of entry to temples.

In the first editorial of *Mook Nayak*, Ambedkar wavered between two possibilities. He wondered whether Untouchables should have their own temples or try to enter the Hindu temples.[85] In the mid-1920s, he was still focussed on the opening of temples to the Untouchables, hence his interest in the Vaikam movement in 1924. In this city in Travancore State (present day Kerala) Untouchables had launched a *satyagraha* to enter a local temple or, at least, to use the road in front of it, which was forbidden them by the Brahmins. The confrontation attracted wide publicity after Gandhi sided with the *satyagrahis* after visiting Vaikam. In 1925, as the conflict continued, Ambedkar declared: 'For us, the most important event in the country today, is *satyagraha* at Vaikam.'[86] The road was finally opened to

Untouchables, but access to the temple was not permitted till 1936, an early date compared to other parts of India.

Meanwhile, the Mahars launched their first movement to enter a temple, at Amraoti, in 1927, under the leadership of G. A. Gavai. Ambedkar supported it but was unable to join it in person because of his brother's death. The movement quickly waned. To begin with, the *satyagraha* at the Parvati temple in Poona in 1929 was of an altogether different dimension. Shivram Janba Kamble led the action and Brahmin reformers participated in it too. Here Ambedkar's role was even more limited than at Amraoti. The movement lost momentum and the temple was not opened to Untouchables till 1947. The most significant attempt finally occurred in 1930 at Nasik.[87] From the outset, Ambedkar was deeply involved in this agitation, which he regarded as an instrument of social change, and not as an end in itself, as his first speech on the spot testifies:

> 'Your problems will not be solved by temple entry. Politics, economics, education, religion—all are part of the problem. Today's satyagraha is a challenge to the Hindu mind. Are the Hindus ready to consider us men or not; we will discover this today ... We know that the god in the temple is of stone. *Darsan* and *puja* will not solve our problems. But we will start out, and try to make a change in the minds of the Hindus.'[88]

Sporadic acts of violence occurred between the demonstrators and members of the upper castes. Then, the latter, contrary to a newly reached agreement, prevented certain Mahars from pulling the processional chariot during the annual temple festival. This incident reinforced Ambedkar's determination but he eventually dissociated himself from the movement in 1934, lest his supporters should attach too much importance to a low priority, religious issue:

> 'I did not launch the temple entry movement because I wanted the Depressed Class to become worshippers of idols which they were prevented from worshipping or because I believed that temple entry would make them equal members in and an integral part of the Hindu society. So far as this aspect of the case is concerned I would advise the Depressed Class to insist upon a complete overhauling of Hindu society and Hindu theology before they consent to become an integral part of Hindu Society. I started temple entry Satyagraha only because I felt that was the best way of energising the Depressed Class and making them conscious of their position. As I believe I have achieved that therefore I have no more use for temple

entry. I want the Depressed Class to concentrate their energy and resources on politics and education and I hope that they will realie the importance of both.'[89]

For Ambedkar, even though it had been an appropriate means of mobilising Untouchables, to claim entry to temples meant asking that they be given a place in a Hinduism whose caste system condemned them to a subordinate position. Ultimately, he preferred to reject this social system in its entirety—including the temple entry issue. Doubtless he was also disappointed by the unwillingness of upper caste representatives in the assemblies to pass laws legalising and enabling the entry of Untouchables to temples. In 1934, Ranga Iyer thus saw his Temple Entry Bill rejected by a majority of the members of the Central Assembly based in Delhi.

As a sociologist, Ambedkar began by analysing the caste system the better to struggle against it. By the end of the 1920s, he had rejected the logic of Sanskritisation which had till then overshadowed the attempts by Untouchables to emancipate themselves. Moreover be gradually came to reject Hinduism in favour of Western values—especially egalitarian individualism—and looked for a new strategy of emancipation. The evolution of the Depressed Classes' Institute was in this respect highly instructive: at the end of the 1920s, its program demanded for political rights. Its administrative council, which Ambedkar continued to chair, contained not even a single upper caste member whereas at the outset there were many of them.[90]

From the 1930s onwards Ambedkar's career was to delineate two strategies of emancipation. The first, which focused on the organisation of political parties, aimed at obtaining a specific representation for Untouchables in India's ruling institutions. The second was none other than the conversion to a religion different from Hinduism. Till the mid-1950s, Ambedkar was to alternate between one or the other solution, according to the context, a strategy that reflected, at one and the same time, a formidable fighting spirit and a healthy dose of pragmatism.

4. In the Political Arena, against Gandhi

'You have now a way of bringing about change, an improvement in your life conditions. That way is through political action, through appropriate laws [...] You can make government provide for you what you are now denied—food, clothing, shelter, education [...] Hence instead of resorting to rosary counting or prayer you should now depend on the political path; that will bring you liberation [...] The conflict hereafter, will not be between the British and the Indians, but between the advanced classes of India and the backward classes. No borrowed or hired person who does not belong to your class can further your welfare by the least degree. You may rid yourself of internal divisions and organise yourself strongly...' (speech by Ambedkar from 1933, quoted in M. S. Gore, *The Social Context of an Ideology*, op. cit., p. 213)

As early as the 1920s Ambedkar had considered political action as one of the Untouchables' instruments of emancipation. In his famous Barshi Takli speech of 1924 he weighed up several strategies, ranging from emigration to conversion to a change of name for the Untouchables, but concluded that winning political rights was his main objective.[1] Nevertheless, till the early 1930s he emphasised social reform at least as much as the struggle for such rights and he did not, in any case, enter the political arena—except to speak to the British as the Untouchables' representative when they organised rounds of consultations. As the decade went on he devoted most of his energy to the political organisation of the Untouchables, through which he hoped to exert decisive pressure on the government.

His political life was over-determined by the institutions of the British Raj. He was initiated into institutional politics in 1919 while the Viceroy Lord Chelmsford and the Secretary of State for India, Edwin Montagu, were preparing a reform for the whole of British India. Their consultations in India encouraged the mobilisation of many Untouchables' organisations, which were eager to obtain various guarantees. In Bombay, the Depressed Classes Mission, which had been founded in 1916 by Narayanrao Chandavarkar, a Brahmin reformer close to Congress, held a meeting in November 1917 attended by 2,500 people. Chandavarkar demanded that Untouchables be granted reserved seats in the Legislative Councils proportionate to their demographic strength.[2] It was on this occasion that Ambedkar began to elaborate his own political programme, which was to bring him into conflict with the Congress and in particular with Gandhi.

Reserved seats or separate electorates?

Ambedkar was consulted in early 1919 by the Southborough Committee, the body that had been entrusted with redefining the electoral franchise within the framework of constitutional reform—a reform which came to be known as the 'Montford' reform, after the names of Montagu and Chelmsford. Unlike the other Dalit leaders who were so consulted, Ambedkar was summoned not because he belonged to any association but because he was the only Untouchable who held a graduate degree in Bombay Presidency.

In his testimony, he explained that the real cleavage among Hindus was not between Brahmins and non-Brahmins (as the Satyashodak Samaj leaders had argued) but between 'touchables' and Untouchables. Ambedkar thus rejected an electoral system based on territorial constituencies because the latter would find themselves in a minority and thus be denied representation; all the more so as the criteria by which the franchise was defined were unfavourable to them. To support his contention he quoted statistics from local authorities of five districts of the Bombay Presidency, in which Brahmins accounted for 9,077 voters, Marathas 4,741, Muslims 1,830 and Mahars 55.[3]

To mitigate this imbalance, Ambedkar first suggested a lowering of the taxable rating level applied to Untouchables. This would allow them to vote in larger numbers and raise their political awareness by accelerating their integration in the electoral process. Above all, he recommended 'either to reserve seats [...] for those minorities that can not, otherwise, secure personal representation or grant communal electorates.'[4] At that time, he regarded the two options as equally valid[5] provided they ensured the presence in the Legislative Councils of a number of Untouchables proportionate to their demographic weight. It was only in an appended document that Ambedkar emphasised the need for a 'community electorate'[6] for Untouchables at the expense of the reserved seats formula.

The difference between the two was nevertheless important. In the reserved seats system, the candidate could only be an Untouchable in a certain number of constituencies (proportionate or not to the Untouchables' demographic weight), but they were never in a majority in any one constituency. In any constituency a coalition of high and intermediate castes could then elect an Untouchable of their choice, for whom the local Untouchables themselves would not have voted. On the contrary, in the separate electorates system only Untouchables could vote for Untouchable candidates. This system was likely to endow Untouchables with their own representatives, thereby constituting themselves into a real political force, whereas the reserved seats left open the possibility of upper caste-dominated parties co-opting Untouchables, handing out tickets during elections and electing them, even when this ran contrary to the wishes of local Untouchables.

In 1919 G. A. Gavai's Depressed Classes' Mission submitted to the British a rival project to Ambedkar's in which it proposed that Untouchable representatives should be co-opted by the elected members of the Legislative Council. For Ambedkar this formula imprisoned Untouchables in their subordinate position, and he vehemently denounced it.[7] Ultimately, the Untouchables obtained only one representative in the Legislative Council of Bombay Presidency within the framework of the 1919 reforms. An additional representative was later appointed in 1924, and Ambedkar joined it in this manner in 1927.

Ambedkar and the Simon Commission: The primacy of national integration and its limitations. The Constitution of India was meant to be reformed every ten years, and hence the British again began in 1928, as they had in 1917–19, to consult representatives of political and social groups. The Simon Commission (named after its president) charged with these consultations had no Indian members, and shocked by this exclusion, the Congress boycotted it. Minority organisations (of Muslims, Sikhs and others) and Dalit associations took part in its deliberations, however.

Ambedkar submitted a memorandum on behalf of the Bahishkrit Hitakarini Sabha which argued for an Untouchable seat quota rather than for separate electorates.[8] It demanded 22 seats in the 140-seat Bombay assembly (only 15 seats would have been their due under the demographic scheme) and for the electoral franchise to be extended to all Untouchables.[9] In his speech to the Simon Commission at Poona, Ambedkar made it clear that if universal suffrage were not granted, he would campaign for separate electorates.[10] The case that he advanced suggests that he still nurtured great hopes of the upper castes and that his nationalist scruples were preventing him from severing his links with the social and political mainstream:

> 'At any rate, this must be said with certainty that a minority gets a larger advantage under joint electorates than it does under a system of separate electorates. With separate electorates the minority gets its own quota of representation and no more. The rest of the house owes no allegiance to it and is therefore not influenced by the desire to meet the wishes of the minority. The minority is thus thrown on its own resources and as no system of representation can convert a minority into a majority, it is bound to be overwhelmed. On the other hand, under a system of joint electorates and reserved seats the minority not only gets its quota of representation but something more. For, every member of the majority who has partly succeeded on the strength of the votes of the minority if not a member of the minority will certainly be a member for the minority.'[11]

His reservations about separate electorates stemmed from his fear that they would divide the Indian nation: 'I do contemplate and I do desire the time when India shall be one; and I believe that a time will come when, for instance, all these things will not be necessary; but all that would depend upon the attitude of the majority towards the minority.'[12]

Thus the choice of joint electorates with reserved seats was a compromise whose aim was to reconcile the defence of a minority and the desire to strengthen the Indian nation. Ambedkar's preference was not, however, that clear cut. During the hearing, the Bengali Muslim leader Suhrawardy asked him whether separate electorates would not offer more protection for Untouchables, for example at polling booths, from upper caste intimidation. Ambedkar readily agreed with him.[13] Thus, in 1928, he was not yet sure which was the best formula. What seems undeniable was his conviction that 'political power is the only solvent' of the problem of Untouchability,[14] and this is why he was so critical of the Nehru Committee's proposals. The committee had been established by Congress and other smaller political organisations in reaction to the appointment of the Simon Commission. It was assigned the task of preparing counter-proposals on the Constitution under the supervision of Motilal Nehru. While the committee consulted Muslim, Sikh, Christian, Parsi, Anglo-Indian and non-Brahmin organisations, Dalit movements were ignored. Above all, the final report of the Nehru committee made no provisions, in the name of national integration, for the protection of Untouchables and Muslims. Its authors, who were inspired by western liberal values, defined the nation as a collection of individuals. In principle Ambedkar followed the same line of reasoning, but he could not accept that Untouchables should be deprived of guarantees such as a separate electorate or reserved seats. Although he was without doubt a modernist, like the Nehrus, as emphasised by Vidhu Verma, and though he yearned for the emergence of an individualistic society free from caste cleavages, he regarded Indian society as being based on a specific hierarchy whereby social equality could be promoted only by relying upon a logic of groups: Untouchables needed to be helped collectively for an unspecified period of transition.[15]

The Simon Commission report finally granted reserved seats to the Depressed Classes, with the proviso that candidates' competence would have to be endorsed by provincial governors, a caveat that incensed Ambedkar. Unfortunately the report remained a dead letter as the Congress had taken no part in its drafting. To break this deadlock, another consultative meeting was held in London in which Ambedkar also took part.

The twists and turns of the Round Table Conferences. The first Round Table Conference in autumn 1930 was again boycotted by Congress, whereas representatives of the Muslims, Sikhs, Christians, Untouchables and the Hindu Mahasabha participated, along with the traditional supporters of the British of the Liberal party. Ambedkar attended accompanied by Rao Bahadur Rettamalle Srinivasan, a Dalit member of the Legislative Council of the Madras Presidency.

In Nagpur, in August 1930, the All-India Depressed Classes' Congress had come out in favour of the same scheme as that defended by Ambedkar before the Simon Commission, one that combined reserved seats and universal suffrage.[16] Ambedkar repeated this demand in London but the Conference reached no conclusion given the absence of the Congress representatives. There followed a Second Round Table Conference, to which Gandhi himself was invited. He was still equivocating about his participation when in Bombay, on August 14, 1931 he met—apparently for the first time—Ambedkar who was about to embark for London. When Ambedkar asked Gandhi what he thought of the debates of the first Round Table, the Mahatma replied that he was 'against the political separation of Untouchables from Hindus',[17] a barely veiled criticism of separate electorates.

Confrontation between the two men took on a more acute form during the second Round Table Conference in London, which Gandhi did eventually attend. They both sat on the Minorities Committee, which was entrusted with discussing the thorny issue of the place of Muslims and Untouchables within the new institutions that the British wished to establish. On October 1st, 1931, Gandhi asked for a suspension of the meeting so as to be able to discuss key issues with leaders of the minorities. The debates resumed on October 8, at which point Gandhi recognised he had failed to engineer a compromise. According to him, this was because of the behaviour of the leaders with whom he had to interact and whose right to speak on behalf of the various communities he doubted. Gandhi disputed, for example, Ambedkar's claim to be the spokesperson of the Untouchables, of whom the Congress, the spearhead of the national movement, was the natural representative, according to him.[18]

Ambedkar had managed to forge closer links, within the Minorities Committee, with the Muslim, Anglo-Indian and European Christian representatives. They drafted a memorandum together. Ambedkar and Srinivasan set down the demand for a separate electorate with reserved seats for the Untouchables, a scheme that they planned to submit to a referendum within twenty years or which would be terminated before that time if universal suffrage were introduced. Gandhi opposed the scheme in no uncertain terms:

> It will create a division in Hinduism which I cannot possibly look forward to with satisfaction whatsoever. I do not mind the Untouchables being

converted to Islam or Christianity. I should tolerate that but I cannot tolerate what is in store for Hinduism if there are these two divisions set up in every village. Those who speak about political rights of the Untouchables do not know India and do not know how Indian society is today constructed. Therefore, I want to say with all the emphasis that I can command that if I was the only person to resist to this thing I will resist it with my life.[19]

The Second Round Table Conference ended inconclusively, without any compromise on the distribution of powers between the various communities. The president of the Minorities Committee, Ramsay MacDonald, asked its members to leave it to him to come up with a means of resolving the deadlock. Hence on their return to India in late 1931 and early 1932, the various protagonists awaited British arbitration, albeit without in the meantime remaining politically inactive, as borne out by the Rajah-Moonje pact.

The Hindu nationalists against Ambedkar. After the Second Round Table conference, the Hindu Mahasabha tried to counter Ambedkar by co-opting other Untouchable leaders, as manifested in the alliance formed between Moonje and G. A. Gavai. The latter was appointed to the Legislative Council of the Bombay Presidency in 1920. In 1929 the Simon Commission had consulted him in his capacity as president of the Depressed Classes' Association of Nagpur. Gavai had then spoken in favour of a separate electorate for Untouchables, but in 1931 he had a change of mind. This *volte-face* was explained by Gavai's opportunism, as he sought to differentiate himself from Ambedkar, his principal rival, but ideological motives were also at stake. As his involvement in the Prarthana Samaj and the Congress amply testifies, Gavai was preoccupied with Hindu unity as defined by upper caste reformers. Hence his coming closer to Moonje ensued as much from ideological motivations as from political calculation.

B. S. Moonje, a Brahmin from Nagpur, began his career in politics as a lieutenant of Tilak before chairing the Hindu Mahasabha from 1927–33. In the early 1930s he tried to use Gavai against Ambedkar, whose demand for a separate Untouchable electorate had worried Moonje as much as it had Gandhi. The result was that Gavai was appointed to the Working Committee of the Hindu Mahasabha and promised a party ticket for the 1934 elections.[20]

After the Second Round Table conference Moonje tried to weaken Ambedkar's stand by mobilising the All India Depressed

Classes' Association of which Gavai was General Secretary. The latter was used as a middle man between Moonje and Rajah, the movement's president. Rao Bahadur M. C. Rajah,[21] who had represented the Untouchables in the Imperial Legislative Council since 1927, had founded the association in 1925.[22] Just as Gavai was Ambedkar's rival in Maharashtra, so Rajah was Srinivasan's in Tamil Nadu. He had moreover followed a similar trajectory to Gavai with regard to separate electorates, again due to his personal conviction and political opportunism. He began moving towards the idea of a separate electorate before the Second Round Table conference but later turned against it, a change of heart that Ambedkar attributed to Rajah's resentment at not having been invited to represent the Untouchables at the Round Table Conferences.

Rajah was certainly disappointed at not having been invited, and he was doubtless irritated to see Ambedkar appearing as the sole representative of the Untouchables. But he was convinced of the need to organise the Untouchables *within* Hindu society and blamed separate electorates for making 'politically untouchable' a community which was 'already socially' ostracised.[23] Rajah, like Gavai, seemed to appreciate the integrating power of the *organicist* model of the Hindu nation propagated by the Hindu Mahasabha.[24]

An agreement was concluded in March 1932 between Rajah and Moonje, who congratulated himself on inflicting a stunning reverse on Ambedkar without having made too many concessions.[25] Indeed this pact contained as its principal measure the perpetuation of a joint electorate in exchange for a percentage of reserved seats proportional to the number of Untouchables. Rajah wrote to the British Prime Minister that he should not worry about Ambedkar's demands as the problem was being settled by an agreement between 'the only central organisation of 'the Depressed Classes'' and 'the organised body of Hindus taken as a whole.'[26] The British ignored the missive: Ambedkar could rest secure in the knowledge that his rivals' influence was at best very weak.

Arm wrestling with Gandhi and the Poona Pact

The colonial power's arbitration following the Second Round Table Conference on the status of communities in the forthcoming Constitution, entitled the *Communal Award*, was announced in August

1932. It recognised the right of Untouchables to have a separate electorate. From now on they were given the right to vote within the framework of general constituencies and within seventy-one separate constituencies which could be filled only by Dalit candidates. Gandhi, who was then in prison at Poona for having revived the civil disobedience movement, immediately went on fast. To understand his response we must consider it within the wider framework of his social thought.

Gandhi and caste. The Mahatma had always contested the opprobrium which blighted the Untouchables by arguing that their occupations were no more demeaning than any other. To set an example he insisted that every resident of his Sabarmati ashram in Ahmedabad had to clean the toilets. Under his guidance, Congress passed a motion declaring the work of Bhangis (sweepers) as respectable.[27]

His increasing concern with the fate of the Untouchables was testified by the many articles published on the subject in 1920–1 in his journal, *Young India*.[28] At the Congress session in Nagpur in 1920 which culminated in his dazzling rise to the head of the party, Gandhi pushed through a motion condemning 'the sin of Untouchability',[29] while at the numerous meetings that he convened to discuss the issue he underlined that, from the age of twelve, he had considered that Untouchability was only a corruption of Hinduism. Moreover he declared that if he had to be reborn, he would like to be reborn among the Untouchables as to share their punishments, insults and sufferings and would try to rescue them from their miserable condition.[30]

However, Gandhi focused on the religious dimension of Untouchability, and in particular on the problem of access to temples. In 1924, as mentioned above, Vaikam's Untouchables launched a *satyagraha* over temple access. Gandhi supported the campaign, even visiting the place in person, but his dialogue with the local Brahmins disturbed him profoundly. His interlocutors rejected all possibilities of compromise and the results of the *satyagraha* were ambivalent: the road was opened to the Untouchables but the temple forbade them entry till 1936,[31] by which point Gandhi had long since withdrawn from the movement.

It seems that his confrontation with the priests of Vaikam eroded Gandhi's convictions simply because the Brahmins believed so forcefully in their own traditions and considered that they enjoyed a position based on the sacred texts.[32] Following this episode, Gandhi declared himself a 'sanatani'; that is a follower of the *Sanatan Dharma*, the eternal religion of the orthodox. He continued to support Untouchable campaigns for access to temples because equality before God was in his eyes a priority, but he would strive to do so in a manner that would not upset the upper castes. Above all, he would refrain from demanding social equality for Untouchables.

This change of heart probably reflected also the resistance of certain Congress leaders, especially those from the upper castes. In 1922 the executive board of the party (the Congress Working Committee), meeting at Bardoli in Gujarat, passed a resolution calling upon Congress activists to help the Untouchables. It was an expression of goodwill that was not followed through in practice: the sub-committee which had been appointed in Bardoli never functioned effectively, largely because it was not being allocated the necessary funds.[33]

However, the limitations of Gandhi's response regarding the Untouchables can be explained more fundamentally by his attachment to the traditional Hindu social order. Questioned on this point by many readers of *Young India*, Gandhi sought to defend certain aspects of the caste system in December 1920:

> I believe that caste has saved Hinduism from disintegration. […]
>
> But like every other institution it has suffered from excrescences. I consider the four divisions alone to be fundamental, natural and essential. The innumerable sub-castes are sometimes a convenience, often a hindrance. The sooner there is fusion the better. […] But I am certainly against any attempt at destroying the fundamental divisions. The caste system is not based on inequality, there is no question of inferiority, and so far as there is any such question arising, as in Madras, Maharashtra or elsewhere, the tendency should undoubtedly be checked. […]
>
> One of my correspondents suggests that we should abolish the caste [system] but adopt the class system of Europe—meaning thereby I suppose that the idea of heredity in caste should be rejected. I am inclined to think that the law of heredity is an eternal law and any attempt to alter that law must lead us, as it has before led, to utter confusion. I can see very great use in considering a Brahmin to be always a Brahmin throughout his life. If he does not behave himself like a Brahmin, he will naturally cease to command the respect that is due to the real Brahmin. It is easy to imagine the

innumerable difficulties if one were to set up a court of punishments and rewards, degradation and promotion. If Hindus believe, as they must believe, in reincarnation, transmigration, they must know that nature will, without any possibility of mistake, adjust the balance by degrading a Brahmin, if he misbehaves himself, by reincarnating him in a lower division, and translating one who lives the life of a Brahmin in his present incarnation to Brahminhood in his next.

Interdrinking, interdining, intermarrying, I hold, are not essential for the promotion of the spirit of democracy. I do not contemplate under a most democratic constitution a universality of manners and customs about eating, drinking and marrying. We shall ever have to seek unity in diversity, and I decline to consider it a sin for a man not to drink or eat with anybody and everybody.[34]

This passage reflects Gandhi's adherence to certain mechanisms of the caste system and even, to some extent, to the spirit of the system: he refers to his belief in reincarnation; he presents the requirement that all members of the upper castes must preserve their rank in society as a positive element of social regulation; and while he rejects the idea of a rigid hierarchy, he views the distribution of men and women across various castes as contributing to social harmony and economic stability. His model is, in many ways that of the *varnas*, which he describes as forming a conflict-free society.[35] The *Varna Vyavastha* indeed appears as an ideal model of organisation which attributes to each individual a social and occupational vocation, thereby assuring that the collectivity functions harmoniously. For Gandhi this emphasis on socio-economic cohesion went hand in hand with a denial of hierarchy in the *varna* system, as evident from another of his articles that was written much later, in 1934:

The four *varnas* have been compared in the *Vedas* to the four members of one body, and no simile could be happier. If they are members of one body, how could one be superior or inferior to another? If the members of the body had the power of expression and each of them were to say that it was higher and better than the rest, the body would go to pieces [...]. It is this canker which is at the root of the various ills of our time, especially class war and civil strife. It should not be difficult, for even the meanest understanding to see that these wars and strives could not be ended except by the observance of the law of *Varna*. For it ordains that every one shall fulfil the law of one's being by doing in a spirit of duty and service that for which one is born.[36]

In sum, Gandhi thought that Hindu society formed almost a harmonious whole provided it was reformed and restored to its pristine order. His approach rested on a metaphor of the body as found in the Hindu collective *imaginaire*, or consciousness, drawn from the *Purusha Shukta*, a hymn from the Rig Veda that Ambedkar analysed differently, as mentioned above. It clearly implies a denegation of caste conflict. Undeniably, Gandhi's views on caste changed from the 1920s to the '40s, and as Guha argues eventually he decided 'to challenge caste directly by accepting and sanctioning inter-marriage itself'.[37] However this 'last and most far-reaching step' not only took place 'only in 1946' but also did not imply the eradication of caste as a social unit. Such a conception is naturally the exact opposite to that of Ambedkar, for whom the individual had to become the basic unit of an egalitarian society, with castes as collective bodies serving only as a temporary means of advancing his politics of equality.

Ambedkar and Gandhi. Ambedkar and Gandhi were not to meet till the early 1930s,[38] but the Mahatma's activities had aroused the interest of Untouchable leaders, including Ambedkar, already in the 1920s. Ambedkar's first comment about Gandhi dates back to 1925 and concerns the Vaikam *satyagraha*. On the occasion of the Depressed Classes' Conference of the Bombay Presidency, he declared:

> 'Before Mahatma Gandhi, no politician in this country maintained that it is necessary to remove social injustice here in order to do away with tension and conflict, and that every Indian should consider it his sacred duty to do so.... However, if one looks closely, one finds there is a slight disharmony...for he does not insist on the removal of untouchability as much as he insists on the propagation of Khaddar [home-spun cloth] or the Hindu-Muslim unity. If he had he would have made the removal of untouchability a precondition of voting in the party. Well, be that as it may, when one is spurned by everyone, even the sympathy shown by Mahatma Gandhi is of no little importance.'[39]

Ambedkar was also attracted to Gandhi's non-violent *modus operandi*. During the 1927 Mahad movement, a photograph of the Mahatma adorned the *pandal* (platform) and Ambedkar explicitly adopted his technique of *satyagraha*, which he defined as an 'affirmation of the right and duty to fight for truth.'[40] The Mahad movement resembled a *satyagraha*. The same thing happened during the 1929 campaign to open Poona's Parvati temple to Untouchables but Gandhi's blessing was not forthcoming. A delegation of the Congress's Anti-Untouchability Sub-Committee set up an inquiry on the spot and concluded that the *satyagraha* had created an 'atmosphere of bitterness and distrust'.[41] The *satyagraha* failed—the Parvati temple would open to Untouchables only in 1947, and the attitude of Gandhi and the Congress aroused Ambedkar's ire. A similar episode occurred in 1930 during a campaign to open a Nasik temple to Untouchables.

However, the rivalry between Gandhi and Ambedkar was to crystallise in 1932 over separate electorates. For the Mahatma, as we already know, such a scheme would fracture the unity of Hindu society. On September 15, he sent the following statement to the Bombay Government in reaction to the Communal Award:

> [The Untouchables] are part of an indivisible family [...] There is a subtle something, quite indefinable in Hinduism which keeps them in it even in spite of themselves. And this fact makes it imperative for a man like me, with a living experience of it, to resist this contemplated separation, even though this effort should cost life itself.[42]

This 'subtle something' that Gandhi called 'a miracle' elsewhere in the same statement was nothing other than integration into the caste system, with its social and economic interdependence and its so-called ritual harmony. But Gandhi could not ignore the fact that in a system of hierarchical integration, this 'subtle something' is manifested also in marks of submission and symbolic—or even physical—violence. Indeed Untouchables are maintained in the system 'in spite of themselves', as the Mahatma rather too candidly admitted. Gandhi did not ignore these flaws since he regarded them as late perversions of an ancient order that could be restored to its original purity by social reform. But he placed his trust in the endeavours of reformers seeking a more egalitarian society in order to reject the measures championed by Ambedkar.

In conversation with Patel on the second day of his fast against the Communal Award, Gandhi made the following statement: '[the Untouchables] do not realise that a separate electorate will create division among Hindus so much that it will lead to bloodshed. "Untouchable" hooligans will make common cause with Muslim hooligans and kill caste Hindus. Has the British Government no idea of all this? I do not think so.'[43] The Mahatma hereby suggests that caste Hindus had to be defended against the British-sponsored solidarity between Muslims and Dalits, an argument the Hindu Mahasabha was already articulating.

The Poona Pact, or the failure of Ambedkar's political plan. Ambedkar was the only Indian politician whom Gandhi contested by resorting to a fast. He did this precisely because he knew Ambedkar would not respond by resorting to violence. In a speech to the Second Round Table Conference, Gandhi had said, 'I have the highest regard for Dr Ambedkar. He has every right to be bitter. That he does not break our heads is an act of self-restraint on his part.' Ambedkar was a lawyer who never turned the law to his advantage and he even adopted the *satyagraha* as his *modus operandi* in Mahar in 1927. Upendra Baxi points out that in 1932 'Gandhi "gambled" on Ambedkar's self-restraint and won'[44]. As soon as he announced that he was beginning his fast to the death in response to the Communal Award, Gandhi received messages of support from all over India. The Mahatma by then embodied a form of holiness which allowed him to reconcile the Great and the little Traditions of Hinduism: he transcended caste and his discourse was therefore acceptable by the majority, including Untouchables. Indeed Untouchables 'voiced their confidence in the leadership of Gandhi' during public meetings at Lahore, Lucknow, Karachi and Nagpur.[45]

Gandhi's fast generated a huge emotional outpouring throughout India.[46] Madan Mohan Malaviya, the Hindu Mahasabha leader who was recognised as the representative of upper caste Hindu opinion in Congress on account of his strict Brahminical orthodoxy, took the initiative of convening a meeting in Bombay on September 19, 1932, the day Gandhi began his fast. Ambedkar was invited in order to renegotiate the terms of the Communal Award. (The title of the meeting, 'Conference of Hindu and Untouchable Leaders', was paradoxical but revealing: even when Gandhi refused to consider the Untouchables as being outside Hinduism, the qualification of 'Hindus' was reserved for the upper caste Congressmen participating in the conference[47]).

The preliminary draft compromises which were successively elaborated by these leaders were submitted to Gandhi, whose physical condition was deteriorating with every day that passed. The recollections of one eye-witness, Kodanda Rao, of the Servants of India Society, an association founded by the 'political guru' of Gandhi, G. K. Gokhale, and which remained close to the Congress, testifies to the pressure exerted at this moment on Ambedkar:

On the sixth day [of the fast] Devdas Gandhi [one the Mahatma's sons] came to the conference from the jail. [...] He said: 'Father is sinking.' The agony of the whole conference was something only you can imagine. Ambedkar had come to Poona, but was staying in a hotel and was speaking somewhat cynically. His point was that he [Ambedkar] was the sole representative of the Untouchables, and not the Mahatma, that the Mahatma had no business to presume that he was the leader of the Untouchables as against himself. And he said, somewhat cynically and somewhat cruelly also: 'Who was the Mahatma to fast? Let him come and have dinner with me.' And these statements outraged people who were all suffering agonies. At that stage Mr M. C. Rajah, another leader of the Untouchables from Madras, who was in the conference. [...] said to Ambedkar: 'For thousands of year we had been treated as Untouchables, downtrodden, insulted, despised. The Mahatma is staking his life for our sake, and if he dies, for the next thousands of years we shall be where we have been, if not worse. There will be such a strong feeling against us that we brought about his death, that the mind of the whole Hindu community and the whole civilised community will kick us downstairs further still. I am not going to stand by you any longer. I will join the conference and find a solution and I will part company from you'.[48] That brought Ambedkar round. He said, 'I am willing to compromise'.[49]

This testimony is useful for qualifying Ravinder Kumar's interpretation, according to which Gandhi succeeded in persuading Ambedkar as a 'true *Satyagrahi*'.[50] The final phase of bargaining took place when Ambedkar came to meet Gandhi at Yeravda prison. The Mahatma then proposed that Untouchables should have more reserved seats than they would have obtained in the framework of separate electorates, in exchange for the renunciation by Ambedkar to this system. 'The Poona Pact' finally established a system of reserved seats, in which 148 seats (instead of 71 as put forward by the Communal Award) were granted to Untouchables in the Legislative Council. But it excluded the principle of separate electorates: in 148 constituencies—those where Untouchables were most numerous—members of the Depressed Classes (the official phrase) would themselves nominate the four Dalit leaders who would be the candidates from whom all voters in the constituency, irrespective of caste, would then have to elect their representative.[51] This scheme was in fact close to that advocated by the Rajah-Moonje pact. For Gandhi, the Poona Pact was much more than an exercise in political engineering: it had wider implications for society as a whole, as evident from his comment to Ambedkar in 1933: 'In accepting the Poona Pact you accept the position that you are Hindus'.[52]

Gandhi, who professed to be above quarrelling interest groups and castes, did not sign the text. It was ratified, on the one hand, by the 'Hindu leaders' of the conference organised by Malaviya, as representatives of the upper castes, and, on the other hand, by the Dalit leaders who participated in it. On 26 September 1932, Gandhi broke his fast. Three days later he approved the setting up, by G. D. Birla, the wealthy and influential Indian industrialist who had already financed many of the Mahatma's pet projects, of an All India Anti-Untouchability League with a budget of 600,000 rupees.[53] Agitations on behalf of Untouchables became one of Gandhi's chief concerns: he launched 'an Untouchability Abolition Week' in September–October, 1932, created a new weekly newspaper, *Harijan* (literally, 'children of God'),[54] in February, 1933, and went on the campaign trail promoting Untouchable interests from November 1933 to August 1934.

During this tour Gandhi had to face down the often violent opposition of orthodox Hindus from the Sanatan Dharma Sabha and the Hindu Mahasabha—which was still part of the Congress at that time. In Nagpur, his starting-point, the Deputy Commissioner reported that 'orthodox Hindus have been conducting strong propaganda against the Temple Entry Bill [see below], the removal of untouchability, and Gandhi's campaign generally'.[55] In Delhi, 'Three sanatanists caused some commotion by throwing black flags into his car'[56]. In South Kanara and Bellary 'on a number of occasions black flags were waved and 'Go back Gandhi' slogans shouted, gestures of hostility which no one would have dreamt of making even two or three years ago when Gandhi was still a popular idol'[57]. In Arrah (Bihar), his 'car was stopped at a canal bridge by a party of Sanatanists who lay down and waved black flags [...]. His followers and the Sanatanists then started a free fight which would have developed into a riot but for the intervention of the police.'[58] In Poona the

Sanatanists—who had for some time been considerably piqued by Gandhi's unorthodox leanings—were apparently responsible for a bomb explosion at the Municipal Hall.[59] In Varanasi, some forty or so Sanatanists carrying black flags assembled on the railway platform and a similar number outside the station when Gandhi's train arrived.[60]

All this mollified Ambedkar's hostility towards Gandhi. In November, 1932, heading for England to take part in the Third Round Table Conference, he began to appreciate Gandhi's public declarations concerning Untouchables. He wrote to his colleagues that he had noticed a gradual convergence with his own position on certain issues, even though he regretted that Gandhi still refused to endorse inter-caste marriage and inter-caste eating. In one of these letters, he indicated, in a very Gandhian manner: 'The Touchables and Untouchables cannot be held together by law, certainly not by any electoral law substituting joint electorate for separate electorates. The only thing that can hold together is love.'[61] In another letter he even quoted Tolstoy, one of Gandhi's main sources of inspiration: 'Only those who love can serve.'[62]

However, the positions of Gandhi and Ambedkar turned out to be irreconcilable during the debates about the legislative abolition of Untouchability, the entry of Untouchables into temples and the role of the Anti-Untouchability League.

The legal abolition of Untouchability. At the end of 1932, several upper caste Congressmen introduced a bill with the aim of abolishing Untouchability in different assemblies. Ranga Iyer, Rajah, Gayaprasad Singh and B. C. Mitra took this matter to the Central Assembly of New Delhi whereas S. K. Bole and Subbarayan did the same in the Legislative Council of Bombay. In February 1933, Gandhi advised Ambedkar to support Iyer's and Subbarayan's bills, but he demurred because neither document condemned untouchability 'as a sin'. He added new arguments in the following weeks to justify and bolster his stance. In an article published in *Harijan*, he underlined the futility of merely abolishing Untouchability: this evil being the product of a social hierarchy of a particular kind, it was the entire caste system that had to be eradicated: 'There will be out castes [Untouchables] as long as there are castes.'[63] He repeated this argument in the Legislative Council of Bombay by indicating that the Chaturvarnya (the system formed by the four *Varnas*) was itself to be abolished. Gandhi responded that, on the contrary, here it was a question of the foundation of Hinduism, a civilisation which, in its original form, in fact ignored hierarchy.[64]

The problem of temple entry. Another debate that emerged at this time concerned Untouchables being allowed to worship in temples. In the wake of the movement launched by Ambedkar for the opening to all of a temple at Nasik, in November 1931, Kelappan, a lieutenant of Ambedkar in Travancore (in today's Kerala) launched his own agitation at the Guruvayur temple in Cochin. He began a fast on September 21, 1932, just after the signing of the Poona Pact. Gandhi managed to persuade him to suspend this drastic step by promising that he himself would begin a fast if the temple were not opened to all by January 1, 1933.[65] He struggled to find a compromise by suggesting an alternate opening of the temple to upper caste Hindus and to Untouchables so that the former were not offended by the presence of the latter. Gandhi was even prepared to accept that the temple would be cleaned after Untouchables had worshipped there. These concessions were not enough to dispel the doubts of the hard core of orthodox Hindus, and therefore the Mahatama abandoned his fast in order not to exert on them moral pressure, which he regarded as an act of violence.[66]

One of the paragraphs in Iyer's bill dealt with opening temples to Untouchables, and it was this provision that precipitated vehement criticism from Hindu traditionalists in Congress, led by Malaviya, who cabled Gandhi and Iyer expressing his opposition to the bill. The text of the bill submitted on March 24, 1933, was never put to the vote.[67] This episode is especially interesting because it reveals how important equal access to God was to Gandhi. He emphasied spiritual egalitarianism more than any other form of parity, assuming that everything would flow from it. In 1933 he told Ambedkar: 'I regard temple entry as a spiritual matter through which everything else will bear fruit.'[68] But he could not impose his views on this issue anyway.

From the Anti-Untouchability League to the Harijan Sevak Sangh. At the outset Ambedkar professed interest in Gandhi's Anti-Untouchability League. In October 1932 he visited Gandhi in prison to suggest that the various committees of the League had to comprise a majority of Untouchables.[69] His recommendation was not followed by any positive action and the League remained dominated by upper caste Hindus, largely because Gandhi wanted to make it 'an organisation of penitent sinners'.[70] Launched on September 30 1932, during an inaugural meeting chaired by M. M. Malaviya in Bombay, the League had G. D. Birla as its president and as its secretary Amritlal Thakkar. (Known as Thakkar Bapa, the latter was a Gujarati social reformer who had set up the Bhil Seva Mandal in the 1920s and was widely respected for his work on behalf of the Servants of India Society.) According to its Constitution, at least three Untouchables (out of nine members) had to sit on the 'central board' of the organisation; they were M. C. Rajah, Rao Bahadur Srinivasan and Ambedkar. The latter wrote to Thakkar suggesting that the League should campaign for the abolition of the caste system and the promotion of inter-caste marriage and dining; this letter seems not to have received any answer. Ambedkar resigned soon afterwards as did all the Dalit representatives of the organisation. The League, which was renamed the Harijan Sevak Sangh (Association for Serving Harijans), focussed its activities—thanks to Birla's funds—on helping Untouchables in a paternalistic manner: it aimed to help their social advancement, notably in the field of education, while promoting a change of heart among the upper castes.[71]

The fate of the HSS and Gandhi's soft-pedalling regarding the Untouchable issue have to be seen in relation to the growing hostility of orthodox Hindus to his policy. In April 1934, British officials thought that his campaigning tour against Untouchability had prompted him to rethink his position: 'Mr Gandhi apparently is getting more and more chary of giving offence to orthodox opposition, the strength of which, it is suggested, he had not fully appreciated, at any rate with regard to temple entry. Congress, as a party, has gained little, if anything, by this tour.'[72] Gandhi's growing reticence regarding the issue was evident from the advice he gave to M. C. Rajah in 1938. Rajah had proposed to move a Temple Entry Bill in the Madras Legislative Council after the 1937 Congress victory in the province, but C. Rajagopalachari, the Chief Minister, asked him to withdraw it.[73] Rajah complained to Gandhi who advised him to 'trust C. R. to do his best. [...] Go to him, reason with him and if you cannot persuade him, bear with him. That is my advice.'[74] The Mahatma was obviously yielding to the conservative bosses of Congress, and Rajah, disappointed, soon joined Ambedkar. Ultimately, the struggle between Gandhi and Ambedkar ended with the former's victory: while the social *status quo* was not totally preserved, the politicisation of Untouchables by means of a separate electorate had been defused. Gandhi's signal success was the Poona Pact, which was to have serious consequences.

First, the reserved seats scheme did not allow Untouchables to benefit from political representation proportional to their demographic weight. The *Government of India Act* of 1935 granted them only 7 seats out of 156 in the Council of State (the Upper House of Parliament at New Delhi), 19 out of 250 in the Central Assembly (the Lower House) and 151 out of 1.585 in the various legislative assemblies of the provinces.[75] Above all, reserved seats thwarted Ambedkar's desire to transform Untouchables into a political force. Given that they never found themselves in a majority in a constituency, an alliance (explicit or tacit) of the upper and intermediate castes could even elect an Untouchable of their choice for whom Untouchables themselves would not have voted. Ultimately, Congress was to become a past master in this kind of co-option.

The debates of 1932–3 eroded the little hope which Ambedkar still had in Gandhi, though he continued to be praised by him. In 1934 he addressed students in Karachi as follows:

> 'The magnitude of [Dr Ambedkar's] sacrifice is great. He is absorbed in his own work. He leads a simple life. He is capable of earning one to two thousand rupees a month. He is also in a position to settle down in Europe if he so desires. But he doesn't want to stay there. He is only concerned about the welfare of the Harijans.'[76]

To be fair to Gandhi, he was the first—and only—Indian politician to make the abolition of Untouchability central to *swaraj* and to act so single-mindedly in order to challenge it. As a result, he was detested by the orthodox Hindus who figured so largely in Congress. Gandhi had to make compromises with these people, who thought he was going too fast. For Ambedkar the Mahatma was going too slowly. He was deeply disappointed and dismayed by Gandhi's actions. This pattern was to repeat itself with the Arya Samaj.

Ambedkar and the Arya Samaj

Some Arya Samajists tended to identify themselves with Ambedkar's plea for the abolition of Untouchability and the eradication of the caste system. One of their number, Sant Ram, invited him to Lahore in late 1935 to clarify what he meant by the necessity 'to finish with the religious notions on which the caste system was founded'.[77] But Sant Ram had to abandon his initiative under pressure of old guard Arya Samajists such as Bhai Parmanand, Hans Raj, Raja Narendra Nath and G. C. Narang, because the text of Ambedkar's speech contained a criticism of the *Vedas* as the cornerstone of caste hierarchy.[78] The invitation was cancelled and Ambedkar's mistrust of the Arya Samajists was further reinforced. The speech which he was unable to deliver in Lahore contained an interesting paragraph about them:

> '…there is a set of reformers who hold out a different ideal [than mine]. They go by the name of the Arya Samajists and their ideal of social organisation is what is called Chaturvanya or the division of society in four classes instead of four thousand castes that we have in India. To make it more attractive and to disarm opposition, the protagonists of Chaturvanya take great care to point that their Chaturvarnya is based not on birth but on *guna* (worth). At the outset, I must confess that notwithstanding the worth basis of this Chaturvarnya, it is an ideal to which I can not reconcile myself.'[79]

For Ambedkar, it was impossible to convert the caste system into Chaturvarnya simply by reducing the divisions of four thousand castes within four *varnas* based on individualistic values, because the high castes would never admit merit as the ultimate determinant of social status. Besides, such a transformation implied that one should first destroy the caste system. But, supposing that the transformation of a caste system into a system of *varnas*, founded on merit, was practicable, the social functions traditionally associated with various *varnas* would continue to create problems because, for example, intellectual activities would remain the monopoly of Brahmins, whereas the Shudras would continue to work the land and to serve the upper orders. Even if membership of a *varna* is not hereditary in this scheme of things, such a specialisation would prove a major obstacle to social mobility.

Even before the rejection of his text by Punjab's Arya Samajists, Ambedkar had his own doubts about them regarding the sincerity of their reformism. Their interpretation of Chaturvarnya appeared to him as a manoeuvre by the upper castes to preserve a fundamentally hierarchical social system. Ambedkar was therefore confronted with two types of reformers—the Arya Samajists and Gandhi—in whom he detected a strong reluctance to put their words into practice, and who, to cap it all, manifested profound hypocrisy in their attempts to preserve caste under another name.

In the 1930s Ambedkar favoured a political strategy based on his demand for a separate electorate for the Untouchables, but he came to question the validity of this approach after Gandhi succeeded in countering his demands. As he was to write in August 1933: 'I am going to withdraw myself from politics and devote myself entirely to my profession, as soon as the work of this Round Table Conference[80] will be finished.'[81]

His faith in political action now eroded, he envisaged at one time converting to another religion as a way of ridding himself of the stigma of Untouchability. Yet Ambedkar was to remain a politician. At Nasik in 1934, in front of 15,000 of his followers, he declared that 'in the coming reforms [the 1935 Government of India Act], they would be called upon to play an important part in moulding their own political future.'[82]

Ambedkar had indeed decided to play the game of new institutions. The reform of 1935, which conferred new responsibilities on the Legislative Councils, also widened the franchise and granted to Untouchables the quota of reserved seats negotiated in the Poona Pact. In view of the impending elections within this system, Ambedkar founded his first political party, the Independent Labour Party in 1936.

5. Searching for an Electoral Strategy

'We are often reminded that the problem of the Depressed Classes is a social problem and that its solution lies elsewhere than in politics. We take strong exception to this view. We hold that the problem of the Depressed Classes will never be solved unless they get political power in their own hands. If this is true, then [the] problem of [the] Depressed Classes is, I submit, eminently a political problem and must be treated as such.' (statement by Ambedkar at the first Round Table Conference, London, 1930)

The Independent Labour Party, as its name indicated, was not intended to be confined to Untouchables. As party president, Ambedkar now tried to set up himself as a leader of the 'labouring masses'. This shift was largely due to his need for an electoral strategy, as he had become aware that he had to widen his social base of support. But to what extend could he carry through this strategy without excessively diluting the identity of his movement? It was indeed to avert this risk that he created in 1942 the Scheduled Castes' Federation, whose name reveals his concern to reorient his political activities towards Untouchables. These two parties, founded at an interval of six years, accurately reflected his dilemma: he was divided between the necessity, on the one hand, of representing Untouchables and, on the other hand, of widening his audience, not only for electoral purposes but also because Untouchables were 'workers' too. Finally, the strategy of Ambedkar's parties posed the problem of the nature of Untouchability and harked back to the key dilemma of his approach: must Untouchables conceive of themselves as an entirely separate group?

The ILP, or how to defend workers without being a Marxist

Ambedkar: workers' leader. The very day he formed the Independent Labour Party, *The Times of India* published an article based on an interview with Ambedkar. Questioned on the name of his party, he replied: 'the word "Labour" was used instead of the words "Depressed Classes" because labour includes Depressed Classes as well.'[1]

Indeed, Untouchables featured only as workers in the ILP's programme, which paid close attention to economic questions and to critiquing capitalism. Ambedkar considered that Indian workers were victims of both Brahminism and of capitalism (*Brahmanshahi* and *Bhandwalshahi*), the two systems being dominated by the same social group.[2] Industrialisation was presented as a priority subject for the State, whose intervention was perceived as indispensable to economic development. The party in its programme, proposed a series of reforms to defend the interests of industrial workers and demanded greater vocational and technical educational opportunities.[3] The ILP even campaigned in favour of appropriate legislation to protect the tenants of 'the lower middle class',[4] among whom there were very few Untouchables! The word 'caste' appeared in fact only in the wording of the last objective of the party:

> The party will also endeavour to prevent the administration from becoming the monopoli [*sic*] of any single caste or community. Consistently with efficiency of administration, the party will endeavour to bring about fair admixture of all caste [*sic*] and communities in the administration of the Presidency [of Bombay].[5]

The question of reservations for the lower castes in the administration did not seem to be a priority objective, another indication of Ambedkar's desire to deal with Untouchability in the broader framework of workers' conditions. This new orientation did not reflect any Marxist influence. On the contrary, Ambedkar constantly criticised the Communists, whom he accused of exploiting the workers' cause to advance their own career,[6] an assessment which could be explained by the fact that the Communist movement was dominated by upper caste leaders. Ambedkar anyway considered Marxism to be of little utility in India; the caste system forbade the formation of antagonistic classes—in his view at least. In *Annihilation of Caste*, a text almost contemporaneous with the formation of the ILP, he underlined that the 'Caste System is not merely division of labour. *It is also a division of labourers*—Ambedkar's emphasis'.[7] This formula conforms to his theory of graded inequality, namely that workers—above all Untouchables—are differentiated according to a hierarchical logic as a function of their *jati* and that the gathering together of all within a 'working class' is an illusion. Indeed Ambedkar met with many difficulties attracting the support of Chambhars or Mangs who considered him to be a Mahar leader. While Marxist-inspired socialism considers, as a criterion of differentiation, the position of each class in relation to the means of production, for Ambedkar the relationship to property was not at the root of the main forms of domination in India:

> Why do millionaires in India obey penniless Sadhus and Fakirs? [...] That religion is the source of power is illustrated by the history of India where the priest holds a sway over the common man often greater than the magistrate and where everything, even such things as strikes and elections, so easily take a religious turn and can so easily be given a religious twist.[8]

Ambedkar, fundamentally sceptical about the aptness of the revolutionary message in India, went on to address the socialists in this vein:

> Men will not join in a revolution for the equalisation of property unless they know that after the revolution is achieved they will be treated equally and that there will be no discrimination of caste and creed. [...] If Socialists are not to be content with the mouthing of fine phrases, if the Socialists wish to make Socialism a definite reality then they must recognise that the problem of social reform is fundamental and that for them there is no escape from it.[9]

Ambedkar's Independent Labour Party was thus an organisation whose leanings were not Marxist but which continued to give priority to the abolition of caste. This social transformation remained Ambedkar's primary objective compared to the revolutionary conquest of the State. The ILP, in this perspective, put forward candidates for the 1937 elections primarily because this event offered an occasion to strengthen the political consciousness of the masses and, of course, to give them true representatives.

The contradiction between the philosophy projected by the ILP and the speeches of Ambedkar justifying his rejection of Marxism is obvious: he claimed to represent workers in general yet he denied a real significance to class analysis and emphasised that caste remained the basic unit of society. This contradiction was evident from the results of the 1937 election. In the Bombay Presidency, the ILP fielded seventeen candidates, thirteen in the constituencies reserved for the Scheduled Castes where they recorded eleven victories, and only four—upper caste candidates—[10] in the general constituencies where it gained three seats. Ambedkar, who had acquired national renown since the Round Table Conferences and his clash with Gandhi, had wished to establish his party beyond the Bombay Presidency. But in the Central Provinces and in Bihar the party gained only three out of twenty seats reserved for Untouchables.[11] These results clearly indicated that, in spite of his efforts, the ILP remained a party of Untouchables centred in Maharashtra, where, incidentally, it owed the lion's share of its success to Ambedkar's own caste, the Mahars. Most ILP candidates belonged to this caste; on the list of candidates, there was only one Mang while the other non-Mahar was an Untouchable from Gujarat. The Chambhars, whose socio-economic development exceeded not only that of the Mangs but also of the Mahars, were hardly represented in the ranks of the party. For them, as for the Mangs, Ambedkar was a Mahar leader and his party represented his caste—not the workers.[12]

With ten seats in the Legislative Council of the Bombay Presidency, the ILP became the second party of opposition to the Congress in the province, behind the Muslim League, and Ambedkar was naturally one of the ten elected members. His interventions in the Legislative Council in 1937–8 focussed mostly on ameliorating workers' socio-economic conditions.

Fighting for the workers. Ambedkar's main objective in the Legislative Council was the abolition of the systems of *vatan* and of *khoti*. On September 17, 1937, he proposed a bill to abolish the *vatan* system[13] under which Mahars were subjugated, but without evicting them from the land which they then occupied as payment for services rendered to the village.[14]

Ambedkar also proposed a bill to abolish the *khoti* system by which land tax was collected by an intermediary, the *khot*. Charged by the State to raise taxes in rural areas, the *khot* could not only keep a part of the revenue accruing, but often set himself up as a local 'minor Rajah'. This process occurred all the more readily as the *khot* was often a member of an upper caste.

Ambedkar sought the abolition of this function in exchange for compensation which should not exceed 1 per cent of the sums collected by the *khot* in his domain.[15] The Congress, which commanded a large majority in the Legislative Council, opposed this demand, arguing that the Revenue Minister had already planned for reform of the *khoti* system[16].

The ILP responded by launching a rural protest movement. It was supported by Untouchable activists but also by Kunbis, many of whom suffered under the *khoti* system. On January 12, 1938, 20,000 farmers from the districts of Thana, Kolaba, Ratnagiri, Satara and Nasik gathered at Bombay for a demonstration that was led by Ambedkar. Communist Party of India members also participated and Ambedkar's speech on this occasion was laden with Marxist overtones:

> 'Really seen, there are only two castes in the world—the first, that of the rich, and the second, that of the poor. [...] Just as we have organised and come here today, so we must forget caste differences and religious differences to make our organisation strong.'[17]

For the attention of his 'Communist friends', he added that in spite of his reservations about Marxist theories 'in regard to the toilers' class struggle, I feel the Communist philosophy to be closer to us.'[18] A delegation led by Ambedkar obtained a meeting with the Congress Chief Minister of the Bombay Presidency, B. G. Kher, but nothing came of it.[19]

This was not the first disappointment associated with the Congress government which had come to power after the 1937 elections. Ten months after Ambedkar had first presented his private bill to abolish *khoti*, no vote had been scheduled on the subject in the Legislative Council. It was a clear indication of Congress's reluctance to incur the hostility of the property-owners, Marathas or Brahmins, who dominated the party. In fact the *khoti* system was to be abolished only in 1949.[20]

Ambedkar's activism against the *vatan* and *khoti* systems tended to project him as the spokesman of those who suffered from the traditional socio-economic organisation in the villages—and more especially of his caste since the Mahars were the only *vetandars* among the Untouchables. But he was eager to reach out to the urban workers too. In 1935, he had formed a trade union for the municipality employees of Bombay, the Bombay Municipal Kamgar Sangh, which grew from 800 members in 1937 to 1,325 in 1938, thereby representing more than 5 per cent of the city's municipal workers.[21]

In September 1938, Ambedkar protested against the *Industrial Disputes Bill* whose aim was to impose a conciliation procedure between employers and workers in dispute. The Congress government justified the measure by citing the growing number of strikes, whereas Ambedkar contested their analysis, emerging as the defender of the right to strike, a fundamental freedom which he did not wish to see curtailed at any rate.[22] When communist circles mooted the idea of a one day general strike, he accepted the proposition with alacrity, and a Council of Action, in which both communists and ILP leaders cooperated, organised the protest.

The meeting of November 6, mainly organised by the ILP, attracted 80,000 participants. The strike the following day evoked a good response. At another meeting, attended by nearly 100,000 people, Ambedkar called for workers to take power by electing their own representatives in the existing legislative bodies—he therefore ruled out any revolutionary agenda. But this stand did not prevent him from sharing the platform with the communist leader, S. A. Dange.[23] The Industrial Dispute Bill was nevertheless passed easily in the Bombay Legislative Council and the agitation subsided.[24]

The ILP gradually established itself as a fully-fledged organisation. In 1940 Ambedkar endowed it with a red flag, in the upper left corner of which were eleven stars symbolising the eleven provinces of British India, a sign of the party's pan-Indian ambitions. In fact the ILP remained confined to the Bombay Presidency but put down roots there: the Bombay city branch had 4,000 members in 1938. Keer emphasises that the organisational efforts of Ambedkar had their limits:

> Ambedkar did not try to organise his political party on modern lines. He had no taste for individual organisation. There were no regular annual conferences or general meetings of the organisations with which he was connected. Where and when he sat was the venue of conference and the time for decision. The President or the Secretary or the Working Committee had to fall in line with his arrangement. [...] When he wanted his people to assemble under his banner, he simply gave them a clarion call, and the organisation sprang up like the crop in the rainy season.[25]

Yet I would argue that Ambedkar's poor organisational skills need to be seen in a more nuanced way. He had no little success in establishing the Samata Sainik Dal ('the party of the fighters for equality') in the 1930s. The Dal provided the ILP with activists for street or door to door agitations as well as muscle men to maintain order during demonstrations. The Dal's uniform included khaki shorts—probably in imitation of the RSS, its great rival in the field—and a red shirt but its flag was blue, the traditional colour of Dalit politics since then. In Nagpur, Vasant Moon recalls that the Dal inculcated a quasi-military discipline among young Dalits. Local members met at sunrise and sunset[26]—as did the RSS members. However, the ILP was not as well structured as the RSS and one has to admit that Ambedkar did not pay enough attention to this issue.

Besides this organisational shortcoming, the ideological contradictions of the ILP mentioned above, gradually became untenable. The party could hardly become the representative of *all* workers whereas it was based on a network of Dalit activists. Not surprisingly, several Kunbi sympathisers gradually distanced themselves from it. Even the poorest considered themselves to be of a naturally superior rank to Untouchables.[27] The line adopted by the ILP thus turned out to be unviable and, in 1942, the party was replaced by the Scheduled Castes' Federation.

The Scheduled Castes' Federation and Caste Politics

Ambedkar founded the Scheduled Castes' Federation (or Dalit Federation, in Marathi) in July, 1942 in order to signal, as the name of the organisation suggests, a shift in political strategy: the emphasis was again on caste. The immediate reason for this decision was the Cripps Mission formula, which was submitted in March 1942 to resolve India's constitutional impasse. It proposed the election of a Constituent Assembly without taking into account any of the demands of Untouchables, whereas Muslims were virtually guaranteed the prospect of a separate state, Pakistan. Ambedkar was not prepared to see his community's interests sacrificed in this manner:

> It is quite obvious that the proposal for a Constituent Assembly is intended to win over the Congress, while the proposal for Pakistan is designed to win over the Muslim League. How do the proposals deal with the Depressed Classes? To put it shortly, they are bound hand and foot and handed over to the caste Hindus. They offer them nothing: stone instead of bread. For the Constituent Assembly is nothing but a betrayal of the Depressed Classes [...]. If they are there, they cannot have a free, independ-

ent decisive vote. In the first place, the representatives of the Depressed Classes will be in a hopeless minority. In the second place, all decisions of the Constituent Assembly are not required by a unanimous vote.[28]

In reaction to Cripps's proposal the All India Depressed Classes' Conference met at Nagpur. It brought together 70,000 delegates from Punjab, the United Provinces, Bengal and Madras Presidency, but in even larger numbers from Bombay Presidency, the Central Provinces and Berar.[29]

The first resolution voted on this occasion demanded a separate electorate for Untouchables; the second sought the establishment of separate villages for Untouchables, 'at a distance from the Hindu villages'; and the third announced the creation of the Scheduled Castes' Federation (SCF).[30]

The creation of the SCF therefore reflected a new mood, a new sense of identity among Untouchables.[31] The Scheduled Castes wished to be recognised as a minority in the same way as Muslims were, and, as a consequence, sought the benefit, not only of a separate electorate, but also of separate territories. From 1926 onwards Ambedkar had suggested that Untouchables should settle new lands; and in 1929, he had even proposed surveying unoccupied but cultivable areas of Sind and of Indore state, whose Maharajah he was close to.[32]

The general guidelines set out in the Nagpur resolutions were clarified by the Executive Committee of the SCF in September 1944, meeting in Madras.[33] One motion reiterated that 'the Scheduled Castes are a distinct and separate element in the national life of India and that they are a religious minority in a sense far more real than the Sikhs and Muslims can be and within the meaning of the Cripps Proposals.'[34] Another resolution stipulated that no Constitution would be deemed acceptable to the Scheduled Castes if it did not have their consent. This proposition was conditional on the fulfilment of several demands: a separate electorate, a guarantee of representation within the executive and a special form of taxation for their own villages.[35] The notion of Dalit villages crystallised around the same time. In 1944 Ambedkar confided to Beverley Nicholas, a British officer:

'In every village there is a tiny minority of Untouchables. I want to gather those minorities together and make them into majorities. This means a tremendous work of organisation—transferring populations, building new villages. But we can do it, if only we are allowed [by the British].'[36]

About the same time, in Madras, Ambedkar met E. V. Ramaswami Naicker, known as Periyar, a leader of low caste Tamils, with whom he discussed the desirability of setting up 'Dravidasthan'—a separate Dravidian political entity in South India. It was, in its way, a variant of the territorial demand formulated by the SCF in the name of the Untouchables.[37] Ambedkar also shared with Periyar a critique of the Justice Party, an anti-Brahmin party which came to power in Madras in 1920. He blamed its leaders for having reintroduced certain features of the Sanskritisation process:

> Instead of abandoning Brahminism, they had been holding on to the spirit of it as being the ideal they ought to reach. And their anger against Brahmins was that the Brahmins gave them only a second class degree. [...] One defect in the political programme of the Non-Brahmin [Justice] party had been that the party made it its chief concern to secure a certain number of jobs for their young men [of the intermediate castes]. [...] During the twenty years the Party had been in office, it forgot the 90 percent of the Non-Brahmins living in the villages.[38]

Ambedkar rightly attributes the decline of the Justice Party to a form of careerism which led it to betray its natural constituency. This critique was in tune with Ambedkar's reorientation towards a greater focus on Untouchables *per se*, a project of which the SCF was the spearhead. As he declared in Madras: 'You should realise what our object is. [...] It is not fighting for a few jobs or a few conveniences. It is the highest cause that we have ever cherished in our hearts. That is to see that we are recognised as the Governing community.'[39] During a meeting organised by the Railway Employees' Union in Madras, he declared in the same vein, according to some press reports, that: 'without minimising the importance of Trade Union, he would like to emphasise the importance of capturing political power.'[40]

The elections of 1945–6 were to reveal that the party still had a long way to go before achieving such ends. They had a dual purpose in that they were about renewing the provincial assemblies and endowing India with a Constituent Assembly. The SCF fared badly in both respects, gaining only two seats in the provincial assemblies, one in Bengal, the other in the Central Provinces and Berar. This setback partly reflected the voting system. In the primaries in which only Untouchables voted, the SCF gained more votes than the Congress in the Presidencies of Madras and Bombay and in the Central Provinces. But these good results could not translate into a commensurate number of seats because of the electoral system. The situation in the United Provinces was especially revealing of the distortions inherent in the electoral system. There twenty seats were reserved for Scheduled Castes, including four urban constituencies, which were the only ones the SCF contested. In the primaries, nine of the party's candidates were successful as against four for Congress—but in the second round the latter won all the seats thanks to the support of non-Dalit voters. The most dramatic result occurred in Agra, where four SCF candidates polled 46.39 per cent of valid votes as against to 27.1 per cent for four Congress candidates.[41] This state of affairs could only strengthen Ambedkar's stance in favour of a separate electorate for the Untouchables. His only hope in this regard lay with the British. He went to England in late 1946 to present his views in this regard. On his return to India, he gave an interview to *Globe Agency*:

> 'A separate electorate would alone guarantee to the Scheduled Castes the possibility of electing to the legislature members of their own who could be trusted at all times to fight in the legislature and in the executive whenever they did anything which had the effect of nullifying the rights granted to Untouchables [...]. It will be noticed that the Congress has been able to elect on its ticket representatives of the Scheduled Castes all throughout India in the different Provincial legislatures. And yet not one of them ever asked a question, moved a resolution or tabled a cut motion in order to ventilate the grievances of the Scheduled Castes [...]. It would be much better not to have representation at all than to have such sham representation in the legislature'.[42]

In spite of pressing his demands, Ambedkar was not heard by the British, who considered that the failure of the SCF in the elections of 1945–6 did not endow it with the status of an important player, or even merit a particular role in the Constituent Assembly.[43]

In addition to the impact made by the electoral system, a much plausible explanation of the SCF's defeat lay in the tiny number of candidates nominated by the party: it did not field any at all in 129 of the 151 seats reserved for Untouchables, reflecting its organisational weakness. As Bandyopadhyay tartly pointed out: 'the Federation had no organisational machinery.'[44] It had no network of party branches and only a handful of cadres. In fact, the party relied very heavily on Ambedkar who was unable to spend much time campaigning given his other commitments as a member of the Viceroy's government. Zelliot underlines that he was also preoccupied in writing *What Congress and Gandhi have done to Untouchables*,[45] one more indication that he was unquestionably as much an intellectual as a politician—at any rate he was not an organisation man.

Besides, the SCF's defeat was also due to the remarkable popularity of Congress, including among Untouchables, because of its dedication to the freedom movement. In contrast, Ambedkar was painted as being 'unpatriotic' for having joined the Viceroy's government. At the local level, he was depicted as a 'traitor', as evident from the election campaign in Nagpur, for instance.[46]

The very modest rise in the influence of the SCF gradually encouraged Ambedkar to revisit the ILP's strategy in order to win support beyond Untouchables, albeit in a very different manner.

From the SCF to the RPI—a return to the ILP?

Ambedkar's oscillations between two party-building strategies, one based on an appeal to the 'labouring classes' and the other relying on a separate Untouchable identity, were still in evidence after independence. The 1951–2 Election Manifesto of the SCF continued to emphasise the need for more equality and stressed the promotion of the backward 'classes' through education and reservations in the administration. It advocated also land reform measures which would benefit Untouchables and 'Other Backward Classes' (the 'backwards', other than Untouchables—essentially Shudras—to which the Constitution of 1950 had just promised special assistance).[47] While it focussed on caste politics, the SCF did not overlook class. In its manifesto the party committed itself to fight 'oppression and exploitation of man by man, of class by class and of nation by nation.'[48] The Marxist overtone of the manifesto was also noticeable in the recommendations regarding agricultural collectivisation and nationalisation of insurance. However, the discourse of caste was counterbalanced not only by an interest in class but also by a universalism which Ambedkar borrowed from Enlightenment philosophers. The equality advocated by the SCF was that of the French republican motto, repeated unambiguously in its Election manifesto which considered 'every Indian as an end in himself with a right to his own development'. The Election Manifesto also referred to the parliamentary form of government which the Constitution—whose text had been drafted by Ambedkar, as we shall see below—had just established and which was described as 'the best form of government, both in the interest of the public and in the interest of the individual'. The SCF wanted to be, moreover 'purely nationalist and modern'.

The SCF seemed to be locked in a contradiction. How could it combine this militant individualism and defending special treatment for the lower castes should it entail granting quotas or implementing agrarian reforms intended to serve a particular group? More important, by continuing to refer only to Untouchables, wasn't it automatically limiting its electoral appeal?[49] Besides, the SCF's manifesto did not include any appealing commitment to the poor and the Scheduled Castes in terms of redistribution. In fact this issue was simply ignored: poverty could only be reduced by increasing production or 'controlling excessive growth of population';[50] no land reform of any sort was advocated. To aid landless peasants, the state should first develop irrigation, fell forests and make waste land available for cultivation thanks to 'modern science.'[51] It is unlikely that poor peasants would have been convinced by such a programme.

Indeed, the elections of 1951–2 delivered no better a result than those of 1946. The SCF won only 2.3% of the valid votes and two seats in the Lok Sabha, one in Hyderabad and the other in Bombay Presidency where Ambedkar was defeated and where the performance of the party was far weaker than expected. On the other hand, the SCF for the first time won representation in the assemblies of Madras, Hyderabad, the State of Mysore, PEPSU (Patiala and East Punjab States Union) and Himachal Pradesh.

Ambedkar drew three conclusions from this electoral setback. First, it reinforced his opposition to the reserved seats system. No longer did he imagine an India endowed with a system of separate electorates but, failing that, he preferred the abolition of reserved seats, which tended to isolate the Untouchable electorate and hampered efforts to tap the votes of other social groups. In August 1955, the Executive committee of the SCF passed a resolution asking for the annulment of the system of reserved seats.[52]

Secondly, Ambedkar realised that the Scheduled Castes' Federation, when it raised the political consciousness of Untouchables, tended also to cut them adrift from the rest of society. Hence in Nagpur, in October 1956, he argued in favour of forming a new party with a broader mandate and encouraged activists to work with the leaders of other communities.[53]

The third lesson he drew from these elections was precisely the absolute necessity of forming alliances with other social and political sectors. He resumed a dialogue with the socialists of the Praja Socialist Party and later with Ram Manohar Lohia's Socialist Party. In 1954, he stood in a by-election at Bhandera (Maharashtra) on the same ticket as Ashok Mehta, a socialist leader—Ambedkar stood for the reserved seat of this dual constituency and Mehta for the general one.

The RPI was to be the end-product of these cogitations. Although it was formally established only in October 1957, the Republican Party of India was conceived by Ambedkar a short while before his death in 1956, when he was concerned with the need to forge an alternative to the Communist Party, whose appeal to the Untouchable electorate he feared. As he declared in 1956,

> Before I die, I must establish a definite political direction for my people. They have remained poor, oppressed and deprived, and because of that, now, a new consciousness and a new anger are growing among them. That is natural. But it is also natural that this type of community becomes attracted to Communism. I do not want my people to fall under the sway of the Communists.[54]

Ambedkar consulted various socialist leaders, among them socialists like Ram Manohar Lohia, P. K. Atre and S. M. Joshi, to seek their support for his plan to form a new political party. He named it the Republican Party of India by reference to both Lincoln's American Republican Party and to the 'republics' of India's Buddhist era.[55] The name also reflected his desire to return to the philosophy of the Independent Labour Party. Ambedkar was apparently able to combine two sets of objectives to represent the low caste groups—mainly Untouchables—so as to broaden his party's appeal to all impoverished sections of society. The RPI in fact projected a program in which the notion of caste faded away behind that of class, but with the aim of appearing as a federation of oppressed populations discriminated against because of their ascribed status, be they Dalits, OBCs or Tribals In the manifests that the SCF produced before the February 1957 elections, the party had already indicated that it was 'prepared to change the name and call itself the Backward Classes Federation so as to include both sections [OBCs and Tribals in additions to the Scheduled Castes] in a common organisation'[56]. The RPI adopted a name which allowed him to accommodate these groups and even more. The constitution of the party endowed the party with the mission of 'organising the down-trodden masses of India particularly the Buddhists [mainly converted Mahars], Scheduled Castes, Scheduled Tribes and Other Backward Classes.'[57] The RPI was to position itself between the defence of Untouchables alone on one side and a politics of class on the other, a delicate balancing act. It had also to establish itself as the spokesperson of social groups which were victims of an oppression related to their status, in the Weberian sense of 'status groups', in this case the Tribes and the lower castes—classified among the Scheduled Castes and Other Backward Classes.[58] In this manner it broadened its audience beyond the Untouchables without falling into the Marxist trap of class or the liberal myth of the individual citizen.

This dilution of Dalit identity also allowed for alliances to be struck with other political parties. This objective was pursued within the framework of the campaign to redefine the state boundaries of the Indian Union according to linguistic criteria. At first Ambedkar had been hostile to the dismemberment of Bombay Province that such a reshaping of the Indian map would entail. From his point of view, the creation of provinces speaking Gujarati, Marathi, Kannada and Telugu could only strengthen the demographic (and, therefore, political) weight of the dominant castes. In Maharashtra, the Marathas would be the first beneficiaries of such a measure; they could in this way consolidate their hold over Untouchables. Yet the strength of linguistic regionalism was such in Maharashtra that Ambedkar, in a somewhat opportunist way, joined the movement. The communists and the socialists had already taken the initiative of forming the Samyukta Maharashtra Samiti (Committee for a United Maharashtra) to press Nehru, who was reluctant to a reorganisation of the administrative map based on communal considerations: the nation, in his opinion, had to be built on the basis of individual allegiance.

Although at heart Ambedkar shared the views of the Prime Minister, he allied with the Samyukta Maharashtra Samiti (SMS) on behalf of the SCF in November 1956.

This agreement, and the support that the SCF brought to the cause of redrawing provincial borders according to linguistic criteria, contributed to its success in the elections of February 1957. The SCF won 4 seats (two of which were reserved for Untouchables) in the Lok Sabha in Bombay Province and fifteen in the Legislative Assembly of the province—most of them in Bombay, to which P. T. Borale, a lieutenant of Ambedkar's, was elected mayor. Ambedkar died three months before the elections but the achievements of the SCF were a posthumous tribute to his pragmatism—one of his distinctive characteristics that we shall consider in the next chapter.

As party leader Ambedkar oscillated between two strategies. He tried first to attract not only Dalits but all kinds of workers by establishing the ILP. But the broad agenda of this party was hard to reconcile with the core Dalit ideology and sociology of Ambedkarism. Hence the launch of the SCF which harked back to the cause of the Untouchables. However, the scope of the party turned out to be too limited and therefore Ambedkar went back to the initial philosophy of the ILP in a different way: with the RPI he tried to set up an organisation representing all those of low status, the Scheduled Castes, the Other Backward Classes and the Scheduled Tribes.

These changes in direction reflected Ambedkar's oscillation between the logic of class and the emphasis, which came more naturally to him, on caste as a basic unit of society. The class option, as is underlined by J. Gokhale, was based on a reading of Untouchability in socio-economic terms which allows Untouchables to seek allies among other castes suffering from similar handicaps. Parties relying on the logic of caste—of which the SCF was the prototype—reflected another strategy: Untouchables were seen as irreducibly separate from the rest of society and the hold of Hinduism on other castes—even the lowest—was such that it was impossible to collaborate with them.[59] Ambedkar's indecisiveness reflected his wavering between the aspiration to rise *within* Hindu society and the urge to sever his links with it. But J. Gokhale, by confining Ambedkar between these two poles—the politics of caste and that of class—

omits to mention a third term, the culmination of his political experiment. Ambedkar eventually conceived of a party which would transcend the logic of class while no longer confining itself to the Untouchable milieu, a party which would become the mouthpiece of all groups comprised of the lower castes and Tribals. Such a project was integral to Ambedkar's analysis according to which Indian society could not be interpreted by means of Marxist categories. But it also envisaged that 'graded inequality' would become blurred, allowing for the emergence of horizontal solidarities between castes and tribes of subordinate status, which in turn could form a block against the elite.

None of Ambedkar's party-building strategies enabled him to project himself as the sole representative of the Untouchables. Even when his party was at its zenith, he never managed to marginalise his opponents and unify the Dalits politically. He was not present at the Nagpur All India Depressed Classes' Leaders' Conference of 1926 which gave birth to the first pan-Indian organisation of Untouchables, the All India Depressed Classes' Association which was a creation of the Congress party. He was appointed as one of its vice-presidents *in absentia*, but the President was M. C. Rajah. Nor did he attend the Delhi annual conference of 1928, at a time when he had been proposed for the presidency. Ultimately, in 1930, he founded his own All India Depressed Classes' Congress as a rival organisation. The opposition between the 'Association' and the 'Congress' peaked in 1932 when Rajah rejected the demand for separate electorates and threw his support behind Gandhi in the Poona Pact episode. Rajah, who had been disillusioned by the Congress governments—including Rajagopalachari's—elected in 1937, joined the Scheduled Castes' Federation in 1942 but at that time Ambedkar had to face another enemy: the All India Depressed Classes' League, which had been founded by Congressmen in 1935. The key figure in this new organisation was Jagjivan Ram, a protégé of the Bihar Congress boss, Rajendra Prasad. The League had been created in order to equip the Congress with 'a political front to mobilise Dalit voters to win the reserved seats provided for in the [1935] new [Government of India] Act'.[60] It did rather well since Congress won 73 out of 151 reserved seats throughout India in the 1937 elections.

However, at that time Ambedkar was still regarded as the Untouchables' representative *par excellence* in the eyes of the British, though he was far from being unrivalled. In 1942, the Cripps Mission did not consult League leaders but rather Ambedkar and Rajah, and Wavell also invited the former to the 1945 Simla Conference.[61] However, the 1945–6 elections had a devastating impact on Ambedkar's credibility *vis-à-vis* the British: with 2 reserved seats out of 151, the SCF could no longer claim to represent the Untouchables. In April 1946 the Cabinet Delegation sent by the British Government to consult Indian political opinion in the run up to the transfer of power met not the Ambedkarites but leaders of the League, including Jagjivan Ram, who was also nominated to the Labour portfolio in the provisional government formed a few months later.[62]

Thus Ambedkar had failed to build a political party to represent the Untouchables. By 1947 he could no longer rely on any substantial organised political support; yet, paradoxically, he was about to have his finest hour as Law Minister in Nehru's Government and Chairman of the Drafting Committee of the Constituent Assembly. How did he bounce back, and how did he perform such an accomplished U-turn to join hands with his former arch-enemies? Pragmatism goes a long way in explaining his resilience. Not only at this critical juncture—1947—but all along it had been one of the watchwords of his career.

6. Opposition or collabortion? Ambedkar's Pragmatism and Resilience

'We must take advantage of the struggle between the two parties [the Congress and the Socialists] and, maintaining our separate identity, cooperate with the one which will accept our conditions, and thus derive the most benefit. Power is the key to social progress.' (statement of Ambedkar in 1948, quoted in M. S. Gore, *The Social Context of an Ideology*, p. 182)

'What I want is power—political power for my people—for if we have power we have social status.' (statement of Ambedkar during the 5th annual conference of the United Provinces Scheduled Castes' Federation, 24–25 April 1948)

The British—objective allies?

Leaders of India's lower castes had traditionally felt an affinity with Europeans, based on their perceptions of Western egalitarianism. Was it not from missionaries and British teachers that they had learnt notions of equality and freedom? Phule, for one, was influenced by his missionary education and his reading of Thomas Paine. Beyond these bonds, Untouchable elites, and the lower castes in general, hoped that the British, as trustees of these values, would aid their emancipation. For instance, the Mahar veterans' petition of 1910 against the exclusion of their caste from the armed forces asked: 'Shall not that nation which emancipated the Negro at infinite self-sacrifice, and enlightened and elevated the poorer people of its own commonwealth, condescend to give us a helping hand?'.[1] The signatories claimed 'the full rights of British citizenship' as recognition of their social equality: 'We are sick of the bondage which the barbarism of Hindu custom imposes upon us; we long to enjoy the perfect freedom that the British nation and British Government desire to offer impartially to all who are connected with them as British subjects'.[2] For this reason lower caste and Untouchable movements were hostile to any indianisation of the State: for them the granting of high positions in the administration to Indians, one of Congress's major demands since its inception, would once again subject the downtrodden to the sole authority of the upper castes. The joint statement of the Depressed India Association and the Servants of Somavamshiya Society before the Simon Commission was unambiguous in this regard: '… no caste Hindu, once he occupies a position of influence, would allow a member of the Depressed Classes, to rise in the social or economic scale but, on the contrary would aim to stabilise his condition as a hewer of wood and drawer of water. We have more to hope from the British officer who, free from communal or caste bias, unfetterred by any wicked tradition, is quick to respond to the prompting of his conscience and the dictates of humanity.'[3]

Ambedkar shared this current of thought. In 1931 his 'Appeal on behalf of the Depressed Classes Institute', by which he tried to raise £40,000, asked 'the Europeans and the Americans' to help a 'deprived humanity'—a part of the human race[4] (Ambedkar often resorted in his Marathi writings to the word *manuski*, in English translated as 'humanness').[5]

The fascination that Europeans exercised over Ambedkar was tempered by his nationalist feelings. But by the late 1930s he moved closer to the British as he realised how the exercise of power by Congress was harming the Untouchable cause.

When nationalism loses its power of inhibition. In 1920–30 Ambedkar was careful not to oppose the Freedom Movement. If he fought against Gandhi and Congress, he usually moderated his criticisms by asserting his attachment to national unity. During the First Round Table Conference, he claimed that Indians should have the right to self-government.[6] There were two principal reasons that explain his stand: first, Ambedkar could not afford to be thought of as a 'traitor to the country', given that participating in the Conference had already prompted such criticism from Congress, all the more so since the first session of the All India Depressed Classes' Congress

(August 8, 1930, at Nagpur) had explicitly opposed the idea of complete independence, whereas it had recently been enshrined in writing in Congress's program, in December 1929, under pressure from Nehru. Ambedkar's organisation meanwhile had demanded Dominion status rather than full independence.[7]

Secondly, Ambedkar had been deeply disappointed by the British as is evident from what he said during the first Round Table Conference:

> 'The depressed classes welcomed the British as their deliverers from age-long tyranny and oppression by the orthodox Hindus [...]. When we compare our present position with the one which it was our lot to bear in Indian society of the pre-British days, we find that, instead of marching on, we are only marking time.'[8]

He blamed this state of things on the colonial power's lack of understanding of India, on its failure to reform society and above all on its decision to establish its authority largely via a network of local notables and an administration dominated by the upper castes. Therefore, during the first Round Table Conference Ambedkar appeared to be in favour of a transfer of power:

> 'We must have a government in which the men in power ... will not be afraid to amend the social and economic code of life which the dictates of justice and expediency so urgently call for. This role, the British Government will never be able to play. [...] We feel that nobody can remove our grievances as well as we can, and we cannot remove them unless we get political power in our own hands.'[9]

Ambedkar entertained such views after 1937, while simultaneously emancipating himself from the nationalist straitjacket and beginning to seek the support of the British. In fact, Congress's accession to power in many parts of India, including the Bombay Presidency, had some impact in radicalising Ambedkar's till then ambivalent position towards the nationalist movement. He considered that rulers indifferent to caste—the British—had been replaced by 'social oppressors'—namely the upper caste Hindus who dominated Congress. The party's political trajectory after its rise to power in 1937 certainly reinforced this opinion. For Ambedkar it pursued very conservative policies in the Bombay Presidency. In response to workers' and peasants' agitation, backed by the Independent Labour Party, the government opted for repression as mentioned above.[10] The *Industrial Dispute Bill* was passed on September 2, 1938, making strikes illegal under certain conditions.[11] Ambedkar was further outraged by Congress's refusal to abolish the *khoti* and *vatan* systems.[12]

There were two parallel trends in Ambedkar's political attitude: his growing opposition to Congress and his rejection of patriotism as an ideology. In the early 1930s he had told Gandhi that Untouchables had no homeland,[13] and in 1939 he reasserted his position, his views having hardened in the intervening years:

> ...whenever there has been a conflict between my personal interests and the interests of the country as a whole, I have always placed the claim of the country above my personal claims [...]. But I will also leave no doubt in the minds of the people of this country that I have another loyalty to which I am bound and which I can never forsake. That loyalty is the community of Untouchables, in which I am born, to which I belong, and which I hope I shall never desert. And I say this to this House [the Legislative Council of Bombay] as strongly as I possibly can, that whenever there is any conflict of interest between the country and Untouchables so far as I am concerned Untouchables' interests will take precedence over the interests of the country.[14]

Ambedkar shared Phule's view, that India did not constitute a nation: 'How can people divided into several thousands of castes be a nation?',[15] he asked again in 1950. He would have perhaps recognised himself as a nationalist had the nation constituted a collection of free and equal individuals, and had intermediate bodies such as castes disappeared. As long as this form of the nation was yet to emerge, Ambedkar concentrated on working on behalf of Untouchables, a decision that in retrospect contributed to the constitution of such a nation of citizens, given that it aimed to promote equality.

Ambedkar had no time for a national movement dominated by an elite and of which the masses were usually the first victims. As he said, in 1943, before the trade union activists, the working classes 'often sacrifice their all to the so-called cause of Nationalism. [But] they have never cared to enquire whether the nationalism for which they are to make their offerings will, when established, give them social and economic equality. More often than not, the free independent national state, which emerges from a successful nationalism and which reared on their sacrifices, turns to be the enemy of the working class under the hegemony of their masters'[16].

Thus Ambedkar eventually dissociated himself from the Congress-led freedom movement because of the way in which Congress administered the provinces. He felt that its early record did not augur well for how it would exercise power if the independence struggle was speedily accomplished. As early as October 1939 he declared in the Bombay Legislative Assembly:

> 'I will not tolerate it. I will shed the last drop of my blood to uproot that position. I will not tolerate it if the social dominance, the economic dominance and the religious dominance which the Hindus exercise over me, is added the political dominance also. I will certainly not tolerate it. I still repeat again that I will never allow it. We shall fight tooth and nail against politics being perverted for the purpose of establishing an oligarchy of a ruling class.'[17]

His priority remained the defence of Untouchables[18] and it led him to cooperate ever more closely with the colonial power.

Working with the British. The British government's involvement of India in the Second World War without having consulted Congress drove the party to resign all the provincial governments where it held power. The British were eager to acquire new Indian interlocutors to mobilise the country on behalf of the war effort, and on October 1939, the Executive Council of the ILP, after lengthy deliberation, voted to cooperate with the British:

> In view of the insurances, given by the H.E. the Viceroy, that immediately after the close of the war His Majesty's Government will enter into consultations with representatives of communities, parties and interests, in framing modification in the Constitution of India and in view of the fact that His Majesty's Government have declared their adherence to Dominion Status as the goal of India and further in view of the fact that the development of the war may take such a turn that the question of defending India may become more important than the question of helping Great Britain, the Executive Council feels that the present is not the proper occasion for withholding its co-operation from Great Britain.[19]

Their justifications for this action all relate, in one way or another, to the national question. Indeed the last of these—to protect India from invasion—could even be interpreted to justify Ambedkar's collaboration with the British in the name of patriotism, a theme he was to develop as the Japanese threat became more acute. It was by virtue of this principle that he opposed Gandhi's decision, in August 1942, to launch the 'Quit India' movement. The 'patriotic duty of all Indians' was rather, according to Ambedkar, to prevent such movements from creating 'anarchy and chaos which would unquestionably help and facilitate the subjugation of this country by Japan.'[20]

Ambedkar was not alone in his views. Within Congress Nehru worried about the consequences of the Quit India movement from an international perspective. To weaken England would play into the hands of the fascists whom the future Prime Minister of India had seen at first hand in Europe in the 1920s and '30s. For Ambedkar the desire to contribute to the British war effort was less compelling than the strategy of collaborating with the colonial power in exchange for concessions for Untouchables. In early 1941 he requested, and was granted, expanded recruitment of Untouchables in the army and, in particular the reinstatement of the Mahar battalion, whereupon he called on members of his caste to enlist en masse.[21] In the same breath he agreed to serve in the British administration; he was nominated, in July 1941, to the Defence Advisory Committee set up by the Viceroy. The aim of this body was to involve Indian politicians in the war effort (M. C. Rajah was one of these) and to lend greater legitimacy to India's coerced participation in the conflict. A year later Ambedkar joined the Viceroy's Executive Council as Member for Labour, a post that he hoped would allow him to improve the conditions of the Untouchables. One of the most significant bills that Ambedkar managed to have passed was the *Indian Trade Unions (Amendment) Bill*, making compulsory the recognition of a trade union in every enterprise provided it fulfilled certain conditions, particularly in terms of representation.

In November 1943, when listing the administrative gains made on behalf of the Untouchables, Ambedkar emphasised above all the fact that henceforth 8.33 per cent of posts in the national administration were reserved for the Scheduled Castes, as had been the case previously in the Madras Presidency, that places were also reserved for them in the institutions of technical education in Britain, that the quota in the Central Assembly had been increased by one seat and that there was now a reserved seat for them in the Council of the State (the Upper House of what was meant to be a Parliament).[22] During his tour of South India in 1944, he also emphasised the beneficial effects of the colonial administration by advocating a technical education project for 68,000 pupils and a law obliging employers to respect certain rules relating to wages and working conditions.[23] As a Labour Member he had initiated the *Payment of Wages (Amendment) Act* and numerous *Factories (Amendment) Acts*.[24] Ambedkar also instigated similar measures to regulate female employment (including a ban on them from working in mines)[25] and improve miners' conditions.[26]

Yet Ambedkar's main expectations from the British side were to be largely disappointed. In October 1942, he presented to the Viceroy a memorandum that set out the Scheduled Castes' demands concerning their place in the assemblies, the administration and the educational system. In the political sphere, the picture which he painted was rather bleak because there were only two Untouchables in the National assembly and only one—Ambedkar himself—in the Executive Council. As regards the administration, out of 1,056 members of the Indian Civil Service, only one was an Untouchable. In the educational field, by 1940 there only 400–500 Untouchable graduates. On this last point the remedy proposed by Ambedkar consisted in granting more scholarships to Untouchable pupils and students. The problems of access to the administrative services remained one of his priorities. He thought that the public sector, the state should give jobs to Scheduled Castes' youths because business and industry were often inaccessible to them. He also emphasised that opening the administration to Untouchables would encourage them to acquire an education. Lastly, he argued that the presence of Untouchables in the administration was a mandatory corollary to legislation because it would allow for the effective implementation of laws.[27]

In order to achieve higher recruitment of Untouchables in the administration, Ambedkar asked that they be categorised as a minority, just as Muslims, Anglo-Indians, Indian Christians, Sikhs and Parsis who had already been granted, in 1934, quotas in the main administrative departments (Indian Civil Service, railroads, customs, post and telegraphs) by the Home Office. However it might not have made much difference: the quota of 8.33 per cent allocated to the Scheduled Castes in the 1936 administration had not been taken up. First, ministerial departments other than Ambedkar's made no effort in this direction; second, it was very difficult to find appropriately qualified candidates among Untouchables.[28] In the political domain, Ambedkar was content with presenting to the government a strangely vague and moderate demand, namely an increase in the number of Untouchable representatives in the National assembly.

The British ignored his proposals, as borne out by the Cripps Mission, which envisaged the election of a Constituent Assembly without giving Untouchables any guarantee. On April 1, 1942, Ambedkar and Rajah made common cause in protest against this project, which they claimed was to subject Untouchables to the diktat of upper caste Hindus: '[It] takes us back to the black days of the ancient past, will never be tolerated by us, and we are all determined to resist any such catastrophe befalling our people with all the means at our command.'[29]

His bitter disappointment did not prompt Ambedkar to leave the Executive Committee. On the contrary, from 1943–5 he redoubled his lobbying of those in power to highlight the Untouchables' predicament in Indian society. In May 1945, he proposed his own plan to designate a Constituent Assembly: he recommended quotas for Untouchables in the assemblies, whereby they would be the real arbiters between Hindus and Muslims. The world ignored his suggestion and the indifference of the British was confirmed by the Wavell Plan. The Viceroy, Lord Wavell, having sought a compromise between Hindus and Muslims in 1945, decided on elections, which had first to test the levels of support enjoyed by the Muslim League, the Congress and other parties. Ambedkar's Scheduled Castes' Federation which achieved poor results in the 1946 elections was the first victim of this decision as mentioned above.

To sum up, Ambedkar's close cooperation with the British did not help him to realise his objectives but did obtain substantial concessions for Untouchables in terms of representation in the administration and the educational system as well as labour laws. The fact that from 1946 India was fast moving towards independence brought him closer to Congress, the obvious candidate for power.

Ambedkar, a Dalit leader in the establishment of post-1947 India

Ambedkar realised that he was losing the British support he had enjoyed for many years when the Cabinet Delegation agreed to Congress's request to meet Jagjivan Ram and other Untouchable leaders from the 'League' in April 1946 but ignored the SCF, considering that it had lost its representational base. The party launched a *satyagraha* in July in Poona, demonstrating in front of the Bombay Legislative Council building[30] in order to win minority status for Untouchables and obtain similar privileges for Muslims. Demonstrations were also held in Central Provinces and Berar and in the United Provinces. In September thousands of Ambedkarites massed in front of the Legislative Council in Nagpur.[31] But most of these agitations were short-lived and Ambedkar therefore 'missed the opportunity of proving, through direct action, his popular support'.[32] The British, consequently, continued to marginalise him.

Ambedkar therefore turned his back on the coloniser and offered his services to an upper caste-dominated Congress. As early as 1942, he announced that, '[i]f the Hindus gave adequate guarantees to the Depressed Classes, they would fight their battles shoulder to shoulder with them. Otherwise, there would be no compromise with them.[33] This doctrine of conditional support accurately reflected his pragmatic approach to politics, which was not to be mistaken for pure opportunism. He was not one to switch allies because of the posts that one or the other might offer him, but according to what would best serve the Untouchables' cause. In this respect, Ambedkar's career differs fundamentally from that of Jagjivan Ram, the key leader of Untouchables in Congress from the 1940s till the 1970s who did not use his position to defend Untouchables as much as he might, but instead helped Congress to project itself as a party representing all layers of society, including Dalits.

The rapprochement between Ambedkar and Congress occurred in the Constituent Assembly. On 17 December 1946, he commented upon the resolution moved by Jawaharlal Nehru regarding the 'Aims and objects' of the Assembly. His speech was met with enthusiastic support from all quarters of the house:

> 'I know today we are divided politically, socially and economically. We are a group of warring camps and I may go even to the extent of confessing that I am probably one of the leaders of such a camp. But, Sir, with all this, I am quite convinced that given time and circumstances nothing in the world will prevent this country from becoming one [applause]. With all our castes and creeds, I have not the slightest hesitation that we shall in some form be a united people [cheers]. I have no hesitation in saying that notwithstanding the agitation of the Muslim League for the partition of India some day enough light would down upon the Muslims themselves and they too

will begin to think that United India is better even for them [loud cheers and applause].'[34]

Ambedkar had no hesitation about questioning the stand of the Muslim League—which had supported his election to the Constituent Assembly—[35] in order to woo the Congress Party: the Congressmen of the assembly could not but be thrilled by his eloquent defence of national unity as they were forging a new India. To rally Ambedkar to this task was a great coup. Incidentally, Rajendra Prasad, the President of the Assembly, had invited him to speak whereas there were more than twenty representatives waiting to do so on the list before him—clearly he wanted Ambedkar to have the floor.

The rapprochement between Ambedkar and Congress continued throughout 1947. First, the former needed the latter's support to retain his seat in the Assembly. In 1946, he had contested elections to join this body, not in Bombay, where Congress was the ruling party, but in Bengal, where he was elected after winning the support of the Muslim League. However, the partition of Bengal stripped the Constituent Assembly of several seats representing the province and Ambedkar lost his seat in 1947. The resignation of an elected member of Bombay Presidency, M. R. Jayakar, allowed him to contest a by-election with the support of the Congress members of the Legislative Assembly who agreed to elect him to the Constituent Assembly at the request of party leaders such as Rajendra Prasad.[36]

In August 1947 Nehru appointed Ambedkar, doubtless under Gandhi's pressure,[37] his Law Minister in the first government of independent India. Ambedkar accepted the invitation of the Prime Minister because, as he said later, 'in the first place the offer was not subject to any condition and secondly it was easier to serve the interests of the Scheduled Castes from inside of the government than from outside.'[38] Yet he was disappointed because he had hoped for the labour or planning[39] portfolios instead of 'an empty soap-box, only good for old lawyers to play with'.[40]

As much in the Constituent Assembly as in the government, Ambedkar promoted the Untouchable cause.[41] He considered the forthcoming Constitution as the privileged instrument to enable a reform of Indian society, and in March 1947 he presented to the Constituent Assembly, on his own initiative, a Constitutional project. In this he demanded a separate electorate for Untouchables as well as a quota proportional to their demographic weight in the Central government and in the state governments; and also in the local, regional and national administrations.[42] Second, he asked that the Constitution should establish a Commission charged with the redistribution of State land in order to settle Untouchables in 'separate villages'.[43] Ambedkar's return to his most intransigent of positions was partially explained by the lessons that he had drawn from the creation of Pakistan. In his memorandum he emphasised that the Muslims of India had been awarded a separate electorate not only because they belonged to a different religion but 'because—and this is the fundamental fact—the social relations between the Hindus and Musalmans are marked by social discrimination.'[44] Why could it not be the same for Untouchables who, if one applied this criterion, were also a minority? In his book *Pakistan or the Partition of India* that went into three editions between 1940 and 1946, he also underlined that the demand of the Muslim League was completely justified.[45] Like the Muslims, Untouchables, in Ambedkar's opinion, were a minority with equal right to their own territory: given that they 'are, as a matter of fact, socially separate [from the rest of the Hindus], [they] should be made separate geographically and territorially also.'[46] After Partition, Ambedkar even declared himself in favour of a division of Kashmir. Furthermore the 1951–2 Election Manifesto of the SCF stipulated that Partition could no longer be questioned. No one should think of undoing it, and the Muslim part of the state of Jammu and Kashmir had to go, definitively, to Pakistan.[47]

Ambedkar's constitutional project was far more radical than that presented by two other Dalit leaders sitting in the Constituent Assembly, H. J. Khandekar and Jagjivan Ram. The first, a Mahar close to Rajah and Gavai who had joined the Congress in the early 1940s, had already clashed with Ambedkar by supporting the Rajah-Moonje pact and by opposing any conversion outside Hinduism.[48] Within the Constituent Assembly he pleaded for joint electorates with reserved seats for Untouchables.[49] As far as Ram was concerned, he took on board this idea and expressed even more clearly his preference for the integration of Untouchables within Hindu society. Indeed he wished 'to accelerate the assimilation of the other minorities (such as the Scheduled Castes) in the parent body by bringing them to an equal level with others in that community'.[50]

Hence he asked that temples be opened to Untouchables and that they be allowed to participate in festivals and other 'social events organised by the Hindus'. This stance was contrary to the views of Ambedkar.

The Constituent Assembly quickly designated within itself specialised sub-committees. The one charged with the problem of minorities—of which Ambedkar, Khandekar and Ram were members—declared itself hostile to the principle of separate electorates by twenty-eight votes to three, and in favour of the reserved seats system by twenty-six votes to three. Vallabhai Patel, the vice-Prime Minister and Home Minister, who chaired the sub-committee, had successfully opposed separate electorates by arguing more or less explicitly that Muslim separatism had been nurtured by this very system. In his view separate electorates would strengthen community divisions, which India had to rid itself of in order to become a strong nation.[51] Ambedkar proposed that at least the candidate of a minority should be declared elected in any constituency only if a substantial proportion of his own group (the Untouchables, for instance) voted for him, but he was not supported by the sub-committee. Patel emphasised that such a scheme would be as harmful as separate electorates.[52]

This issue was discussed again during the following plenary session when Patel submitted the sub-committee's report to the Constituent Assembly. On August 28, 1947, one of Ambedkar's lieutenants, S. Nagappa, proposed an amendment which reflected his leader's position. He stipulated that in constituencies reserved for Scheduled Castes, only the candidates who obtained at least 35 per cent of the Dalit votes could be returned. This provision avoided the danger, in the assemblies, of Dalit representatives being mainly elected by the upper castes, as established by the Poona Pact. In support of his motion, Nagappa declared that Untouchables at the grass roots level did not generally acknowledge the leadership of the elected members of the reserved seats, and even that these deputies, when they sought their votes on the occasion of election campaigns, were told: 'Get out, man! You are the henchmen and show boys of the caste Hindus. You have sold our community and you have come here on their behalf in order to cut our throats. We don't accept you as our representative.'[53]

The amendment was welcomed with a perverse irony by Sardar Patel who had obtained, in advance, the promise of its withdrawal from Nagappa. Earnestly, bud amid laughter, Patel said that Nagappa was 'moving it only to make a speech and then withdraw it.'[54] He went on and on in the same vein: '...Mr Nagappa was allowed to move the amendment on condition that he will withdraw it. There is no use in carrying on the debate. He only wanted to show to his community that he has not sold himself away. If you take it seriously and give importance to this business, then it would show that there is some substance in it.'[55]

Wrapping up the debate, Patel called on Untouchables to 'forget what Dr Ambedkar or his group have done', adding, '...I feel that the vast majority of the Hindu population wish you well. Without them where will you be? Therefore, secure their confidence and forget that you are a Scheduled Caste [*sic*].'[56]

Nagappa withdrew his amendment, which had been signed by four representatives, including Ambedkar, who strangely enough was absent on this occasion. In fact, he had given up after the subcommittee's debate. In all probability he thought that separate electorates were subject to such opprobrium that it would be futile to demand them again in the plenary session. For one thing Congressmen may have felt they were betraying Gandhi by accepting separate electorates given that he had rejected them by putting his life at stake in 1932 in Poona. For another, Partition, which had just taken place, and had resulted in unprecedented communal violence, had been attributed by Congress to the granting of a separate electorate to Muslims decades before. Moreover, the legitimacy of Nagappa's plea was eroded by the attitude of some Muslim representatives. Taking advantage of the fact that he had asked for a block minority vote of 35 per cent, they demanded a similar conditions for their own community. Anti-Muslim feeling was running so high that Dalit leaders could only lose out for being associated with making the same demands. Ambedkar also abandoned the demand for separate electorates because most Dalit representatives were against it. This was how Patel at least perceived the issue, for he said that his conversations with the elected representatives had convinced him that it had the support of only two or three of them.[57]

Ambedkar undoubtedly hoped to compensate for this tactical retreat by the radically modernising character of the Constitution that he was drafting. On November 4, 1948, in his capacity as the president of the 'Drafting Committee', he set out the constitutional project, much of which he had written.

If none of its articles abolished caste, they did outlaw discrimination based on religion, race, caste, sex and place of birth, given the paramount importance of the right to equality, which was to become Article 15 of the 1950 Constitution. It also prohibited any such discrimination pertaining to access to shops, restaurants, hotels, leisure facilities, wells, streets and other public places benefiting from any financial support by the State. Above all, Article 17 abolished Untouchability. Hard labour and any other *begar* (forms of servitude, often hereditary, of which Dalits were the principal victims) were declared illegal by Article 23. The modernisation of India that the new Constitution was supposed to usher in therefore raised Ambedkar's hopes of the advent of a more egalitarian society. His benign neglect regarding separate electorates probably reflected his faith in the modernisation process more than hard-headed realism (i.e. his realisation that the balance of power was such that a vote on his cherished separate electorates could only fail). On November 4, he declared in this connection:

> 'In this country, both the minorities and the majorities have followed a wrong path. It is wrong for the majority to deny the existence of minorities. It is equally wrong for the minorities to perpetuate themselves. A solution must be found which will reserve a double purpose. It must recognise the existence of the minorities to start with. It must also be such that it will enable majorities and minorities to merge some day into one.'[58]

Ultimately, Ambedkar rallied around the temporary reserved seats scheme; the Indian Constitution contented itself with establishing a quota of reserved seats for Untouchables, renewable after ten years if need be and in proportion to their numbers.

From the 1930s onwards, Ambedkar chose to collaborate with the British once his nationalist scruples had been set aside. To a large extent, this shift was due to the attitude of Congress. But he continued in this pragmatic vein when Congress led the country after independence. In January 1950 he advised the Scheduled Castes to cooperate with Congress.[59] We can interpret his approach as having been less opportunistic than pragmatic because on each occasion, it was, for him, a matter of using his office to promote the Untouchable cause rather than his own self-interest. While Congress tried to co-opt him—and hence defuse his capacity to mobilise against the social status quo—he remained a free man and continued to advocate social reform. When the Congress government refused to implement one of the measures he considered most important—the Hindu Code Bill—he preferred to resign in order to carry on his campaign as we shall see below. Ambedkar was not for sale; nor was he after *kursi* (an official position) for the sake of it. In the 1951 election he said as much during a speech in Punjab:

> 'If I wanted I could remain in the Congress for ever and would have definitely got a good place there, but I would have done it only if I had selfish motives and not any regards for my community. I would have remained there, if I was in need of any licence or permit for myself. The man seeking licences and permits can do so at the expense of his community. This the experience I have gained during the period I remained in the Congress Government.'[60]

His pragmatic attitude to power also explained his resilience: while he looked completely isolated in 1946, he bounced back in 1947 and was, once again, able to work for the same cause in the political arena. The balance sheet of his achievements may seem modest but in no way was it unimportant. Due to Ambedkar, Untouchables doubtless obtained larger quotas in the administration than the British would have granted on their own initiative. As for the Indian Constitution, the gap between the memorandum that Ambedkar had submitted in 1947 and the final text where Scheduled Castes achieved only reserved seats suggests that he had failed miserably. But Ambedkar exercised a considerable influence on many other aspects of the constitutional draft, which is enough to justify his choice of pragmatism.

7. Shaping the Indian Constitution

'Tall, well built and dark, he is known for deftness and agility of mind. An intellectual giant he has a rough exterior but he is intensively humane from within. Although he has been spurred on by difficulties never bending and yielding. There was a time when he did not get a place in the locality of higher strata of society, because he was a low caste. But his courage of conviction carried him through.' (Hari Sharan Chhabra (ed.), *Opposition in the Parliament*, Delhi: New Publishers, 1952, p. 142)

This extract from a bibliographical note drafted by a Brahmin writer in the early 1950s is evidence enough of the fact that Ambedkar was then at the zenith of his political career. He owed this recognition to his appointment as Law Minister in the first government of Independent India, but still more to his designation as the head of the famous 'Drafting Committee', responsible for formulating the nation's Constitution. There he achieved apotheosis as a statesman. It was Ambedkar's hour of glory, of which the image remains fixed in the public eye: tight-fitting suit, tie, horn-rimmed spectacles, hair carefully combed, the Constitution of India in his hand; thus was he to be sculpted and depicted.[1]

That an Untouchable found himself in a position to exercise a considerable influence on national politics aroused bitter criticism from upper caste Hindus. Some even tried to deny retrospectively that he had played a significant role in the Constituent Assembly.

The 'False Manu'?

His appointment as the head of the Drafting Committee won him the title of 'the new Manu', after the legendary author of the Laws of Manu. This was rather piquant given that in 1927 Ambedkar had set fire to this very text during the Mahad *satyagraha*.

In his indictment of Ambedkar, Arun Shourie labels him 'the false Manu', maintaining that he was in no position to influence the constitutional text given that the Drafting Committee was responsible only for shaping the articles drafted by the specialised sub-committees, whose suggestions were anyway discussed later in plenary sessions. Besides, Shourie writes, Ambedkar was outside the Congress Party, where the important guidelines for each article were decided.[2] Lastly, Shourie argues, Ambedkar found himself in a minority on numerous occasions, in the sub-committees, in the Drafting Committee and during the plenary sessions. It is our contention that Shourie's conclusion underestimates Ambedkar's role in the Constituent Assembly. He did far more than shepherd through clauses that had been framed by others, even though he occasionally complained about how Congress leaders consulted each other in advance in order to hasten the passing of certain articles.[3]

In taking issue with Shourie's interpretation, H. S. Verma and Neeta Verma oppose the way he depicted Ambedkar by arguing that, in fact, he had been selected by the Constituent Assembly on account of his administrative competence and political influence.[4] They demonstrate that his election to the helm of the Drafting Committee was the result of one of his first interventions in the Constituent Assembly, in 1946. After Nehru spelled out before the assembly the objectives of the Constitution, another member, Jayakar, suggested that such a resolution could not be voted on as long as one ignored whether representatives of the Muslim League—who still wavered between demands for Pakistan and loyalty to India—would or would not join the Assembly. In a very balanced speech, which impressed many Congressmen by its moderation and the perfect command of law that it demonstrated, Ambedkar proposed a compromise solution. For the Vermas, therefore, it was only by virtue of his competence that Ambedkar was appointed head of the Drafting Committee.

Moreover, we must also re-assess the role of the Drafting Committee which, while not responsible for drafting the primary texts, had to knock these into shape on the basis of articles proposed by Committees, before submitting them to the Constituent Assembly. The Assembly read several drafts and, each time, Drafting Committee members—more often than not its chairman, Ambedkar—guided and channelled the discussion. Ambedkar was also one of the few members of the Constituent Assembly who belonged, besides the Drafting Committee, to more than one of the fifteen Committees.[5] Hence he could follow closely all the debates on articles as vital as those concerning the rights of the minorities.

Above all, as president of the Drafting Committee, he was sent all the propositions of the various committees and it was his responsibility, and that of the committee secretary, S. N. Mukherjee, to whom he would later pay warm homage, to reformulate these articles—many of which required clarification. These editorial tasks also rested largely on his shoulders because of the chronic absenteeism that plagued the Drafting Committee suffered. One of its members, T. T. Krishnamachari, declared subsequently, in November 1948, before the Constituent Assembly:

> 'The House is perhaps aware that of the seven members nominated by you [to the Drafting Committee], one had resigned from the House and was replaced. One died and was not replaced. One was away in America and his place was not filled up and another person was engaged in State affairs and there was a void to that extent. One or two people were far away from Delhi and perhaps for reasons of health did not permit them to attend. So it happened ultimately that the burden of drafting this Constitution fell on Dr Ambedkar and I have no doubt that we are grateful to him for having achieved this task in a manner which is undoubtedly commendable.'[6]

If Ambedkar was not the author of the Constitution, he was always at hand throughout its formulation. Not only did he alter the committee's propositions; he also followed them through to the bitter end, in the plenary sessions, defending one formulation rather than another, repeatedly shaping the debates and so on. Ambedkar therefore played a determining role in the shaping of India's Constitution, and it explains why Shourie is so critical of him! With some justification he blames him, in particular, for having marginalised Gandhi's ideas.

The revenge on Gandhi of a westernised democrat

Ambedkar defended in the Constituent Assembly values and political models that he had imbibed in his youth while studying abroad. He believed in liberal democracy. He opposed the Left, which wanted to redefine the Indian Republic, from the first article of the Constitution onwards, as 'socialist'. He thought this would have had the effect 'simply of destroying democracy',[7] because it was for the government designated by the people to choose the best form of social organisation, as he explained on November 19, 1948:

> The reason why we have established in this Constitution a political democracy is because we do not install by any means whatsoever a perpetual dictatorship of any particular body of people. While we have established political democracy it is also the desire that we should lay down as our ideal economic democracy. [...] [Now], there are various ways in which people believe that economic democracy can be brought about; there are those who believe in individualism as the best form of economic democracy; there are those who believe in having a socialistic state as the best form of economic democracy; there are those who believe in the communistic ideas as the most perfect form of economic democracy [...]. [In these conditions] we have deliberately introduced in the language that we have used, in the Directive Principles, something which is not fixed or rigid. We have left enough room for people of different ways of thinking, with regard to the reaching of the ideal of economic democracy, to strive in their own way, to persuade the electorate that it is the best way of reaching economic democracy.[8]

Faithful to this line of argument, he opposed a constitutional amendment to nationalise natural resources—it was eventually not put to the vote, another sign of Ambedkar's 'constituent power', as if he had the moral authority to dictate whether an amendment could be considered or not.[9] Another indication of his attachment to liberal democracy was manifest in his proposing an amendment in the plenary session—a rare occurrence because his principal role was to defend the text of the Drafting Committee—in favour of a strict separation of executive power and the judiciary.[10] Some representatives opposed it in the name of the authority of the State, by arguing that too strict a legal control would weaken it. Nehru participated in the debate even though his responsibilities as Prime Minister allowed him little time, because he wanted to support Ambedkar's amendment.[11] Ultimately it was adopted and became Article 50 of the Directive Principles. Ambedkar later defended the setting up of a judicial system of British inspiration;[12] in his view, separation of powers would on no account weaken the State.

Ambedkar was in any case a supporter of a strong Centre, on the grounds that too much federalism would hamper the uniform application of the Constitution across the entire territory of India. He argued, for example, that the article abolishing Untouchability would not be evenly enforced if the states enjoyed too much autonomy[13]. This centralising option naturally offended Gandhi's supporters, who had always been very concerned about decentralising power right down to the village level. In the Constituent Assembly Ambedkar took his posthumous revenge on the Mahatma when he succeeded in brushing aside the propositions of the most radical Gandhians, or at least attenuated their influence.

The texts on the basis of which the Drafting Committee prepared its Constitutional project were hardly Gandhian in tone. The resolution on objectives proposed by Nehru on day one of the Constituent Assembly was inspired only at one remove by the Mahatma, while the reports of committees and sub-committees—the most important of which were chaired by Nehru and Patel—no longer referred to Gandhi. But it was of course not the only reason why the first outline of the Constitution that Ambedkar submitted to the Constituent Assembly in November 1948 bore hardly any Gandhian stamp. It was a monumental tome of 315 articles, of which, he said—not without evident satisfaction—that 'the Constitution of no country is so voluminous.'[14] He then had to defuse the Gandhians' criticism about the place of villages in the overall architecture of the project:

> 'Another criticism against the Draft Constitution is that that no part of it represents the ancient polity of India. It is said that the new Constitution should have been drafted on the ancient Hindu model of a State and that instead of incorporating Western theories the new Constitution should have been raised and built on village panchayats and district panchayats. There are others, who have taken a more extreme view. They do not want any Central or Provincial Governments. They just want India to contain so many villages Governments. The love of the intellectual Indians for the village community is of course infinite if not pathetic [...]. What is the village but a sink of localism, a den of ignorance, narrow mindedness and communalism? I am glad that the Draft Constitution has discarded the village and adopted the individual as its unit.'[15]

Many Gandhians regarded the speech as a provocation, and H. V. Kamath, one of the most active elected members of the Constituent Assembly, responded:

> 'I listened to his [Ambedkar's] speech with considerable pleasure and not a little profit. But I expected him to tell us what, if any, had been borrowed

from our own political past, from the political and spiritual genius of the Indian people [...]. If we do not cultivate sympathy and love and affection for our villages and rural folk I do not see how we can uplift our country. Mahatma Gandhi taught us in almost the last mantra[16] that he gave in the last days of his life to strive for panchayat raj. If Dr Ambedkar cannot see his way to accept this, I do not see what remedy or panacea he has got for uplifting our villages [...] Sir, it was with considerable pain that I heard Dr Ambedkar refer to our villages in that fashion with dislike, if not with contempt. Perhaps the fault lies with the Drafting Committee, among the members of which no one, with the exception of Sriyut [K. M.] Munshi, has taken any part in the struggle for our country's freedom. None of them is therefore capable of entering into the spirit of our struggle, the spirit that animated us.'[17]

The notion that the Drafting Committee had betrayed Gandhian thinking about the village's role in the state because it sidelined senior figures in the independence movement, was taken up by Arun Shourie, who attacked Ambedkar's life and works under the pretext that he was a collaborator with the British. Other members of the Constituent Assembly were even more offensive. Arun Chandra Guha, a Bengali, questioned the overall framework of the Constitutional project:

'... Dr Ambedkar has passed some remarks about the village units. We have been in the Congress for years. We have been taught to think of the village panchayats as the future of administrative machinery. The Gandhian and the Congress outlook has been that the future constitution of India would be a pyramidal structure and its basis would be the village panchayats [...]. I admit that we require a strong center; but that does not mean that its limbs should be weak [...]. I yet request the House that it may incorporate some clauses so that village panchayats may be allowed to play some effective part in the future administration of the country.'[18]

This demand was reiterated by Gokulbhai Daulatram Bhatt, another senior Congressman.[19] An amendment to the project submitted by Ambedkar was introduced by Professor K. T. Shah who considered that 'in the long run, this Union must consist of locally autonomous units equal inter se, which will be the strength as well as the salvation of this country.'[20] The amendment said that 'member States of the Union of India shall be organised on a uniform basis of groups of village Panchayats co-operatively organised *inter se* and functioning as democratic units within the Union.'[21] K. T. Shah wanted to insert this provision in the first article of the Constitution where the various entities comprising the Indian federation were described: one could hardly attribute more importance to the village! Ambedkar opposed this amendment which seemed also too extreme to at least three other members of the Constituent Assembly, and it was rejected. Another amendment concerning Article 31 was proposed a few days later by a Tamil representative. It read: '...the State shall take steps to organise village panchayats and endow them with such powers and authority as may be necessary to function as units of self-government.'[22]

Ambedkar immediately accepted this amendment, to the great relief of the top rank Congress leaders, such as Rajendra Prasad (the President of the Assembly) and Seth Govind Das.[23] Gandhians were delighted, loudly citing idealised evocations of ancient India and of the villages which were the repository of this tradition;[24] they quoted the Mahatma and thanked Ambedkar.[25] Their speeches were ample evidence of the central role played by the latter in getting these amendments passed, but they were wrong in believing that Ambedkar had admitted defeat (or had been convinced by their speeches): his backtracking was only a façade. While he resisted greater emphasis on villages in Article 1, he gracefully accepted it thirty articles below, because Article 31 occurred in the Constitution's Directive Principles, namely a list of recommendations made to the States of the Union for the conduct of day to day policies. These were mere blandishments lavished on the States, notably so that they pursued more determined social policies. The main point is that non compliance with the Directive Principles could not be taken to the courts: in contrast with the Fundamental Rights codified by the first articles of the Constitution, they are 'not justiciable'. Ambedkar himself seemed to have been behind the category of 'Directive Principles', a concept that he is said to have tracked down, within parliamentary democracies, only in the independent Ireland. He considered the 'Directive Principles' as 'instructions' but underlined that they 'had no legal value'[26]. Hence Ambedkar accepted an emphatic reference to the village in a section of the Constitution whose articles had no practical implication. In this manner he succeeded in defusing a very strong Gandhian demand that could have questioned the overall framework of his project.

In the same manner he sealed the fate of many other Gandhian propositions. For instance, he accepted an amendment to Article 34 according to which 'the State shall endeavour to promote cottage industries on cooperative lines in rural areas.'[27] The same scenario occurred later in relation to prohibition. Again, Congress members drew their inspiration from the Mahatma. Mahavir Tyagi, for instance, said: 'I submit that Gandhiji's foremost plank of constructive programme was prohibition [cheers], and we all stand pledged to this programme.'[28] Ambedkar accepted an amendment calling on the State 'to take necessary measures for the prohibition of the consumption of intoxicating drinks and drugs'. This would become Article 47 of the Directive Principles, whose subordinate character Ambedkar once again emphasised: 'There is therefore no compulsion on the State to act on this principle. Whether to act on this principle and when to do so are left to the State and public opinion. Therefore, if the State thinks that the time has not come for introducing prohibition or that it might be introduced gradually or partially, under these Directive Principles it has full liberty to act.'[29]

The last such debate concerned the cow, which Gandhi—like so many Hindus—considered sacred and whose slaughter had to be forbidden according to him. Seth Govind Das wanted to register the ban on cow slaughter within the Fundamental Rights of the Constitution,[30] but Ambedkar deftly defused his demand by drafting himself an amendment with a close associate of Das's, Thakur Das Bhargava, which they submitted on November 24, 1948. It presented cow protection as being part and parcel of a project of modernisation, one that was dear to Ambedkar:

> The State shall endeavour to organise agriculture and animal husbandry on modern and scientific lines and shall in particular take steps for preserving and improving the breeds of cattle and prohibit the slaughter of cow and other useful cattle, specially milk-yielding and draught cattle and their young stock.[31]

Thus drafted, the article took its place among the Directive Principles. T. Bhargava admitted that the amendment owed much to Ambedkar, and even that it was 'his work'. Consequently, he commented, 'in a way, this is an agreed amendment'. This is a clear indication that once approved by Ambedkar, an amendment was almost certain to be accepted. In this instance the Gandhians capitulated to his pressure only with great reluctance, as admitted by T. Bhargava:

> 'While moving this amendment, I have no hesitation in stating that for people like me and those that do not agree with the point of Dr Ambedkar

and others, this entails, in a way, a sort of sacrifice. Seth Govind Das had sent one such amendment to be included in the Fundamental Rights and other members also sent similar amendments. To my mind it would have been much better if this could have been incorporated in the Fundamental Rights, but some of my Assembly friends differed and it is the desire of Dr Ambedkar that this matter, instead of being in the Fundamental Rights should be incorporated in the Directive Principles.'[32]

Contrary to Shourie's views, Dr Ambedkar was clearly one of the principal architects of the Indian Constitution, along with draughtsmen such as Sri B. N. Rau. While it is undeniable that the Constitution drew a great deal on the 1935 Government of India Act and the 1928 Nehru Report, Ambedkar's influence throughout its preparation was considerable, as exemplified in the sidelining of the Gandhian approach, which was not solely the result of Nehru's aversion to its traditionalist, village-oriented, flavour. Ambedkar was however aware that the Indian Constitution was only a skeleton still to be fleshed out. In the final debate which preceded the adoption of the Constitution, in January, 1950, he underlined the scope of these issues:

'On January 26, 1950 [the date when the Constitution would be proclaimed], we are going to enter into a life of contradictions. In politics, we will have equality and in the social and economic life, we will have inequality [...]. We must remove this contradiction at the earliest possible moment, or else those who suffer from inequality will blow up the structure of political democracy which this assembly has so laboriously built.'[33]

He declared also that political democracy would have no meaning if it did not go hand in hand with social democracy, a remark that amply demonstrates that Ambedkar was not seduced by the practical efficacy of the Constitution to which he had devoted so much energy. Nor does it mean that he doubted the importance of such reform 'from above'. Put simply, he believed that further steps needed to be taken, which is why he was so staunch in defence of the Hindu Code Bill.

The Hindu Code Bill and the break with Nehru

During the debates in the Constituent Assembly, Ambedkar demonstrated his determination to reform Indian society by recommending the adoption of a western-inspired Civil Code and opposing delegates who wished to maintain personal laws, especially Muslim representatives who were very concerned about the fate of Sharia:

> 'I personally do not understand why religion should be given this vast, expansive jurisdiction, so as to cover the whole of life and to prevent the legislature from encroaching upon that field. After all, what are we having this liberty for? We are having this liberty in order to reform our social system, which is so full of inequities, discriminations and other things, which conflict with our fundamental rights.'[34]

However, Ambedkar obtained nothing more than an article of the Directive Principles stipulating that: 'The State shall endeavour to secure for the citizens a uniform civil code throughout the territory of India.' This recommendation was to remain a dead letter, notably because the minorities—to begin with, Muslims—adopted a hard line on their personal laws. Many Congress members also opposed any reform of Hindu practices concerning inheritance, marriage (and divorce) and adoption, as shown by the fate of the Hindu Code Bill.

This phrase refers to a long-term project, the aim of which was to reform the traditions of Hindu society. After more than a century of legislation—ranging from the Abolition of Sati (1829) to the Hindu Women's Right to Property Act (1937)—the British decided to consolidate these reformed Hindu personal laws in one code. In 1941 a Hindu Law Committee was appointed under B. N. Rau's chairmanship, and by August 1944 it had published a draft Hindu Code. According to its main provisions daughters as well as sons were given a share of the inheritance upon the deaths of their parents, widows were granted absolute estate, monogamy was a rule of law and divorce was allowed under certain circumstances. The Code was introduced in the legislature in April 1947 but the political circumstances—Independence and Partition—did not allow for discussion of the text. In 1948, Nehru entrusted the drafting of the new code to a sub-committee of the Assembly and nominated Ambedkar as its head.[35] The latter got written in it essential principles such as equality between men and women on the question of property and adoption, the granting of legal status to monogamous marriage only, the elimination of the 'caste bar in civil marriage'[36] and the need to justify concretely a petition for divorce—a procedure which till then was usually just a case of a woman being repudiated by her husband.[37] This questioning of the customs governing the private lives of Hindus stirred great emotion, not only among the traditionalists of the Hindu Mahasabha but also among leaders of Congress, including Rajendra Prasad. In a letter to Patel, who revealed strong reservations *vis-à-vis* such reforms, Prasad railed against a project whose 'new concepts and new ideas are not only foreign to the Hindu law but are susceptible of dividing every family'.[38] Many Congress bosses, including the party president Pattabhi Sitaramayya, opposed the bill and feared that it could alienate local notables—mostly conservative landholders—before the general elections of 1951–2. Prasad did not use such arguments in public; instead he campaigned against the bill in private, stating that members of the provisional Parliament had no popular mandate to address such issues.

Jawaharlal Nehru set great store by the code, which he saw, as did Ambedkar, as one of the cornerstones of the modernisation of India. He even announced that his government would resign if this bill were not passed,[39] and Ambedkar pressed him to submit it to Parliament with all speed. The Prime Minister asked him for a little time and even split the Code into four sub-sets to defuse the opposition before submitting it to the Assembly on September 17, 1951. The debate that followed confirmed how hostile to it were most traditionalist Congressmen. After four days of discussions, Ambedkar gave an impassioned speech where he mentioned that the extramarital relationship of Krishna and Radha was as indication of the degraded condition in which Hinduism maintained its womenfolk. Not surprisingly, this infuriated the most conservative MPs. T. Bhargava claimed that Ambedkar wanted this law passed in order to legalise his recent union with a Brahmin nurse.[40] He had indeed married, in April 1948, Dr Sharda Kabir, one of the doctors whom he had consulted, in 1947, when his work as head of the Drafting Committee had precipitated a rapid deterioration in his health.

Finally, on September 25, the portion of the Hindu Code Bill concerning marriage and divorce was mauled by a series of amendments and finally buried without Nehru uttering a word of protest. Ambedkar considered that he had not been supported enough by the Prime Minister and tendered his resignation from his government on September 27.[41]

In a statement published a little later, Ambedkar attributed Nehru's back-tracking to pressure from Congress: 'I have never seen a case of chief whip so disloyal to the Prime Minister and the Prime Minister so loyal to a disloyal whip.'[42] In fact Nehru feared that Congress MPs would reject the project en masse and/or that the President of the Republic, Rajendra Prasad, would indeed carry out his threat to refuse to promulgate it as a law.[43]

Certainly, the Hindu Code Bill was only one of the reasons adduced by Ambedkar for his resignation. He also reproached Nehru for his refusal to allot him a planning portfolio of any sort; and he differed with him over Kashmir too since he thought the territory should have gone to Pakistan. Beyond all these stated reasons, there was an unstated one—namely, Independent India's first general elections were approaching and Ambedkar wanted to fight these on his own party platform. Yet, it is highly significant that Ambedkar chose to leave Nehru's government over the Hindu Code Bill. It shows above all that, while he believed in the political path of social reform from above, this approach should consist of more than a simple constitutional frame; it also implied concrete implementation of measures that would necessarily alter time-honoured social customs. Now, if many Congressmen approved of the constitutional framework of Indian democracy, they were not prepared to support tangible advances that questioned the social status quo.

From the late 1930s till the 1950s, Ambedkar devoted all his energy to seeking a political solution to the Untouchables' predicament. He had tried hard at first to build political parties willing to defend the latter—and even the workers in general. He then cooperated with the British in return for some guarantees for his people and finally collaborated with the Congress government in the same spirit. This approach allowed him to keep at bay the Gandhian ideas that without doubt would have been better represented in the final text had he not been there to put a check on them. But he tested the limits of his influence in the state apparatus during the debates on separate electorates and more especially the Hindu Code Bill. He chose this Bill as his battleground because, in his view, beyond the constitutional frame, Indian society was in desperate need of thoroughgoing social reforms, reforms for which Congress was not yet ready.

Although he expressed a certain contempt for politics after leaving Nehru's government, Ambedkar was not to withdraw from political life. He took part in the 1951–2 election campaign and a short while later, before his death in 1956, launched the idea of the Republican Party of India. At the same time he began a religious, even spiritual, quest, focused on Buddhism, a religion in which he gradually found the only acceptable solution to Untouchability.

8. The 'Solution' of Conversion

'I don't want to have anything to do with these false political elections. With such false elections I could be a Prime Minister but I do not value it [...]. I have embraced Buddhism. I would like you to do so too—not Untouchables alone but the whole of India and even the world. [...] This religion tells me to work for the well being of all, for their happiness and the fostering of love for all. This religion should be accepted not only by men but by the Gods as well [...]. If we leave aside a few communists, there is no one in the world who does not want some religion. That which promises equal opportunity to all is the true religion. The rest are all false religions.' (Ambedkar's speech of Jan. 14, 1955 in Bombay, cited in M. S. Gore, *The Social Context of an Ideology*, op. cit., p. 220)

Conversion as a means of escaping the caste system had already been tried by many Untouchables; nor had Christian missionaries been slow to employ this argument in their drive to evangelise. Most Christian converts in late nineteenth-century Maharashtra were Mahars, a symptom of the famines of 1876 and 1879 when missionaries came to the rescue of the most deprived sections of society.[1] But Ambedkar had no need to refer to this precedent in justifying his decision to desert Hinduism. It ensued logically from his analysis of the caste system, the originality and force of which lay in its demonstration that social hierarchy was consubstantial to the Hindu religion. To leave it was thus the only means to attain equality.

Ambedkar's first reference to conversion to another religion dates back to 1927. During the Mahad Conference he said: 'We want equal rights in society. We will achieve them as far as possible while remaining within the Hindu fold or, if necessary by kicking away this worthless Hindu identity. And if it becomes necessary to give up Hinduism it would no longer be necessary for us to bother about temples.'[2] Earlier that year at the Jalgaon (Berar) Depressed Classes' Conference, which he chaired, a resolution in this vein was passed. Some days later, a dozen Mahars converted to Islam, to the great displeasure of many orthodox Hindus who tried to defuse the new movement by allowing Untouchables access to new wells. The spectre of mass conversion prompted thoughts of blackmail, the orthodox arguing that if they remained within the Hindu fold, caste Hindus might relax some of the religious rules from which they were suffering.[3] Ambedkar embraced conversion as a strategy only in the early 1930s.

Conversion, a strategy of social emancipation?

Changing religion in pursuit of greater equality. In the spring of 1933, Ambedkar told Gavai, with whom he represented the Untouchables at the third Round Table Conference, that he intended to leave the Hindu fold. He added that Islam repelled him and he was inclined to opt for Buddhism.[4] He gave no further signs of making a move till 1935 when in October he presided over a meeting of representatives of the Depressed Classes at Yeola, which he had convened to assess ten years of struggle. It was significant in that he considered that the movement had reaching a turning point and had to be relaunched afresh. He then announced his decision to convert,[5] which followed from an admission of failure in his attempts for closer integration with Hinduism, through the movement for temple entry:[6]

> 'The disabilities we have suffered, and the indignities we had to put up with, were the result of our being the members of the Hindu community. Will it not be better for us to leave that fold and embrace a new faith that would give us equal status, a secure position and rightful treatment? I advise you to severe your connection with Hinduism and to embrace any other religion. But, in doing so, be careful in choosing the new faith and see that equality of treatment, status and opportunities will be guaranteed to you unreservedly. [...] Unfortunately for me I was born a Hindu Untouchable. It was beyond my power to prevent that, but I declare that it is within my power to refuse to live under ignoble and humiliating conditions. I solemnly assure you that I will not die a Hindu.'[7]

The participants then unanimously adopted a resolution calling for the abandonment of the Hindu religion. Ten months later, on May 31, 1936, Ambedkar organised in Bombay a new meeting to win support for conversion. This strategy was limited to Mahars for, as he explained, he preferred to sound out the views of Untouchables caste by caste. This choice reflected the deep-seated considerations of caste when it came to conversion. In the past, entire castes had indeed converted to another religion. Ambedkar declared in Bombay:

'Our aim is to gain freedom. We are not interested in anything else at the moment. If we can gain freedom by conversion, why should we shoulder the responsibility of the reform of Hindu religion? And why should we waste our energy, time, labour and money on that? Let there be no misunderstanding that the object of our struggle is our liberation from Hinduism and not reform of Hinduism.

The aim of our movement is to achieve freedom, social, economic and religious for Untouchables. So far as Untouchables are concerned, this freedom can not be achieved except through conversion.'[8]

Here Ambedkar closed a chapter in his political career before opening a new one. On the one hand, he gives up reforming Hinduism, having made every effort over many years, yet concluding that the struggle was pointless and now he had no option other than to leave the religion of his birth. On the other hand, and in a more implicit manner, he shifted the debate away from faith but towards other issues—social, economic and religious—concerning Hinduism and religion in general.

Ambedkar's Bombay speech is important also for the comparison which it establishes between religions in India from the point of view of social systems. While he does not ignore the existence of caste in the Christian and Muslim communities, he draws a sharp distinction between these social systems and what he has observed of caste's role in Hinduism: '… if the Muslims and Christians start a movement for the abolition of the caste system in their respective religion, their religions would cause no obstruction. Hindus cannot destroy their caste system without destroying their religion.'[9]

This analysis reflects the central idea in the thought of Ambedkar, namely that Hinduism was a religion which implied hierarchy, whereas other religions authorise equality. In an open letter written in 1936,[10] he set out the choice of conversion between three religions—Islam, Christianity and Sikhism—each of which had different advantages.

Comparing these three, Islam seems to give the Depressed Classes all that [*sic*] they need. Financially the resources behind Islam are boundless. Socially the Mohammedans are spread all over India. […] Politically the Depressed Classes will get all the rights which the Mohammedans are entitled to [...] Christianity seems equally attractive. If Indian Christians are too small numerically to provide the financial resources necessary for the conversion of the Depressed Classes, the Christian countries such as America and England will pour immense resources if the Depressed Classes show their readiness to embrace Christianity. Socially, the Christian community is numerically too weak to render much support to the converts from the Depressed Classes, but Christianity has Government behind it. Politically, Christianity will give them the same rights which Islam gives [...] Compared to Christianity and Islam, Sikhism has few attractions. Being a small community of 40 lakhs, the Sikhs cannot provide the finance. [...] They are confined to the Punjab, and as for the majority of the Depressed Classes the Sikhs can give them no social support. Politically, Sikhism is at a positive disadvantage as compared with Islam or Christianity. Outside the Punjab, Sikhs are not recognised for special representation in the Legislature and in the services. [...] What the consequences of conversion will be to the country as a whole is well worth bearing in mind. Conversion to Islam or Christianity will denationalise the Depressed Classes. If they go to Islam the number of Muslims will be doubled and the danger of Muslim domination also becomes real. If they go to Christianity, the numerical strength of christians becomes 5 to 6 crores. It will help to strengthen the hold of the British on this country. On the other, if they embrace Sikhism they will not only not harm the destiny of the country, but they will help the destiny of the country. They will not be denationalised. On the contrary, they will help in the political advancement of the country.[11]

The simple fact that Ambedkar saw conversion to Islam and to Christianity as a factor contributing to 'denationalisation' and one likely to attenuate the freedom struggle, is evidence that still he had not completely embraced the 'separatist' discourse which he was to articulate later.[12] He was therefore prompted to suggest to caste Hindus who were anxious to halt the conversion of Untouchables to a 'foreign' religion to make Sikhism as attractive as Islam and Christianity by granting reserved seats to Untouchables who converted to that faith: 'All that is necessary is to add to the list of Scheduled Castes in each province other than the Punjab the word "Sikh" as that of a person from the Depressed Classes who becomes a convert to Sikhism will not lose his political rights he would have had if he had remained a Depressed Classes.'[13]

In November 1935, 800 Depressed Classes youth from villages in Nasik district had met in Nasik and reaffirmed their will to leave

Hinduism. They had burnt the Manu Smriti and passed a resolution asking Untouchables not to participate in Hindu *yatras* (pilgrimages), visit Hindu holy places, give money to Hindu priests or observe Hindu festivities.[14] In May 1936 a meeting of Mahars in Bombay passed three resolutions which testified to the influence of Ambedkar's new strategy over members of his caste:

(1) conversion is only a means by which Mahars may achieve freedom and equality;
(2) Mahars are ready to convert en masse;
(3) As a first step towards conversion, Mahars will refrain from worshipping Hindu deities, observing Hindu holidays and visiting Hindu sacred sites.[15]

Between the Yeola meeting of October 1935 and that held in Bombay in May 1936, Ambedkar clarified his intentions and reaffirmed his will to forge ahead. The reactions he encountered, as much from potentially 'receiving' minorities as from among upper caste Hindus or other Untouchable leaders, led him, however, to revise his plans.

Reactions, counter-offensives and divisions among Untouchables. Unfortunately for Ambedkar's mass conversion project, Indian Christians were not slow to air their misgivings about it. Officially, their representatives disapproved of any idea of an instrumental conversion which, devoid of any spiritual content, would have served only the upward social mobility of Untouchables. In reality, these kind of massive conversions were dreaded because of the intra-community tensions which they were likely to engender. 'Old Christians'—notably the Syrians—who thought of themselves as an elite, disapproved of this sudden inflow of the lower orders.[16] In any case Ambedkar no longer favoured this option precisely because of the persistence of caste prejudice among Christians. That this religion was foreign to India may also have diverted Ambedkar from Christianity, according to Zelliot.[17]

Buddhist leaders were more welcoming, although Buddhism did not feature among the solutions that Ambedkar contemplated at that time—at least in his public speeches. The secretary of the Mahabodhi Society, an association based in Varanasi, indicated a little after the Yeola speech that Untouchables would be welcomed by his community. He reaffirmed the absence of caste distinctions within Buddhism with all the zeal of an advertisement: 'We guarantee an equal status to all converts.'[18]

Muslim leaders reacted positively too, including those outside India: the Arab press expressed its interest in Ambedkar's plans while the vice-chancellor of Al Azhar University in Cairo—which raised funds to facilitate a possible mass conversion—explained that it was not necessary to be circumcised or to wear the veil to become a Muslim. He even sent a delegation to India in December 1936.[19] From October 1935, Maulana Mohammed Irfan, a representative of India's Khilafat Central Committee, assured Ambedkar that Islam was an egalitarian religion and conversion would allow him to become a leader of India's largest minority. The same month, Maulana Ahmed Sa'id, the head of the Indian Association of Ulemas, sent him a similar message.[20] The Muslims of Punjab entrusted a new convert—Kanhiya Lal Gauba—, a member of the Legislative Assembly, to persuade Ambedkar to opt for Islam. Many ulemas, in particular in the Muslim princely states, appealed to Untouchables with the same objective.[21]

The most eagerly awaited reaction of all was from the Sikhs. Ambedkar had for some time been in touch with representatives of this community who had opened a management college in Bombay that welcomed Untouchables.[22] As soon as Ambedkar made clear his plan to convert to another religion, Sardar Dalip Singh Doabia, the vice-president of the Golden Temple's Managing Committee based in Amritsar wrote to him that Sikhism corresponded completely to what he expected from a religion and that Untouchables would be welcomed.[23]

In January 1936, while Ambedkar chaired a two day meeting of Untouchable youths in Poona, he took part in a recitation of Sikh religious songs (*bhajans*) and was then invited by these Sikhs to join their community. In the same week two Muslim delegations also presented him with similar pleas.[24] That April he participated in a Sikh Mission Conference at Amritsar with Untouchables from Punjab, Kerala, the United Provinces and the Central Provinces, at which more than fifty people converted to Sikhism. In May, his son Yashwant and his nephew went to Amritsar and lived for six weeks in the Golden Temple. More significantly, in mid-September Ambedkar 'dispatched a group of thirteen followers, whom he called the vanguard of the conversion movement, to study at the Sikh mission in Amritsar'.[25]

The Hindu Mahasabha feared that by converting to another religion, Untouchables would weaken the majority community demographically—and therefore electorally. They also were wary that such a move might lead to a convergence of Untouchables with India's religious minorities. At the second Round Table Conference Ambedkar had already co-authored with Muslim and other minorities' leaders a Minorities Pact which demanded separate electorates and weightage for Muslims, Christians, Anglo-Indians, Europeans and Depressed Classes. Through conversion Ambedkar could consolidate this coalition at the expense of Hinduism.

Less than a fortnight after the Yeola meeting, a delegation from the Hindu Sabha of Bombay met Ambedkar, who assured them that before making 'any final decision he would confer with the leaders of the Hindu Mahasabha and other Hindu organisations.'[26] The Hindu Mahasabha then convened an extraordinary session in Bombay, on October 29, 1935, with 1,000 delegates attending under the chairmanship of its most orthodox leader, Madan Mohan Malaviya. N. C. Kelkar, one of the chief figures of its Maharashtrian branch, protested against Ambedkar's ingratitude towards Gandhi, who, he said, had concerned himself with the Untouchable problem since 1932. He elaborated on the same theme in December, at the annual session of the Hindu Mahasabha.[27] At that time the Mahasabha coopted many Untouchable leaders in order further to isolate Ambedkar: Jagjivan Ram, J. M. Mandal (a Bengali Namasudra leader), Rasiklal Biswas (another Namasudra who had first been part of Ambedkar's All India Depressed Classes' Congress), a UP Chamar leader, Dharma Prakash, P. N. Rajbhoj, a Poona Chambhar who had been one of Ambedkar's lieutenants, M. C. Rajah and Palwankar Baloo—a Chamar leader and former cricketer[28]—were all appointed to the Hindu Mahasabha's Committee for the Uplift of the Depressed Classes.[29]

The revival of the movement for mass conversions of Mahars, debated at a meeting in Bombay in 1936, was a cause of great concern to the Hindu Mahasabha. As the latter's press release put it, the prospect of Untouchables crossing over to Islam aroused in its members the dread 'of being eliminated from its own land'.[30] This apprehension had become a familiar motif since the early twentieth century because of the divergent demographic trends of Hindus and Muslims, which were reflected in the ten-yearly census figures.[31] It was fostered by the 'undeniable' existence of a Muslim plot: according to Hindu nationalist leaders, the financial largesse of the Nizam of Hyderabad, the ruler of India's largest princely state, lay at the root of the problem. They claimed that he had offered 40 million rupees to Ambedkar if he converted to Islam—an unverifiable assertion.[32] Interestingly, Mahar leaders in Nagpur were thinking along similar lines. V. Moon cites one of them who said: 'If we become Muslims, we'll get the help of the Nizam of Hyderabad!'[33] Moon points out that 'Many people thought we should become Muslims' because of old cultural affinities: 'There were many in the community [i.e. Mahars] who honoured the [Muslim] godmen, who went to the Muslim durgahs, who gave vows to Tajuddin Baba [...] There were some who spoke unblemished Urdu and recited poetry.'[34]

Moonje—the Nagpur-based leader of the Hindu Mahasabha, the group most directly affected by this primarily Maharashtrian issue—held three days of secret talks with Ambedkar in Bombay, with J. K. Birla,[35] a rich orthodox Marwari brother of G. D. Birla. Interestingly, Moonje empathised with Ambedkar's viewpoint, namely that one could not realistically expect any reform of orthodox Hinduism.[36] Instead, he suggested, with the approval of the Shankaracharya of Karweer Pith, a religious dignitary of Maharashtra, that Untouchables 'join the Sikhs or the Arya Samaj who have completely eliminated the caste system',[37] thereby allowing them to remain within the fold of 'Hindu culture'.

The Shankaracharya's contribution deserves to be outlined in greater detail. A Sanskritist whose thesis had been accepted by the Oriental University of Washington, he headed the Karweer pith (monastery), a dissident Maharashtrian branch of a prestigious Hindu congregation based at Sringeri (Karnataka).[38] As president of the Lahore session of the Hindu Mahasabha, in October 1936 he defended Moonje's proposal in a significant manner:

'The temple satyagraha at Nasik revealed to me two salient facts. Firstly, a large section of Untouchables has grown militant during recent years and it is clamouring for immediate relief. Secondly, it is futile to coax the so-called Sanatanists into agreeing to concede to Untouchables their legitimate rights This revelation prompted me to advise Dr Ambedkar and his followers to stop wasting their energies in trying to persuade the orthodox, and to found a sect of their own, or to go over to one of the existing sects of Hinduism which does not flourish on Untouchability. [...] Conversion implies one embracing an alien faith. Nothing could be more ridiculous than to suppose that Sikhism is alien to Hinduism. [...] It is one of the many protestant sects of Hinduism.'[39]

Like Moonje, the Shankaracharya did not subscribe to a reform of Hinduism of which Untouchables would be the beneficiaries—we may even assume that he was set against it. He simply tried to defuse their new militancy as a means of keeping them in the Hindu fold, hence his pleas for a sectarian solution or Sikhism.

Ambedkar weighed up very carefully the possibility of a conversion to Sikhism after some Muslim leaders began to voice their opposition to a massive rallying of Untouchables to Islam, arguing that it would deny them the advantages borne of their minority status and risked fomenting mobilisation by lower caste Muslims against the established social order.[40] He therefore added a rider to his agreement: namely, that Untouchables converting to Sikhism would maintain the privileges gained by the Poona Pact.[41] Moonje accepted this provision during talks with Ambedkar on June 19, 1936. He then won the approval of the Maharajah of Patiala, the most influential Sikh prince of India, to get the agreement ratified by Ambedkar and Sikh dignitaries.[42]

Then in August 1936 Ambedkar announced that he would abandon the prospect of Untouchables converting to Islam, something Moonje regarded as a personal victory.[43] According to what later became known as the 'Ambedkar-Moonje Pact', the former 'agreed to lead a Sikh conversion movement and to join Hindus and Sikhs in countering Muslim and Christian proselytising among Untouchables.' In return, Moonje pledged the Hindu Mahasabha's support for Sikh converts retaining the political rights accorded to them as (Hindu) Untouchables under the 1932 Poona Pact'.[44] However, Moonje and Ambedkar were to be countered by the opposition of Gandhi and of other Untouchable leaders.

After Ambedkar's speech at the Yeola conference, Gandhi had set himself against the idea of a mass conversion of Untouchables, bringing two key arguments to bear. First, he asserted that Untouchability had begun to wither away because of the activities of reformers who would be demoralised by such conversions; second, religion being a spiritual matter, one could not change it as one moves house or buys a new coat.[45] These arguments were taken up by other Untouchable leaders. Gavai criticised Ambedkar's indifference to the spiritual dimension of Hinduism: 'This clearly shows he does not have any faith in God or in religion. And then it is only for achieving equality that he is thinking of changing from one religion to another'.[46] This position was elaborated by another of his rivals, Rajah, who had dissociated himself from Ambedkar's conversion initiative as early as November 12, 1935, by reaffirming his faith in upper caste reformers and his attachment to Hinduism.

> 'The Congress, under the inspiration of Gandhiji, has taken up the question of removal of Untouchability and the Hindu Mahasabha has followed suit. It is our duty to help them in their endeavour and not to throw obstacles in their way. [...] Hinduism is our religion and it is sacred to us. It is our duty to preserve it and purify it. We do not want to cut away form the Hindu fold. We want better recognition—a recognition of the fact that we are men equally with the caste-Hindus.'[47]

Rajah, with whom Moonje wanted to ratify the agreement with the Sikhs at the same time as Ambedkar, leaked news of the secret ongoing negotiations. He claimed that a massive conversion to Sikhism would reduce a Hindu socio-religious problem to a question of 'community migration'.[48] Rajah also criticised Moonje, claiming that he was contradicting his reformist rhetoric aiming to integrate Untouchables into the Hindu nationalist project, and regretting that he had found no other solution to the problem raised by Ambedkar than their transfer to the Sikh community which already contained Untouchables to whom these converts would become assimilated. Sensing Moonje's strategy, Rajah launched a head-on attack against him:

> 'One would expect you, as President of the Hindu Mahasabha, to ameliorate the social condition of the Depressed Classes by removing civic and social disabilities of these classes, not to speak of securing for them the right of worship in Hindu temples on an equal footing with other worshippers, and to further the Harijan movement started by Gandhiji all over the country. Instead of doing this, what is it that you are doing? You are dissecting the Depressed Classes and affiliating them religiously to the Sikhs while retaining them politically as Hindus.'[49]

M. C. Rajah was not the only Untouchable leader to oppose conversion; Rao Bahadur R. Srinivasan, as well as Jagjivan Ram, declared themselves hostile to such a move. The latter organised a meeting of the Depressed Classes' League on behalf of the Congress, just after its April 1936 Lucknow session. Rajah was appointed as president of the league, Gavai as vice-president and Rajbhoj as General Secretary.[50] The meeting unanimously condemned Ambedkar's decision as regards conversion. The latter hit back despite the opposition of certain Mahars, such as P. G. Solanki, an elected member of the Legislative Council of Bombay who ten years earlier had converted to Christianity and, having noted that the condition of Christian Untouchables was no better than that of Hindu Untouchables, had returned to the fold of Hinduism.[51] Meetings for or against conversion multiplied in the spring of 1936 and an anti-conversion conference was organised in Bombay on May 30 by Untouchable—above all Chambhar—supporters of Gandhi.[52] That same month the All India Depressed Classes' Conference held a meeting in Lucknow which one hundred or so delegates attended. These were the representatives of the creeds to which Ambedkar had intended to convert (Islam, Sikhism, Christianity, Buddhism, the Arya Samaj...). The assembly began by passing a motion in support of Ambedkar's speech at Yeola. He, being ill, was absent, but excerpts of his book *Annihilation of Caste* were read from the platform.[53]

Ambedkar announced his choice of Sikhism in August 1936, because he preferred 'to have some responsibility as for the future of the Hindu culture and civilisation'[54] and did not want to break with the majority community. In September he sent a delegation of thirteen of his supporters to Amritsar to study Sikhism.[55] In November he travelled to London to sound out British political opinion about the guarantees which they would be willing to grant in the new Constitution to Untouchables who would convert to Sikhism.[56] The authorities replied that such provisions would apply only to the Sikhs of Punjab, which, in his view, was an irrelevant proposition. In early 1937 negotiations between Ambedkar and the Sikh leaders continued but meetings became less frequent and by the end of the year Ambedkar no longer mentioned the idea of conversion. This volte-face cannot be explained only by the disappointing British response to his demand to extend the Sikh quota to converts.

Among other factors accounting for his decision were, first, that Sikh Dalits had told Ambedkar of the atrocities they had suffered at the hands of the Jats—which undermined all hope of emancipation—[57]; and, second, the opposition to such mass conversions of the Sikh political class: the Akalis—including Master Tara Singh—feared that the leadership of the community would be wrested from them or, at the very least, that their authority would be diminished.[58] The challenge that a mass conversion would have posed to upper caste Hindus also made Ambedkar afraid of retaliatory measures, some of which, as testified by the threats of social boycott, had already materialised in 1935–6. Ambedkar now seemed very isolated in the face of a coalition of Congress and Untouchable leaders and circumstances were conspiring against him since 1937 was to be an important election year. A mass conversion, in this context, could have provoked even more violence, and Ambedkar, resuming his see-saw political style, redirected his energies towards the political battle, as evident from the founding of the Independent Labour Party in August 1936. The election fight was bound to be tough. In Maharashtra, his campaign for conversion had made his adversaries, from the Congress but also from the Hindu Mahasabha, more determined than ever. During the election campaign, Moonje set out to field his best candidates against Ambedkar. He asked Madan Mohan Malaviya for the necessary funds to finance the candidacy of Khandekar, a Dalit rival of Ambedkar in Maharashtrian politics—and later in the Constituent Assembly.[59]

Thus Ambedkar's first attempt to abandon Hinduism proved short-lived and he returned to the political struggle immediately afterwards. He contested the elections of 1937, participated in the Viceroy's Council, later in Nehru's government and was in charge of drafting the Constitution. However politically he encountered many disappointments, such as the defeat of the Hindu Code Bill which prompted him, as mentioned above, to resign his ministerial post in 1950. This disappointment was followed by another, his defeat in the election of 1951. Appointed in 1952 to the Upper House (Council of States) due to the goodwill of Congress, the speeches he gave there manifested his intense bitterness. Then, in May 1954, he was defeated by a Congress candidate at a by-election for the Lok Sabha seat of Bhandera (near Nagpur). If that were not enough, the SCF was then disintegrating in the wake of its electoral defeats in 1951–2. Ambedkar's chief lieutenants, among them Rajbhoj and N. Shivraj, abandoned the movement one after another. Meanwhile in 1956 Ambedkar founded a school to train Untouchable political leaders and, later that year, established the Republican Party. But all the while he manifested a far greater interest in religion in general and in Buddhism in particular.

The choice of Buddhism as an egalitarian creed

Ambedkar converted to Buddhism in 1956, exactly twenty years after he had opted in favour of Sikhism. This shift need to be explained, but before doing that we must emphasise that during this period the Ambedkarites had not completely neglected religious issues. In fact they had prepared the ground for conversion to Buddhism by abandoning Hindu rites. As Wamanrao—the organisational brains behind the 1956 conversion—said as early as the mid-1930s: 'Before we adopt another religion, we have to wipe out the culture of this religion [Hinduism]'.[60] Ambedkar's young followers stopped doing puja, boycotted Hindu festivals—including Krishna's birthday—and broke idols. In Nagpur, and probably elsewhere, they even harassed and ostracised caste fellows who took part in Hindu processions—to such an extent that some of them could not find a girl to marry from their community. Vasant Moon considers that 'By 1942 we had given up our celebration of nearly all the Hindu festivals.'[61] Moreover Nagpur's Mahars had begun celebrating Buddha Jayanti (the anniversary of the Buddha's birth) even before the 1956 conversions because of Ambedkar's growing inclination towards this religion.[62]

His familiarity with Buddhism went back to his youth. In 1908 one of his teachers, K. A. (*alias* Dada) Keluskar, impressed by his aptitude, gave him a biography of Lord Buddha he had published ten years before. It had a profound influence on his young mind,[63] even though for years he never referred to it. In 1934 he built a house at Dadar (Bombay) that he called 'Rajgriha', the name of the capital of the ancient Buddhist kings of Bihar.

In 1935–6, during the first conversion movement, he never envisaged leaving Hinduism for Buddhism, but his interest in the religion grew in the mid-1940s—as manifested in the name he chose for his first college, 'Siddharth', after the Buddha.[64] In 1948 he republished *The Essence of Buddhism* whose author, Lakshman Narasu, as he emphasised in the foreword, fought against caste and against British authoritarianism. That year he published *Untouchables*, a work where—as we have noted—he presented Untouchables as the descendants of the Buddhists who had been marginalised when the rest of society crossed over to Hinduism. At the same time, his activities within the Constituent Assembly prepared the ground for his conversion to Buddhism and the official recognition of the religion. In May 1947 he opposed K. M. Munshi's amendment which sought to forbid the conversion of minors, thus possibly preventing any conversion.[65] He also lobbied for Buddha Jayanti, the anniversary festival of Lord Buddha, to feature in India's calendar of official holidays. Lastly, he was involved in the adoption of the many Buddhist symbols with which the Indian Republic endowed itself between 1947 and 1950: the *chakra* (the wheel of Dharma) on the Indian flag, the lions of Ashoka—the Buddhist emperor of ancient India—as the national emblem and the inscription of a Buddhist aphorism on the pediment of Rashtrapati Bhavan, the residence of the President of the Republic.[66] In 1950, he went to Sri Lanka and began a compilation of Buddha's writings and called upon Untouchables to convert to Buddhism,[67] an appeal he repeated on his return to India.[68]

Ambedkar's interest in Buddhism is quite consistent with his personality, as Valerian Rodrigues has shown in a remarkable piece of writing. On the one hand, he believed in 'the need for religion on the part of man and society'[69] but on the other hand, he adhered to the values of Enlightenment: Buddhism, therefore, was an ideal choice because it was more susceptible to reinterpretation and adaptation to the modern world than other religions. At least this was how Ambedkar saw it. For him, there were no 'canonical texts that were the authentic teachings of the Buddha himself'.[70] Thus he could chose to redefine Buddhism according to his own needs. According to Ambedkar 'In contrast to religion, dhamma was a secular ideology, understanding the world, man and society, and transforming them in the light of reason and on the basis of morality. To test its veracity no exterior but purely human criteria were required.'[71] In his reinterpretation of Buddhism, Ambedkar emphasised a social, egalitarian dimension which may be present in its teaching but in a much less prominent manner. As Rodrigues points out, in the *Buddha and his Dhamma* 'Ambedkar put a lot of his earlier arguments elaborated in his other writings, in the mouth of Buddha to hammer home this criticism of Hinduism.'[72] He says, for instance: 'Graded inequality, the Buddha thought, might produce a society on ascending scale of hatred and descending scale of contempt [one of Ambedkar's favorite phrases] and might be a source of perpetual conflict'[73].

Buddhism certainly offered the best possible choice because it was an egalitarian religion entertaining relations with Hinduism.[74] During an All India Radio broadcast on October 3, 1954, Ambedkar declared:

> 'Positively, my social philosophy may be said to be enshrined in three words: liberty, equality and fraternity. Let no one however say that I borrowed my philosophy from the French Revolution. I have not. My philosophy has roots in religion and not in political science. I have derived them from the teachings of my master, the Buddha [...]. My philosophy has a mission. I have to do the work of conversion [to Buddhism].'[75]

This statement is in concert with the procedures of 'building of tradition',[76] consisting in legitimising cultural borrowings (here the republican formula) by referring them back to a prestigious, native past. In this way, imported notions are vernacularised, and reinterpreted. In this case, Ambedkar selected, within Buddhism, the values which he found in western republican doctrine. He legitimately highlights the egalitarian meaning of Buddhism, but he undoubtedly goes too far when deducing from it a message of social justice. The egalitarianism of the Buddha comes more from a religious and spiritual logic—above all it is the equality of human beings before God. But the fact that Buddhism was perceived by Ambedkar as an alternative to Hindu social hierarchy is clearly reflected in the practical details of his conversion.

The Conversions of 1956. In 1956 Ambedkar wrote to the General Secretary of the Maha Bodhi Society, D. Valinsinha, saying that he was preparing the conversion of India's Untouchables to Buddhism. A first wave of conversions occurred on March 18, not in Maharashtra, but in another stronghold of Ambedkarism, Agra, where the

Jatavs formed the main Untouchable caste; on that occasion 2,000 of them renounced Hinduism.[77] But Ambedkar wanted to proceed methodically and particularly to finalise a specific rite of initiation (*Dhamma diksha*) that was more concerned with a social critique than the procedure generally used by Buddhist monks.

On May 24, 1956, he announced that he would convert to Buddhism in October of the same year and called upon all Untouchables to join him in doing likewise. He adopted for the occasion the tone of a Christian clergyman: 'I am a shepherd. This may be an exaggeration. You are sheep and I am a shepherd. If you follow me, you will shed your ignorance after some days and understand things better.'[78]

On September 23 he confirmed that the ceremony would take place on October 14, the day of the Hindu festival of Dasahara. He invited the head of the Buddhist monks of India, the Burmese Bhikku Mahasthaveer Chandramani, to carry out the ritual. The conversions took place at Nagpur, where several hundred thousands Untouchables, responding to Ambedkar's appeal, came dressed in white, some of them bearing ochre flags, the colour of Buddhism. Ambedkar and his second wife were the first to convert, which they did beneath a canopy, in front of the crowd. The Bhikku made them take the oath to Buddha, to Dhamma (the doctrine of the Buddha) and to Sangh (the community of the monks). He then asked them to avow allegiance to Panchsheel (the Five principles which are the refusal to kill, to steal, to lie, to have illegitimate sexual relations and to drink). Ambedkar and his wife repeated in Marathi the words of the Bhikku in Pali (the language of the Buddhist canon) then bowed three times before the statue of Buddha. Finally, Ambedkar pronounced these words:

> 'By discarding my ancient religion which stood for inequality and oppression today I am reborn. I have no faith in the philosophy of incarnation; and it is wrong and mischievous to say that Buddha was an incarnation of Vishnu. I am no more a devotee of any Hindu god or goddess. I will not perform Shraddha [the Hindu funeral rite]. I will strictly follow the eightfold path of Buddha. Buddhism is a true religion and I will lead a life guided by the three principles of knowledge, right path and compassion.'[79]

These words reflected the anti-Hindu motives that underpinned Ambedkar's conversion, and they were followed by twenty two oaths, of which the first six, the eighth and the nineteenth were aimed directly at Hinduism:

1. I shall not recognise Brahma, Vishnu and Mahesh as gods, nor shall I worship them.
2. I shall not recognise Ram and Krishna as Gods, nor shall I worship them.
3. I shall not recognise Gauri and Ganapati as gods nor shall I worship them.
4. I do not believe in the theory of incarnation of god.
5. I do not consider Buddha as the incarnation of Vishnu.
6. I shall not perform Shraddha [a Hindu rite that one carries out for the safety of the deceased] nor shall I give offerings to god.
7. I shall not do anything which is detrimental to Buddhism.
8. I shall not perform any religious rites through the agency of a Brahmin.
9. I believe that all human beings are equal.
10. I shall endeavour to establish equality.
11. I shall follow the eight fold path of the Buddha.
12. I shall observe the ten Paramitas (observances) of the Buddha [the virtues in which a follower of the Buddha has to restrain himself].
13. I shall be compassionate to all living beings and I shall nurture them with care.
14. I shall not steal.
15. I shall not lie.
16. I shall not commit adultery.
17. I shall not drink liquor.
18. I shall lead my life striving to cultivate a harmonious blend of the three basic principles of Buddhism [Enlightment, Precepts and Compassion].
19. I thereby reject my old religion, Hinduism, which is detrimental to the prosperity of human kind and which discriminates between man and man and which treats me as inferior.
20. I fully believe that Buddhism is Saddhamma.
21. By my embracing Buddhism I am being reborn.
22. I hereby pledge to conduct myself hereafter in accordance with the teaching of the Buddha.[80]

Ambedkar then asked the hundreds of thousands of Untouchables[81] awaiting conversion to stand. He then administered the three refugees (*tisarana*), the five vows (*pancha shila*) and the 24 oaths 'of his own devising to the assembled multitude'.[82]

Ambedkar died a short while afterwards, on December 6, 1956: the funeral procession was the biggest Bombay had ever seen[83] and the cremation was the occasion for a new wave of mass conversions numbering some 100,000 people.

In Maharashtra, the anti-Hindu dimension of these waves of mass conversion was reconfirmed, subsequently, by the removal of Hindu deities from Untouchable localities, sometimes as a means of provoking the upper castes. The palanquin of the village goddess, which Mahars usually maintained, was returned to upper caste Hindus. Similarly, Untouchables increasingly rejected the obligations and functions attached to their ritual status, which did not occur in practice without precipitating tension and often violence.[84]

These conversions were appreciated by some and criticised by others, sometimes unexpectedly. The journal *Maha Bodhi* contested the analysis of Buddhism conveyed by Ambedkar, particularly in *The Buddha and his Dhamma*, where he is especially interested in the social, egalitarian, aspect of Buddhism at the expense of its spiritual dimension.[85]

Conversions were tacitly, if not explicitly, disapproved of by the leaders of Congress and the Hindu Mahasabha, but many of them were relieved at the choice of Buddhism rather than of Islam or Christianity. The Hindu nationalist leader, V. D. Savarkar, considered that the converts had not changed religion at all. The *Indian Express* (Bombay) was more precise:

> One is glad however, that even while recoiling from the traditional Hindu social order, he [Ambedkar] chose another essentially Indian way which, like Sikhism, Brahmoism and the Arya Samaj, is only a variant of Hinduism.[86]

This analysis reveals the limitations of his conversion to Buddhism as a solution to the problem of Untouchability.

Buddhism, a pseudo-remedy? Ambedkar opted for Buddhism because of its egalitarian philosophy but also because, like Sikhism, which had been his first choice during the 1935–6 movement, it was a compromise solution which spared him a break with Hinduism. He is said to have declared one day to Gandhi: 'I will choose only the least harmful way for the country'. The day before his conversion he added: 'And that is the greatest benefit I am conferring on the country by embracing Buddhism; for Buddhism is a part and parcel of Bhartiya culture. I have taken care that my conversion will not harm the tradition of the culture and history of this land.'[87]

This concern partly explains the limited implications of his decision. Ambedkar's Buddhism became integrated, almost in the form of a sect, into Hinduism. Sects, as we have noted above, appeared in the past, in a recurring way, as a solution to Untouchability inasmuch they constituted the only egalitarian institution within Hinduism. Yet it was precisely this sociological aspect that Ambedkar appreciated most in Buddhism, the religion which played a pioneer role in the development of renunciation and therefore of the sectarian phenomenon in India. The Buddhism of the newly converted Untouchables was also similar to that of a sect because Ambedkar played in it the role of the *guru*. He even appeared as a sect founder during the conversions of 1956, since he modified on his own initiative the Buddhist rites by adding to them, after his initiation according to classic procedures, the formulae which were his own and that he himself repeated (recourse to a Bhikhu here was brushed aside) to his crowds of followers. Moreover, after his death Ambedkar was to be worshipped as a *bodhisattva*, an embodiment of Lord Buddha, as much in Maharashtra[88] as among the Jatavs of Northern India.[89] This is why he is often represented dressed in a saffron coloured robe. Many homes of converts worship only Ambedkar and the Buddha and celebrate only their two birthdays as religious holidays.

Though limited, this conversion movement offered Ambedkar an excellent means of passing on his message of equality, as shown in Baby Kamble's recollections:

> Just as Gautam became Buddha by the concentration of spirit, Bhim became Buddha by the persevering exercise of knowledge. Strength, intelligence and Baba[saheb] Ambedkar's principles brought us life, magnificence and immortality. The speeches of Baba spoke about personality, about righteousness of spirit, justice and integrity. It was the moment when we begin to understand his speeches. I resolved to make mine these principles and to shape my life to come by them.[90]

Ambedkar's appeal to Untouchables to rise in dignity was clearly all the better received as it used the idiom of spirituality. A woman who converted in 1956, though she found it hard to abandon her Hindu gods, immediately felt that she was suddenly 'beam[ing] with her new identity',[91] a very sophisticated choice of words for an illiterate Mahar. Another convert's testimony suggested in the same way that Buddhism brought to Untouchables a new self-esteem and an acute sense of their separate identity. Karat, an intellectual of Mahar origin, confides as much: 'I have accepted the Buddhist Damma [doctrine]. I am a Buddhist now. I am not a Mahar, nor an Untouchable nor even a Hindu. I have become a human being. I am now equal with high caste Hindus. I am equal with all. I am not lowborn or inferior now.'[92]

A survey conducted in 1964–5 among sixteen to twenty-two year old college students in Poona showed that 'through conversions the "ex-Untouchables" have not only acquired a high evaluation of themselves, but have raised themselves in the esteem of others',[93] including the local Brahmins and the non-Buddhist Mahars.

Another survey conducted thirty years later in the same city revealed that Buddhist Mahars have achieved a remarkable leap forward in terms of social mobility: an overwhelming majority of the 270 heads of households selected for interview emphasised that they have not only 'broken their link with their past, as polluted Untouchables, by converting to Buddhism, but also developed a new educational awareness.'[94] As a result, no more than 11 per cent of the interviewees were illiterate—as against 79 per cent of their fathers. Consequently, whereas 63 per cent of these fathers were villagers, there was none among the interviewees: more than 50 per cent were white-collar workers.[95] Interestingly, this upward mobility has enabled Mahar Buddhists to overcome old caste barriers: about half of the interviewees declared that they mixed freely with upper caste people socially—including marriages and eating together on occasion.[96]

The case of the Chamars of Uttar Pradesh illustrates well the process of identity-formation that is conducive to upward social mobility. This shoemaking caste had for years forged its identity according to the old logic of Sanskritisation by claiming that it descended from a Kshatriya (warrior) caste. This explains the name they adopted, Jatav, a deformation of Yadav, the name of the Kshatriya dynasty founded by Krishna according to their own reading of what they considered to be history. Believing in this myth of origin, Chamars did not reject the caste system but instead tried to rise within it by seeking recognition as Kshatriyas. Ambedkar's propaganda had a strong impact on them in the 1940s, so much so that 'The initiative to form a new party was taken by the Jatav Mahasabha in Agra, the Chamar Mahasabha in Kanpur, the Adi-Hindu Ravidas Mahasabha in Allahabad and many other similar organisations'.[97] Then conversion to Buddhism endowed the Jatavs with a new identity, of an ethnic type. In this alternative identity they found both a new self-esteem and feelings of solidarity. The Jatavs adopted it as a message of equality after Ambedkar toured Northern India in the 1940s[98] and they were to become the most ardent supporters of the SCF and later the RPI in Northern India.[99]

Gail Omvedt concludes that 'With the conversion to Buddhism Ambedkar achieved what Phule and Periyar for all their resistance to Hinduism had failed to achieve: making a conscious non-Hindu identity a collective material and radicalising force in India.'[100] It was an achievement due not only to conversion to Buddhism, but also to the growing popularity of Ambedkar's notion that Dalits were the autochthons of India. Militant autochthony in this context does not reflect the usual xenophobic leanings but instead carries an emancipatory power. As a result, being a Mahar became a source of pride since it seemed to be synonymous with 'son of the soil'—*dharniche*. Baby Kamble, for instance, writes in her autobiography:

> This term [Mahar] makes blush with shame those people of my caste who have today become enlightened. What shame is there in this term? On the contrary, it makes us hold high our head. I vouch highly for the fact that I, a Mahar, am a native of this land of Maharashtra. I am not a vagabond who arrived here and doesn't know from where. This land is my home and the Mahar is the mother who bears testimony to this. Because even today, this country, this *rashtra* takes its name from us, Mahar.[102]

Thus pride may arise from a reinvention of local roots as much as from conversion to the religion which was that of India's indigenous people. In both cases it reflects the impact of the ethnicisation of caste set in motion by Phule, Periyar and Ambedkar, indeed, as suggested by Gail Omvedt.

However, the impact of conversion to Buddhism varies according to groups (even individuals) and places. In Maharashtra, the conversion of the Mahars had mixed consequences. Their break with Hinduism seemed quite relative and the converts therefore did not get emancipated from caste hierarchy. Their name changed. They now called themselves 'bauddha' in Marathi, but this move was only slowly and partially reflected in the emergence of a new collective identity. Zelliot highlights that conversion freed the *bauddha* 'from the sense of being a polluting person',[103] but this outcome remained abstract enough because 'the mass of Buddhists in the slums of cities or the landless in the rural area, live in much the same fashion as the desperately poor in any culture'.[104] However Zelliot admits that the glass is half full:

> What has happened is that even in areas where observers report 'no change at all', one finds that Buddhists no longer carry out what they feel are ritually submissive, degrading, or impure duties; that some young people, far more than in other Untouchable and backward communities, become educated; and that Buddhists do not participate in the Hindu public practices so long denied to them, not now out of a prohibition but out of a sense of separateness.[105]

The result is particularly mixed because the conversions of 1956, and those which followed, concerned almost exclusively Mahars: if, in 1956, 55 per cent of the Untouchables of Maharashtra converted to Buddhism—so that Buddhists rose in number from 2,500 in 1951 to 2.5 million in 1961—but almost all the *bauddhas* were drawn from the Mahar milieu. The coincidence between this new religious community and the frontiers of caste made it more difficult, for the former, to become emancipated from the status of the latter. Above all, this phenomenon complicated the emergence of an identity common to all Untouchables, transcending the cleavages of caste. The Chambhars not only did not convert to Buddhism but opposed any project seeking to bestow the benefits of the politics of positive discrimination to *bauddhas*. Moreover several converted Mahars continued to observe Hindu customs, particularly when they were too poor to afford a break with their original locale.[106]

Perhaps because of this coincidence between caste and 'sect', Ambedkar sometimes resorted to mechanisms of Sanskritisation to promote socio-cultural reform among Untouchables. In his preliminary speech at the conversion meeting of 1956, he evoked parables exhorting Mahars to no longer touch carcasses nor to let their womenfolk prostitute themselves. Zelliot thus deduces hat 'the Mahar, now Buddhist life, is to be pure by both Hindu and elite standards.'[107] She identified in the process of conversion a type of 'Palisation', a notion built on the root 'Pali', the language of the Buddhist canon that was copied on the model of Sanskritisation. In practice some *bauddhas* foreswore alcohol, as they were encouraged to do in one of the oaths sworn during conversion.[108] The logic of caste continued to play a role here in a new way.

Conversion, the last strategy of emancipation implemented by Ambedkar, had been envisaged by him from the 1930s onwards. It was then put on the back burner because of external pressures and because of his hopes for the future, born of other strategies. But it ensued so logically from Ambedkar's analysis of Hindu society that it was bound to be reactivated after alternative strategies eventually failed. In 1956, Ambedkar returned to it and fulfilled, twenty-one years later, his prophecy of 1935. However, conversion has not been a panacea. The choice of Buddhism by millions of Dalits helped them to become mentally emancipated from Brahmin domination but its sociological impact has been negligible. Buddhism supplied a new ethnic identity, with which Ambedkar had begun to endow them through his original myth of the 'Broken men'. Such an identity could have provided the basis of a horizontal solidarity appropriate to transcend cleavages among *jatis.* Unfortunately, however, divisions remained, setting Mahars against Mangs and against Chambhars, to speak only of Maharashtra.

These deep caste roots are all the more pervasive as the logic of caste has also been used by Ambedkarites to force Mahars to give up their traditional roles. To cite one example, they encouraged his supporters to resort to forms of social boycott based on old caste practices to compel recalcitrant Mahars to fall in line. Baby Kamble recalls:

> The young fast agreed to give up the collection of carrions. But the older persons who had the taste of it found it difficult. They did not however dare to openly protest in front of the younger lot. Families ate it in secret. As a custom they began to be boycotted. One did not invite them any more to

marriages. If inadvertently, one had allowed one of them to sit down among the guests, one served him in broken earthen pots for that. He was treated with contempt even at the marriage site, in front of everybody. He surrendered obviously and resumed then his place in society.[109]

Such a process was a double-edged sword. On one side, it allowed Mahars to free themselves from degrading tasks to which the systems of *baluta* and *vatan* had subjected them even before these were abolished after independence. And many of them made big sacrifices, because, as highlighted by Pawar, Mahars did not have 'any other means to live by.'[110] The search for new jobs was difficult but it proved a saving grace, among other things, because it accelerated the drift away from village life. On the other hand, this forsaking of the traditional Mahar functions occurred under the aegis of collective pressure: here the logic of caste was to prevail.

9. The Impact and Relevance of Ambedkar Today

The modest sociological effect of conversions to Buddhism must not mask the overall impact of Ambedkar's achievement. If Mahars who turned Buddhist remained Untouchable and failed to form long-lasting alliances with other castes of similar status, Ambedkar accelerated, and even initiated real social change within his caste, at least in Maharashtra. But Ambedkar made a strong impact in many other provinces, so much so that he was arguably the first pan-Indian Dalit leader. In the Punjab, Jürgensmeyer describes how the emancipation process among Untouchables in the 1940s was due to the 'Ambedkar Alternative';[1] in the United Provinces, Lynch analyses the impact of Ambedkar's ideas on the Jatavs of Agra as a 'turning point' in their socio-political mobilisation.[2]

In fact, the very impact of Ambedkar explains the efforts of the upper castes and, more generally, of the wider Indian establishment to marginalise him. Official speeches ignored him for decades and he was only awarded India's highest honour, the 'Bharat Ratna', in 1990, while V. P. Singh was Prime Minister. Even though he had been the architect of the Indian Constitution, it also took till 1990 before his portrait appeared in Parliament alongside India's other 'Great Men', who had long received lavish official praise. Even the government of Maharashtra hesitated for years before naming one of its state universities after Ambedkar. As early as 1978, Untouchable activists lobbied for Marathwada University in Aurangabad to be renamed after Ambedkar, but upper caste students resorted to violence in response: about 1,000 Untouchable dwellings were partly destroyed and two people died.[3] The Congress government of Maharashtra began to act only in 1993, when the party realised that a new political mobilisation was gaining momentum among Dalits and understood that such a gesture would bring dividends electorally speaking.

Its decision to publish his complete works was also laboriously arrived at in the 1970s. And then it was strongly resented. In 1987 the appearance of *Riddles in Hinduism*, which had not yet been published because of its provocative tone, prompted violent protests.[4] It is noteworthy that the million of rupees reserved by central government for the project remained unclaimed for many years because no university wished to be associated with such a publication.[5] Similarly, the first film of Ambedkar's life was made only in the 1990s.

When he was not met with indifference, Ambedkar was the subject of acerbic criticism by Gandhians and Hindu nationalists.

The target of Gandhians and Hindu nationalists

From the outset Gandhians were naturally the first to attack Ambedkar because of his opposition to the Mahatma. This antagonism crystallised at the Second Round Table Conference and later because of Ambedkar's attempts to marginalise the ideas of the Mahatma during the Constituent Assembly debates. A persistent critique also emanated from Gandhians who opposed Ambedkar's plans for the modernisation of India; in their opinion he drew too heavily on the West for inspiration. D. R. Nagaraj epitomised this stand of opinion. For him, Gandhi was certainly a 'romantic and a starry-eyed [*sic*] in his portrayal of rural India, but he had a better intuitive understanding of the modern civilisation.'[6] By contrast, Ambedkar was mistaken in thinking that the modernisation of India, and the political centralisation which accompanied it, were pre-conditions for the emancipation of Untouchables who would otherwise remain condemned to their traditional hierarchies. In fact 'the newly emerging centres of modern development had prompted a system of collaborative mechanism with superior castes allowing the subaltern communities and castes only a marginal role. Institutions of capitalism, science and technology were taken over by upper castes whereas in traditional society, lower and artisan castes were in possession of indigenous technologies.'[7]

This analysis is certainly not free of romanticism, because to mourn the passing of the traditional division of labour is to be blind to the stigmas which were attached to tasks perceived as degrading by the upper castes. Artisanal castes possessed useful skills that the mechanisation of work threatened to eliminate but their traditional tasks were also the root cause of their lowly status. Nagaraj's approach echoes the way in which Mahatma Gandhi strove to improve conditions in rural leather tanning enterprises without giving the least indication of being willing to rid 'one of the most useful industries'[8] of the stigmas which were associated with it and of the ritual pollution that it engendered. At best, the Gandhian idea of a conflict-free society reflects a form of naivety; at worst it is a discourse intended to make more palatable the strategy of maintaining the social status quo.

Most Gandhians however sought to reconcile Ambedkar with the Mahatma, rather than subjecting the former to systematic criticism. Suhas Palshikar established a very interesting list of parallels between these two towering figures of Indian history who 'strived to visualise a community based on justice and fraternity': they both 'believed that social transformation could come about only by social action'; they both 'would have no difficulty in agreeing upon the value of non-violence' and they were both 'concerned with the question of emancipation.'[9] This argument is typical of a spontaneous Gandhian underplaying of conflict. Palshikar was criticised by Ambedkar's supporters who felt that the Mahatma did not regard the emancipation of the lower castes as a priority.[10]

However, the most determined adversaries of Ambedkar are found today among the ranks of Hindu nationalists. It is undeniable that the RSS tries to co-opt him into its pantheon of great men—as the picture on page 147 makes clear—and that the main political representative of this ideological strand, the Bharatiya Janata Party (BJP), displays his portrait at its meetings so as to woo Untouchables—who comprise one fifth of the electorate in the Hindi-speaking zone, the party's stronghold. But in reality, the upper castes that dominate the BJP have made Ambedkar one of their favourite targets.

Arun Shourie, who was appointed minister of disinvestment in A. B. Vajpayee's government in 2003, has been leading the charge against Ambedkar's growing popularity for some time. For Shourie this popularity is unwarranted because it is blind, a standpoint reflected in the title of his book, published in 1997, *Worshipping False Gods: Ambedkar and the Facts which have been Erased*. The hidden facts that Shourie wishes Indians to recall are divided into three categories which in turn are reflected in the book's three sections: the first concerns Ambedkar's long association with the British; the second, the counter-productive nature of his methods in relation to upper caste social reformers; and last, his role in the drafting of the Indian Constitution a subject to which we do not need to return here.

Collaborator with the British and gravedigger of social reform?

For Shourie, Ambedkar played into the hands of the British because he was motivated by selfish careerist interests, regardless of any nationalist sentiment. Ambedkar's appointment to the Viceroy's Council in 1942 thus allowed the colonial power to benefit from the support of some Indians while simultaneously harshly repressing the Quit India movement.[11] For Shourie, 'Ambedkar and Jinnah became not just accomplices of Imperial politics; they became the best of agents, agents who had been so flattered into self importance that they did not see that they had made the cause of the Imperial rulers their own.'[12]

Shourie insists on placing Ambedkar and Jinnah, the founding father of Pakistan, on the same footing. He highlights that the first participated in meetings with the second during 'Deliverance Day' when the Muslim League celebrated the dismissal of the Congress governments in 1939.[13] He depicts Ambedkar as a collaborator devoid not only of any nationalist sense but above all of any scruples: he allowed himself to be co-opted by pure ruthless ambition. He quotes in support of this thesis a letter which the Governor of Bombay sent to the Viceroy in 1942, soon before Ambedkar's appointment to the Council of the latter:

> As you know, too, he has been, for some time, anxious to obtain a position in the High Court or elsewhere, in which he could have a chance of providing for his own future. He has given me, for some time the impression of a man who is no longer really interested in the work he is been doing for his own followers, and is anxious to reach a different sphere.[14]

It is true that Ambedkar was plagued by financial difficulties throughout his life, but does this allow Shourie to assert that he was prepared to betray his caste fellows and that his struggle to free Untouchables was not the reason why Ambedkar supported the British? If his true motives had been careerist, why then did he resign from Nehru's government in 1951?

Picture distributed by the Rashtriya Swayamsevak Sangh, a Hindu nationalist organisation eager to co-opt Dr Ambedkar by including him among a galaxy of historic Hindu heroes.

Shourie's accusation regarding Ambedkar's lack of nationalist commitment drew a passionate response from Dalits and their supporters. S. M. Gaikwad underlines that Ambedkar 'never opposed to India gaining freedom at any time';[15] he turned down any form of independence that did not guarantee political representation to Untouchables. Moreover Ambedkar contributed to nation-building, given that he favoured the elimination of caste considerations, such as Untouchability, 'which was preventing India from constituting itself as a unified and a modern nation'.[16] Gaikwad also hits back by arguing that Congress 'represented the Indian national bourgeoisie's drive for an overall political and economic control; while people like Ambedkar, representing the most underdeveloped, servile segment of the "Indian nation", tried desperately to secure for themselves some foothold in the newly emerging power structure.'[17] At most, Congress was only an elitist movement whereas Ambedkar launched a politicisation of the masses without which the Indian nation would never have been able to move forward.

As well as describing Ambedkar as a collaborator, Shourie also accused him of being the gravedigger of social reform by exaggerating the stigma of Untouchability. He downplays what Ambedkar had endured by arguing that 'the privations or humiliations he suffered were no greater than, they were in fact so much less than the trials that Ramakrishna Paramhansa, Swami Vivekananda, Gandhiji and countless others had to wade through.'[18] The men he cited were religious or public figures engaged in a spiritual quest whose sufferings were either bound up with the nationalist struggle or with their decision to embrace asceticism (including in the political arena). Such personal choices hardly merit comparison with the stigma of Untouchability that afflicted Ambedkar. Shourie's attack reflects the upper caste outlook that, from Gandhi to the Hindu nationalists, had always called for a reformist approach. For most of the proponents of this approach, social reform was likely to improve the condition of the lower castes without questioning the basic structure of the social system—even to strengthen its cohesion because it was, in their opinion, a means of reinforcing the nation.

Shourie then sees in Ambedkar the troublemaker who hampered both social reform launched by the 'really' enlightened spirits, such as 'Swami Dayananda, Swami Vivekananda, Lokmanya Tilak, Sri Aurobindo, Gandhiji, Ramana Maharshi [who] were engaged in a mighty effort to roll back the debilitating effects of the calumnies about our culture and religion which British rulers implanted into our minds.'[19] He establishes a link between nationalism and social reform by taking the risk of an ideological shift: he defends Hinduism from a nationalist point of view by claiming that the degradation of this religion date back to the British influence and that, implicitly, Untouchability is not part of Hindu culture. Well-intentioned upper caste reformers were about to remedy this so-called plague when Ambedkar came on the scene and ruined their plans by radicalising caste conflicts.

Shourie also blames Ambedkar for stirring up Untouchables, for altering their mindset towards a purely confrontational mentality. He compares him with Narayan Guru (1854–1928), an Untouchable religious preacher from Kerala, who managed to help members of his caste by encouraging them to relinquish their most impure practices:

> Whereas Ambedkar taught his followers to make demands on others, Narayan Guru taught them to make demands on themselves: just as the Guru persuaded persons of the higher castes to open the temples to devotees of all castes, he strove as hard to ensure that the people of his own caste—the then lowly Ezhavas—stopped their discrimination against the Untouchables, that they too opened *their* temples to devotees from the still lower castes. Instead of pandering to the practices of the lower castes, he preached temperance to castes and tribes whose very mode of living and livelihood revolved around toddy-tapping. He asked his preachers to educate the lower castes to the importance of truth, cleanliness as to instil in them fear of unrighteousness, to instil in them faith in God.[20]

Shourie therefore rejects Ambedkar's egalitarian and purely social claim and argues instead in favour of a reformist pattern. He clearly draws his inspiration from Gandhi, but also from the contemporary discourse of Hindu nationalism.[21] And the criticisms that he levelled against Ambedkar regarding positive discrimination is framed in this perspective. Shourie argues that Ambedkar introduced 'the evil' of quotas which extended bit by bit to the elected assemblies, to the administration and to the university and created a mentality of the assisted 'in which jobs are a matter of right, not something for which a person must work and excel.'[22] He describes the beneficiaries of 'reservations' as privileged, almost affluent, citizens:

> They have been weaned on the belief that the positions they have reached are their entitlement because of the oppression to which their group has

been subjected in the past, they neither aspire to acquire the skills to discharge the responsibilities well nor is their conduct such as befits the positions which they have been accorded. The job is ill done, and so society is harmed.[23]

Here he echoes the growing rejection of positive discrimination by the urban (upper caste) middle class. This fast-expanding social group which has benefited enormously from the economic liberalisation of India since 1991, is increasingly hostile to the 'privileged rights' which the lower castes enjoy. The development of the private sector thus goes hand in hand with a form of meritocratic mentality where the progeny of the upper caste elites think of themselves as 'self-made men'. While this new class dreams of America, it expresses its ambitions in the idiom of nationalism and pride in Hindu culture and is very sensitive about being faithful to 'tradition'. It also forms the hard core of Hindu nationalist voters, yet occasionally refers back to Gandhi, as does Shourie, who concludes:

The essence of Gandhiji's way to political advance [*sic*], to social reform was that each group, that each person must make demands not on others but on oneself: [...] Ambedkar's way, that of the Communists, that of our 'activists' today is to make demands on the other, in particular on the Government of the day.[24]

Arun Shourie's harsh judgement of Ambedkar is, I would argue, primarily a response to the increasing popularity of Ambedkarism and to the recent rise to power of Untouchables who question the social status quo. Indeed, the parties who look to Ambedkar for inspiration, after having shown themselves incapable of playing a significant political role, achieved an electoral breakthrough of major proportions in the 1990s.

The political legacy of Ambedkar: posterity or treason?

The marginalisation of the RPI. In the first decade of its existence, the RPI, the last party founded—posthumously—by Ambedkar, had some encouraging results. Not only did it capitalise on the movement for the creation of Maharashtra according to linguistic criteria in 1957 by implanting itself on the state's political scene, but it made its first breakthrough in Northern India in the 1960s, as shown in the Table 9.1.

Table 9.1 THE RPI AND THE ELECTIONS OF 1962 AND 1967

	Seats gained and percentage of votes polled			
	1962		*1967*	
	Lok Sabha	*Vidhan Sabha*	*Lok Sabha*	*Vidhan Sabha*
Andhra Pradesh	0 (0.96)	0 (0.40)	0 (0.50)	1 (0.27)
Gujarat	0 (0.89)	0 (0.41)	0 (2.02)	0 (0.08)
Madhya Pradesh	0 (1.84)	0 (1.26)	0 (1.70)	0 (0.84)
Tamil Nadu	0 (1.54)	0 (0.45)	0 (0.20)	0 (0.20)
Maharashtra	0 (11.66)	3 (5.38)	0 (12.71)	5 (6.66)
Karnataka	0 (3.86)	0 (0.82)	0 (3.1)	1 (0.77)
Punjab	0 (6.25)	0 (2.15)	0 (2.63)	3 (1.79)
Uttar Pradesh	3 (4.27)	8 (3.74)	1 (4.07)	10 (4.14)
Delhi	0 (3.14)	–	0 (5.68)	–
Himachal Pradesh	0 (6.56)	–	0 (2.33)	–
Bihar	–	–	–	1 (0.18)
Rajasthan	–	–	0 (0.18)	0 (0.13)
Haryana	–	–	0 (2.32)	2 (2.9)
West Bengal	–	–	0 (0.66)	0 (0.01)

Although Maharashtra remained the stronghold of the RPI in terms of votes polled, it was in Uttar Pradesh that it gained the largest number of seats in 1962 and 1967. Interestingly, two out of three RPI MPs returned in Uttar Pradesh in 1962 and seven out of eight RPI MLAs in the UP Vidhan Sabha were elected in constituencies which were not reserved for the Scheduled Castes, a clear indication of its increasing capacity to attract support beyond Dalits. In fact the party benefited from the votes of Muslims whose confidence in the Congress party—to which they usually gave their support—had been shaken by a communal riot in Aligarh, to which the government responded hardly at all. Muslims felt the need to organise themselves and hence allied with Untouchables against upper caste Hindus, the traditional support base of Congress.

The RPI also tried to broaden its base by emphasising the socio-economic side of its programme. In 1959, the party's Maharashtrian branch campaigned for land redistribution to landless labourers. This proved relatively successful, even though the government gave in to its demand verbally but maintained the status quo ante.[25] In 1964, the fourth session of the party met at Ahmedabad, once again putting this question at the core of its program. A year later the RPI published a Charter in which socio-economic questions loomed large. It demanded the effective implementation of the 1948 law on minimum wages, the strict control of grain prices and the fulfilment of administrative job quotas for the Scheduled Castes and Scheduled Tribes.[26] The 1962 Election Manifesto of the RPI advocated nationalisation of land and the development of collective agriculture.[27]

This focus on socio-economic issues displeased the old guard comprising Ambedkar's former lieutenants who remained faithful to the philosophy of the SCF. They considered the problems of Untouchables as specific and regretted that the RPI had turned away from them or, at the very least, had conflated them with other issues.[28] This dilution was particularly badly received by B. K. Gaekwad (1902–71), a Mahar from Nasik district who had been entrusted by Ambedkar with developing the SCF in rural Maharashtra and who was recognised as the architect of the party in the state. Gaekwad was typical of the Mahar old guard who had joined Ambedkar in the early days. It was a group largely rural in background whose levels of education were not very high.

From the late 1950s these figures began to clash with the new generation of urban, better educated leaders epitomised by B. C. Kamble—a Bombay lawyer. However, their differences of doctrine and social background do not suffice to explain these tensions: the RPI was also a victim of factionalism and a crisis of leadership that followed Ambedkar's death. He alone embodied the spirit of the SCF but had not designated a successor. The conflict between Gaekwad and Kamble became personal and resulted in 1959 in a split, with Kamble forming the Durushta RPI which ultimately joined Congress.

This was only the first of many such splits. Another occurred in 1969 when Khobragade formed his own party after R. S. Gavai had been chosen—over Khobragade—as RPI (Gaekwad) candidate for the Upper House of Maharashtra. Gawai succeeded Gaekwad a short while later. Finally, Ambedkar's son, Bhaiyyasaheb, anxious to cash in on his name despite his lack of organisational skills, created his own party. Thus by the early 1970s there were four RPI factions, led by Gavai, Kamble, Khobragade and Bhaiyyasaheb Ambedkar respectively. Their competition largely explains the party's electoral decline. In 1967 the two RPIs won only 2.48 per cent of valid votes at the national level and only 5 MLA seats, all located in Maharashtra. In 1971, the four RPI factions regained one seat in the Lok Sabha but managed to get elected only three MLAs in Maharashtra.

The RPI also failed in its efforts to put down roots beyond Maharashtra and to widen its base. Not only did it eventually attract very few non-Dalit voters, but even among Dalits it was often confined to one caste in each region. In Maharashtra, the cleavage between Mahars and other Untouchables was reflected in voting patterns. The RPI was thought of very much as a Mahar party; accordingly the other Untouchable castes, in particular Chambhars, preferred to lend their support to Congress. Moreover, their leaders were opposed to Mahars who had converted to Buddhism when it was suggested that reservations—till then confined to Untouchable Hindus and Sikhs—should be extended to them. Chambhar leaders feared the competition of a caste more numerous than their own in sharing Untouchables quotas. In Uttar Pradesh, the RPI was easily identified with the Jatavs.

To these liabilities was added the strategy of Congress, which was a past master in co-opting 'Dalit leaders'. Jagjivan Ram drew to him 'Ambedkarites' whose desertion further weakened the RPI. Soon after the death of Ambedkar, P. N. Rajbhoj became the first significant renegade. He joined Congress in order to win election, in 1957, to the Upper House of Parliament, on that party's ticket.[29]. After the formation of the RPI, the first major leader of the party to join Congress, in 1965, was R. D. Bandhare, the leader of the party's Bombay branch, who ignored Gaekwad's leadership and had long suggested that the RPI should merge with Congress. In Uttar Pradesh, B. P. Maurya, the main leader of the RPI in the region, crossed over to Congress after the collapse of the RPI in the state elections of 1969. In exchange, he was rewarded with a ministerial post in the government of Indira Gandhi.[30]

If Congress undermined the RPI by encouraging such defections, the latter also discredited itself by 'running after' the dominant party. From the late 1960s onwards, Gaekwad and Maurya were the main advocates of such a policy. Gaekwad succeeded in imposing this line in 1971, when his party could be nothing more than a small junior adjunct of Congress. The four RPIs collaborated with Indira

Gandhi during the 1977 elections but without profiting from their strategy.

From 1980 till the mid-1990s, no offshoot or faction of the RPI gained a single seat; Dalit party politics seemed to be dying. However, the grandson of Ambedkar, Prakash, who took over from his father, who died in 1978, tried hard to reunite the various political heirs of the RPI, the number of which continued to increase. For instance Ramdas Athavale had seceded from the RPI (Ambedkar) and eventually joined Congress. In February 1996, different groups converged under the aegis of Prakash Ambedkar and opted for a loose organisational structure with a collective leadership. During the general elections organised three months later, the party joined hands with the Janata Dal in order to form a third force in Maharashtra—between Congress and the Hindu nationalists (the Shiv Sena and BJP)—but it did not gain a single seat. Two years later, however, the efforts of Prakash began to bear fruit: at the twelfth general election, the RPI gained four seats—all in non-reserved constituencies—thanks to its alliance with Congress and the Samajwadi Party, an organisation born of the split in the Janata Dal. In this manner the strategy of alliance with socialist forces which Bhim Rao Ambedkar had initiated forty-five years earlier had at last found its reward. The RPI, however, remained a regional force, confined to Maharashtra. In 1999 political recidivism drew it back to its past mistakes, to faction fighting. Soon, there were three Dalit parties again: one was led by Athavale, who allied with Sharad Pawar's Nationalist Congress Party; another one was led by Prakash Ambedkar, who remained associated with Congress (I); and a third, with R. S. Gavai at the helm, remained a separate group.[31] Thus in 1999 the factions emanating from the RPI retained no more than a single seat. The same result was registered in 2004 when the RPI (A) of Athavale, a component of the Congress—led alliance, could only win one seat.

The Rise of the BSP party of the Untouchables or architect of the Bahujan Samaj? Another organisation that claimed its roots were to be found in Ambedkarism was the Bahujan Samaj Party, which acquired considerable influence in North India in the 1990s. It has appropriated the electoral symbol of the parties of Ambedkar, the elephant on a blue base, and its activists greet each other with 'Jai

Bhim!' (Victory to Bhim—Ambedkar's first name). One of its slogans proclaims plainly: '*Baba [Saheb Ambedkar] tera mission adhura Kanshi Ram karenge pura*' (Baba, your mission remains unfulfilled, Kanshi Ram [the founder of the party] will complete it.) But is this man really a political heir of Ambedkar?

Kanshi Ram is from a Punjabi Chamar family which, like that of Ambedkar and Jagjivan Ram, benefited from the recruitment of Untouchables to the British Indian army, his father and his uncles also having been employed by the military. Kanshi Ram took advantage of positive discrimination policies to gain a BSc in science and in 1953 was hired as a chemist in a Defence Ministry laboratory.

His Ambedkarite connections were forged when he was posted to Poona, where he discovered that the miserable condition of Mahars and Mangs was far worse than that of Untouchables in Punjab.[32] Immersed in the political culture of Maharashtra, he read two of Ambedkar's classics, *Annihilation of Caste* and *What Gandhi and the Congress have done to the Untouchables.* These texts, together with his interaction with RPI activists, prompted him to get closely involved with the party. He left the RPI a little later, demoralised by factional squabbling and the alliance with Congress.

In 1971 Kanshi Ram launched the 'Scheduled Castes and Scheduled Tribes, Other Backward Classes and Minority Communities Employees' Association' by applying the strategy initiated by Ambedkar to aggregate all castes and tribes who were victims of discrimination relating to their social status. Sudhai Pai points out that 'His idea of joining hands with the BCs [Backward Classes] and forming a Bahujan Samaj drew inspiration from Ambedkar's conception of an autonomous Dalit movement with a constantly attempted alliance of Dalit and Shudra.'[33] But Kanshi Ram added to this social coalition other ascriptive groups, namely religious minorities (Muslims and Christians). He appointed at the head of the organisation five vice-presidents representing each of these five communities. According to him, they formed what he termed the *bahujan samaj* (lit. 'society of those in the majority'), a coalition intent on opposing the *alpjan*, or the *savarna*, the upper castes. Like Ambedkar, Kanshi Ram considered that Dalits were the most politically aware component of this social coalition—also because he regarded them, as did Ambedkar, as an ethnic group, India's original autochthons.

In the same spirit in 1973 Kanshi Ram launched set up the All India Backward (Scheduled Castes, Scheduled Tribes, Other Backward Classes) and Minority Communities Employees' Federation. Known by its acronym BAMCEF, it was intended to defend the interests of *bahujan* civil servants. In this context it generated a significant response as the implementation of positive discrimination policies had given rise to a small but substantial Dalit elite. In Uttar Pradesh, for example, Scheduled Castes form the largest contingent of high-ranking civil servants, after Brahmins and Kayasths[34] (BAMCEF claimed to have up to 200,000 members).[35] It was a development that perturbed the authorities, who resorted to intimidatory measures, including harassing BAMCEF members. This reaction prompted Kanshi Ram to transform it into a 'ghost organisation' in the 1980s. His early focus on the emerging Dalit middle class and his correlative relative neglect of peasants' interests is also reminiscent of Ambedkar. In fact, the SCF election manifesto of 1951 reflected the same imbalance.

Studying the public career of Ambedkar, Sudhai Pai points out that 'Parallel to his attempt to work among educated Dalit employees, he also tried to spread the message of Ambedkar among the masses'[36] through political means. Indeed, like Ambedkar, he was increasingly convinced of the need to reorient his actions and to enter politics. BAMCEF provided him with the cadres of a new party, the Dalit Shoshit Samaj Sangharsh Samiti (DSSSS—or DS4—Committee for the Struggle of the Society of Dalits and the oppressed). The reference to Dalits in the name of the organisation—as in the case of the Scheduled Castes' Federation almost forty years earlier—showed that Kanshi Ram wanted to refocus his actions on his own social milieu. However, in 1984 he founded a new organisation, the Bahujan Samaj Party (BSP—Party of the plebeian masses), the name of which was more closely related to his original project: to rally around the party all the ascriptive groups among India's lower social orders.

The BSP has done increasingly well at the polls. It rose from 2.07 per cent of valid votes in the 1989 general election to 4.2 per cent in 1999 and to 5.3 per cent in 2004. Its geographical heartland is in Uttar Pradesh, where it grew from 12 MLA seats in 1989 to 66 in 1993. This achievement allowed it to form a coalition government with the Samajwadi Party (SP, the Socialist Party). The alliance fractured two years later not only because of personal rivalries between the leaders of the BSP and the SP, but also, and perhaps more significantly, because of genuine class conflict between OBCs—the main support base of the SP (especially Yadavs)—and Dalits in rural areas, where, very often, the latter are farm labourers for the former.

The BSP then displayed a strong sense of pragmatism by brokering an alliance with the BJP. It was approached by the BSP and agreed to support a government steered by Mayawati, a Dalit-Jatav-woman, who was leading the BSP in Uttar Pradesh. For the first time in India a state—in this particular case its largest one—was governed by a Dalit woman. The feeling of pride which the *bahujan samaj* derived from this experience strengthened the electoral base of the BSP, especially since the politics of Mayawati benefited above all these social groups. Anxious to contain the growing influence of the BSP, the BJP withdrew its support from Mayawati in 1995, but the elections that took place the following year saw Kanshi Ram reap the benefits of his strategy, since the party jumped from 11 to 20 per cent of the votes polled in the state elections. With its sixty-seven seats the BSP once again convinced the BJP to lend its backing to a new Mayawati government. This time the alliance between the two parties lasted only a few months, with the BJP succeeding in taking power on its own after having provoking a split in the ranks of the BSP.

In spite of this setback, Kanshi Ram was to reap the benefits of the alliances which he had brokered in the '90s. These had permitted him to capture power and, by doing so, to widen still further his party's social base. In 1999 the BSP gained as many as fourteen seats in the Lok Sabha elections and nineteen in 2004. All these seats, however, were won in UP, where the BSP continued to make gains in the state elections. For the first time in 2002 it won more seats than the BJP—98 as against 88. Once again both parties formed a ruling coalition: Mayawati became Chief Minister for the third time and succeeded in the novelty of completing more than one year in office for the first time. However she was dislodged from power in 2003.

The BSP's rise to power in UP can be explained by the implementation of a program and a strategy broadly inspired by Ambedkar's political legacy. Kanshi Ram advocates a pragmatic approach to politics which recalls Ambedkar's. Indeed the BSP's collaboration with the BJP is reminiscent of Ambedkar's collaboration with the British and Congress. In both cases, the aim of Dalit leaders was to allow Scheduled Castes to have access to power in order to implement Dalit-oriented policies. Moreover, Kanshi Ram's effort to transform the *bahujan samaj* into a political force was parallel with Ambedkar's policy. He also put into practice the same desire (as that of Ambedkar) to widen the base of the party to communities other than Dalits. Kanshi Ram thus tried to defend the interests of OBCs whom he considered, for example, to be under-represented in the administration and took the necessary measures.[37] The BSP also tried to cater to the needs of Tribals and Muslims. During the state elections of 1996 in Uttar Pradesh, more than 30 per cent of its candidates came from OBC castes, which therefore were better represented than Dalits (29 per cent). In addition, 18 per cent of the candidates were Muslims and 17 per cent from the upper castes.[38] In the general election of 1996, Koeris (market gardeners) voted in relatively large numbers for the BSP in Uttar Pradesh. According to reliable surveys, nearly a quarter of them did so, against 74 per cent of Chamars.[39] During the state elections of September 1996 in Uttar Pradesh, an opinion poll revealed that 27 per cent of Kurmis—another OBC caste—and 19 per cent of lower-ranking OBCs—the Most Backward Classes—voted for the BSP. These figures are much lower than those of Dalits—sixty-five per cent of whom voted BSP[40]—but they prove that the party was expanding its influence beyond the Scheduled Castes vote bank. This success was achieved without resorting to a Marxist discourse of class struggle but by returning to Ambedkar's project of uniting ascriptive groups which were victims of discrimination rather than only those who suffered from economic hardship.

The close relations and descendants of Ambedkar nevertheless criticised Kanshi Ram, either because he opposed the RPI, or because they regarded him as intellectually and culturally inferior to 'Babasaheb'. Or indeed because their dominant image of Ambedkar is as the architect of the Indian Constitution, as the man of principles, whose pragmatism they often conveniently overlook. Others blame the BSP for not trying hard any more neither to analyse caste society as formerly done by Ambedkar nor to give enough emphasis to education as a priority for the emancipation of the Dalits, as Ambedkar had done.[41] Kanshi Ram, without being artless or uncultivated, certainly does not have Ambedkar's intellectual sophistication. But he has read his works and shares his interpretation of the caste system. Above all, he puts into practice entire swathes of Ambedkar's strategy. Like him, he considers that access to power has to be a priority for Dalits and that in the pursuit of this end one can be utterly pragmatic. Sudhai Pai substantiates this interpretation while commenting upon her research in Uttar Pradesh:

> There are strong parallels between the attitude of the leaders of the UPSCF in the 1940s and the BSP in mid-1990s: both believed that political power rather than a grass-root level revolution is essential to improve the socio-economic conditions of the lower castes.[42]

Unlike the leaders of the RPI, Kanshi Ram has never allowed himself to be co-opted and has remained faithful to his mission, as did Ambedkar.

The BSP's main weakness also reminds us of Ambedkar's political parties, namely their mediocre grasp of organisation, which goes with a disturbing personalisation of power: the BSP is very closely identified only with one leader (and with Mayawati). Even though in 1997, for the first time, the chiefs of state units of the BSP were elected, Kanshi Ram continues to appoint district heads and even party functionaries in charge at the *tehsil* and block level in UP. Hence the slogan 'the BSP is Kanshi Ram, and Kanshi Ram is the BSP'.[43] This peculiar feature threatens to affect it permanently, just as Ambedkar's parties were debilitated by poor organisation.

Ambedkar has always been the bogeyman of Gandhians, not only because of the hostility accumulated since the Poona Pact but, more fundamentally, because of the ideological assumptions which distinguish the two great personalities. Beyond the Gandhians, Ambedkar antagonised the Indian establishment in its entirety and in particular the Congress party, not least because he never allowed himself to be co-opted. He remained committed to the Untouchables' cause and a sworn enemy of the social *status quo* which the dominant party maintained so adroitly—particularly because the hierarchical structure of the Hindu world lent itself to the implementation of a truly clientelistic network. If Ambedkar was the object of acerbic criticism, he was above all blacklisted by everyone: he was ignored and his ideas have been deliberately marginalised for years.

Ambedkar's name reappeared in the Indian political discourse in the 1980s. At the time of writing, all political parties, including the BJP, refer to him and cite him as the icon that nobody can ignore. Ambedkar symbolises the political mobilisation of Untouchables, which has never been so formidable, as shown by the electoral successes of the BSP. One manifestation of the changing mood occurred in 1997, with the election of Kocheril Raman Narayanan, an Untouchable, to the post of President of the Republic.[44] While a man of Congress and one of extreme moderation in his views—which his diplomatic career helped him to refine—he referred gladly to Ambedkar who he had the opportunity to meet in New York in 1943.[45]

In face of the political rise of Untouchables, the party which is also the most popular among the upper castes, the BJP, seems to vacillate between two discourses. On the one hand it praises Ambedkar, the symbol of the Dalit movement because it cannot alienate the lower castes—a considerable portion of the electorate. On the other hand, it tries hard, as exemplified by Arun Shourie's writings, to tarnish Ambedkar's reputation. It is a contradiction that says much about the nature of the challenge that India's political establishment must stand up to.

Conclusion

Before Ambedkar some Shudras such as Phule had rebelled in the name of egalitarianism against the caste system, but no Untouchables had done so, except for saints who extolled the virtues of salvation via spiritual discipline out of this world.

As a pioneer, to Ambedkar fell the task of elaborating a strategy of emancipation specially intended for his own social milieu and others like him. At the outset the mechanisms of Sanskritisation appealed to him and he was drawn to upper caste reformers, including Gandhi, and motivated by issues such as temple entry. Later, the dangers of such an approach—which conformed hardly at all with the values of equality and personal freedom in which he had been trained in the West—became plain. He deepened his reflection on the caste system and discovered that 'graded inequality', its structuring principle, gravely endangered the unity of the lower castes and hence their capacity for mobilisation.

But which strategy should be implemented to surmount this obstacle? Ambedkar sought institutional guarantees to protect the interests of Untouchables and to this end pursued several strategies. The first was to obtain a separate electorate, an option shut out by Gandhi in 1932, and later by debates in the Constituent Assembly. This obliged Ambedkar to fight for a system of reserved seats and implied collaboration with those in power, whether the colonial authorities or the Congress regime.

Ambedkar was also at the forefront of political parties whose aim was to organise the most deprived sections of society and to influence the political process. He wavered between efforts to widen his social base to all workers—as manifested in the Independent Labour Party in 1937—and a desire to focus only on Dalits, as born out by the Scheduled Castes' Federation, founded in 1942. However the electoral setbacks suffered by the SCF in 1946 and in the early 1950s brought Ambedkar back to his original plan by a different route. A few months before his death he launched the idea a 'republican party' which was intended to represent the interests of the lower castes and workers. In fact, the RPI was to represent Dalits, the Other Backward Classes and Tribes, that is ascriptive groups, victims of discrimination based on their ritual status. Ambedkar had thus arrived at a formula allowing him to escape the competing pulls of caste (Untouchables) and class.

His dilemma reflected a deeper question about the status of Untouchables: are they 'separate' from the rest, or can they be integrated into Hindu society through alliances with other, higher, castes? Ambedkar never found a clear-cut and definitive answer to this question. Even after he renounced Sanskritisation, however, he never went as far as to break with the Hindu world altogether, hence the persistence of class in his ideology and his demand for reserved seats. But all through Ambedkar's career, this strategy ran counter to another one relying on three fundamental projects: a separate electorate for Dalits, their own space or territory and a party that represented them.

In practice, whatever the strategy he implemented, neither the ILP, the SCF nor the RPI represented the Untouchables in their entirety. Moreover none of the so-called 'Ambedkarite' organisations widened its sphere of influence beyond the Mahars of Maharashtra, the only region where they had some success. Other Dalit castes, such as Mangs and Chambars, became jealous of the rise in importance of Ambedkar's caste. Hence he failed to surmount the handicaps of 'graded inequality': not only did the lower castes opt out of a common front but among Untouchables also divisions remained very distinct.

The outcome of Ambedkar's political career was definitely mixed: certainly he obtained major concessions from the British by collaborating with them—including a new policy of positive discrimination in favour of the Untouchables—and his politics made an impact during the constitutional debates when he gained more concessions for the Dalits and succeeded in marginalising some Gandhian propositions. But he did not get the separate electorate he wanted for the Scheduled Castes, he failed to have concrete social reforms adopted, such as the Hindu Code Bill, and he was not able to establish a party representing the interests of the Untouchables of India as a whole.

These failures explain why Ambedkar from time to time envisaged implementing an alternative strategy, that of conversion. This option presented itself to him for the first time after the setback that was the Poona Pact. But he hesitated between many options—Islam, Christianity and Sikhism—and eventually postponed a definitive decision and again allowed himself to be sucked into the political maelstrom with the creation of the ILP. Disappointed by his experience within the Nehru government, in the mid-1950s he returned to the conversion option. This time a choice was forced upon him, from the inner self: that of Buddhism, a doctrine that he had discovered in his youth and had adopted as his personal philosophy.

His conversion was not an escape; nor was it *purely* an individual step. Collective conversion was also the expression of a social revolt: in 1956, mass conversions were explicitly directed against the hierarchical structure of Hindu society. It was a strategy of emancipation which went along with the 'separatist' aspect of his approach, although by choosing Buddhism, Ambedkar limited the scope of his break with Hinduism.

The intermediary nature of this break goes on a par with the post-conversion persistence of the logic of caste. Indeed, the deep roots of caste were such that new converts often remained Untouchable in the eyes of other castes, all the more so as these Buddhists came, almost exclusively, from among Mahars. After the mass conversions of the 1950s and '60s, the stream of converts quickly dried up, partly because to embrace Buddhism meant foregoing the quota from which Untouchable Hindus benefited in administration, education and elected assemblies. The *bauddhas* had to wait till 1990 for this dissuasive provision to be removed by Prime Minister V. P. Singh.

If the final outcome of Ambedkar's actions was rather mixed, the significance of his achievement must be seen within the wider scope of the pioneering objective that he had set himself. However, he would have had a bigger impact had he devoted more time to the organisational structures of the movements and parties which he engendered. Ambedkar's strengths were those of his weaknesses: nothing he achieved would have been possible without his strength of character which was so manifest and explains his tremendous charisma. Unfortunately his individualism and his very personal exercise of power adapted badly to organisational constraints.

Ambedkar's death destabilised the movement he had inaugurated. None of his lieutenants was capable of assuming the leadership—especially so after they joined battle in a vicious cycle of factional infighting. On the other hand, the Congress Party, expert in the co-option of Untouchable leaders, lured several of them. Former lieutenants of Ambedkar allowed themselves to be tempted by the spoils of office, the price of which was nothing less than their compliance.

The disgust of educated Dalit elites at their so-called leaders and representatives prompted many of them to desert politics. Some opted for literature, and Maharashtra became the heartland of Dalit poetry.[1] Others, often drawn from such literary circles, took the revolutionary path by forming, in the early 1970s, the Dalit Panthers, a movement inspired by the American Black Panthers, that did not shirk from violence as a means of countering upper caste oppression—hence the frequency of riots, particularly linked to the change of name of Marathwada University. The movement quickly split between, on the one hand, a school of thought influenced by Communist ideology, and, on the other hand, a group faithful to Ambedkar's teachings.[2]

Finally, a third category of Ambedkar's followers devoted themselves to organising Untouchables outside the political arena, and in this manner Kanshi Ram formed BAMCEF. However, this group also established parties, the DS4 and then finally the BSP, whose steady growth in certain states of North India is evidence of the durability of the movement started by Ambedkar. The BSP developed in the image of Ambedkar's achievements, even though it did not resume all of its dimensions. Ambedkar even became the symbol of the political mobilization of the lower castes.

The long-term, entrenched neglect of Ambedkar soon became something of the past. In August 1999, history textbooks which till then contained no mention of his name were augmented by an additional two pages outlining his contribution to the drafting of the Constitution—this too at the request of Dalit movements.[3] Dalit leaders also showed their growing assertiveness and militancy, especially in reaction to Shourie's book on Ambedkar: Dalit MPs burned several copies of it in Parliament.[4] But nothing illustrates better Ambedkar's central place in the conflict between Dalits and Hindu nationalists than the controversies surrounding the statues raised in his honour.[5] Mayawati had as many as 15,000 of them erected in her second term as Chief Minister of Uttar Pradesh,[6] signifying that Ambedkar had become the Dalit symbol *par excellence* through which Untouchables could assert their presence in India's public space. Places reserved for these statues were sometimes surreptitiously occupied by others,[7] but more often Ambedkar's statues were 'dishonoured', the commonest provocation consisting in 'decorating' them with a garland of shoes. Such deeds precipitated countless riots, not only in the north and in Maharashtra but also in the south, especially in Karnataka and Tamil Nadu.[9] That Ambedkar should be at the heart of this contest for public space is at least proof that he has become the symbol of confrontation between the lower castes and the upper castes, at a time when the former are growing in strength.

Notes

Introduction The First Dalit Leader in India

1. The Nagpur-based editor of Ambedkar's collected works, Vasant Moon, another Ambedkarite Mahar, conveys the same testimony in his autobiography. As soon as he learnt of Ambedkar's death he filed a petition for leave drafted as follows: 'I feel many times the sorrow I felt at the death of my father. I want to go to his funeral procession in Mumbai (then Bombay). So please approve the leave.' (V. Moon, *Growing up Untouchable in India: A Dalit Autobiography*, London: Rowman & Littlefield, 2001, p. 159)
2. In this book I use the word Untouchable more often than Dalit simply because the latter was not in common usage during Ambedkar's lifetime—even though he introduced the term with its modern connotations in the 1920s.
3. U. Baxi, 'Emancipation as Justice: Legacy and Vision of Dr Ambedkar' in K. C. Yadav, (ed.), *From Periphery to Centre Stage: Ambedkar, Ambedkarism and Dalit Future*, Delhi: Manohar, 2000, p. 49.
4. Books on Ambedkar's life and work have multiplied over the last decade, following the political rise of the Dalits.
5. The pioneering biography by Dhananjay Keer, *Dr Ambedkar: Life and mission*, Bombay: Popular Prakashan, 1954, has gone into three editions and many reprints. The best biography of Ambedkar is Eleanor Zelliot's unpublished PhD thesis, 'Dr Ambedkar and the Mahar Movement', University of Pennsylvania, 1969. Three other biographies may also be mentioned: D. N. Shikare, *Dr Ambedkar*, Poona: Jayant and Co., 1963; W. N. Kuber, *B. R. Ambedkar*, New Delhi: Government of India, 1978 and *The Life of Dr Ambedkar*, Hyderabad: Babasaheb Dr Ambedkar Memorial Society, 1979. Interestingly, many more biographies of Ambedkar have been published in vernacular languages. In Marathi, C. B. Khairmode's *Dr Bhimrao Ramji Ambedkar* runs to over 14 volumes (the first was published in 1952); in Hindi, C. P. Jigyasu published *Dr Babasaheb Ambedkar ka jivan sangharsh*, Lucknow: Hindu Samaj Sudhar Karyalaya, as early as 1961.
6. The government of Maharashtra set up an advisory committee under the chairmanship of the State's Education Minister. The Committee appointed an Editorial Board of which Vasant Moon was the key officer. The first volume of the series called *Dr Babasaheb Ambedkar Writings and Speeches* came out in 1979.
7. See Ramachandra Guha, 'A bare cupboard: Why biography doesn't flourish in South Asia', *Times Literary Supplement*, 30 Aug. 2002, p. 12. I will content myself with citing the opening sentences of this article: 'In contrast to the art of the novel, the art of biography remains undeveloped in South Asia. We know how

to bury our dead with reverence or bury them through neglect, but not to honour or judge them [...] This is a world governed by deference, not discrimination.'

8. The ruling dynasty of Indore, the Holkars, as that of Gwalior (the Scindias), of Baroda (the Gaekwars) and of Nagpur (the Bhonsles) had established their respective kingdoms following the eighteenth-century conquests of these areas by a warrior leader of the Maratha caste, Shivaji. Marathas were originally a middle-ranking farming caste of which the élite, following these military successes, claimed a Kshatriya status. While the Scindias, the Gaekwars and the Bhonsles were Marathas, the Holkars belonged to a shepherd caste, the Dhangars.
9. Ambedkar himself recognised the fact that, because he lived in a cantonment, he had little contact with the wider world and, consequently, was hardly conscious of the plague of Untouchability (see Bhagawan Das (ed.), *Thus spoke Ambedkar*, vol. 4, Bangalore: Ambedkar Sahithya Prakashana [s.d.], p. 65).
10. Such an attitude was not rare, even at the beginning of the twentieth century. Daya Pawar reports that his village barber had for many years refused to cut the hair of the Mahars (his caste and that of Ambedkar) and of the Chambhars another Untouchable caste. It was said that 'he could very well shave the buffaloes; and [an Untouchable] did not value more than a buffalo. The barber was afraid of losing his clientele if he touched us.' (D. Pawar, op. cit., p. 96.)
11. These recollections of Ambedkar come from a speech given on May 17, 1936 when he spoke about some episodes of his life that shaped his decision to struggle against Untouchability (Bhagawan Das (ed.), *Thus Spoke Ambedkar*, vol. 4, *op. cit.*, p. 67)
12. Cited in V. Rodrigues, 'Introduction' in V. Rodrigues (ed.), *The Essential Writings of B. R. Ambedkar*, Delhi: Oxford University Press, 2002, p. 9. Gail Omvedt recently pointed out that Ambedkar was 'above all a man of strategy, of practical politics, even with his most radical public statements'. G. Omvedt, 'Undoing the Bondage: Dr Ambedkar's Theory of Dalit Liberation' in K. C. Yadav (ed.), *From Periphery to Centre Stage*, op. cit., p. 137.

Chapter 1 Maharashtra Between Social Reform and anti-Brahmin Mobilisation

1. Iyothee Dass—a Dalit activist turned Buddhist—who hailed from Madras—was a contemporary of J. Phule (see V. Geetha and S. V. Rajadurai, *Towards a Non-Brahmin Millennium: From Iyothee Thass to Periyar*, Calcutta: Samya, 1998).
2. After 1956, Untouchables who converted to Buddhism and declared this identity to the Census enumerators were no longer considered as Scheduled Castes. Therefore, according to the Census of 1971, for instance, the Scheduled Castes represented 12.48 per cent of the population of Maharashtra and the Mahars alone 8 per cent, which still accounted for 35 per cent of the Untouchables of Maharashtra.
3. The numerical weakness of the trading castes in fact prompted some Brahmins to play the money-lenders' role and this strengthened their holding of landed

property given that defaulting debtors had no choice other than to mortgage and later to sell their land.

4. The proportion of Brahmin delegates to the Congress sessions of 1889, 1895 and 1915 who declared 'business' as their profession was 22.9 per cent whereas those that designated themselves as farmers was 10.2 per cent. (G. Omvedt 'Development of the Maharashtrian Class structures, 1818 to 1931', *Economic and Political Weekly* [Hereafter EPW], Special Number, August, 1973, p. 1418)
5. Karve differentiates both systems by arguing that the *balutedars*, however low they may have been in the caste hierarchy, were always village servants performing certain duties for the entire cultivating population whereas the *prija* (dependents) of the *jajmani* system were bound to a certain family from generation to generation (I. Karve, *Maharashtra State Gazetteer: Maharashtra—Land and its People*, Bombay, 1968, p. 140). While the *balutedar's* services were, in theory, intended for the village as a whole, they were often secured by the *patil* and the *kulkarni*. The *patil* could moreover exact *corvée*, a form of forced labour, from the Untouchables. (J. Lele, 'Caste, Class and Dominance: Political Mobilisation in Maharashtra' in F. R. Frankel and M. S. A. Rao (eds), *Dominance and State Power in Modern India: Decline of a Social Order*, vol. 2, Delhi: Oxford University Press, 1990, p. 119). The diversion of Mahars' services by the *patil* is testified by many witnesses. Baby Kamble, a Mahar woman who owed her fighting spirit to the teachings of Ambedkar, thus confides in her autobiography: 'During the entire day, the Mahar servant was at the disposal of the *patil* of the village. With other persons of his family he performed all the chores which this latter gave to do in the hamlets and in the village localities' (Shantabai Kamble and Baby Kamble, *Parole de femme intouchable*, Paris: Côté-femmes éditions, 1991, p. 213).' A selection of the life stories of these two women, Shantabai Kamble and Baby Kamble, has been published in English in chapter four of G. Poitevin (ed.), *The Voice and the Will Subaltern Agency: Forms and Motives*, New Delhi: Manohar/CSH, 2002.
6. T. Pillai-Vetshera points out: 'We speak of twelve *balutedars* since in every village there were theoretically twelve castes of artisans and village servants. In smaller villages, however, there were often less, and in bigger settlements more than twelve.' (T. Pillai-Vetschera, *The Mahars: A Study of their Culture, Religion and Socio-economic Life*, New Delhi: Intercultural Publications, 1994, p. 287).
7. The notion of '*baluta*' is so central in the life of Mahars that it is the title that Daya Pawar had given to his original autobiography in Marathi.
8. M. R. Jayakar, one of the most illustrious Kayasth Prabhus of the Bombay Presidency in the 1930 and '40 tells, in his autobiography, how he was prevented from learning Sanskrit at the prestigious Elphinstone High School by the professor who taught this subject, a Brahmin who reserved this privilege only to the 'twice borns'. (M. R. Jayakar, *The Story of My Life*, Bombay: Asian Publishing House, 1958, vol. 1, p. 13)
9. See, for example, the situation of Mahars of the Central Provinces as it is described in R. V. Russell and Hira Lal, *The Tribes and Castes of the Provinces of India*, vol. 4, New Delhi/Madras: Asian Educational Services, 1993 (1916), p. 142.
10. J. Gokhale, *From Concessions to Confrontation, The Politics of an Indian Untouchable Community*, Bombay: Popular Prakashan, 1993, p. 52.

11. In the 1940s, Vasant Moon was the only non-Brahmin pupil in the Normal School of Nagpur (V. Moon, *Growing up Untouchable in India*, op. cit., p. 14).
12. Being an élite corps, the 'covenanted service', which implied the signing of a contract between the British state and the civil servant, was largely reserved to the British.
13. A. Seal, *The Emergence of Indian Nationalism: Competition and collaboration in the Later Nineteenth Century*, Cambridge University Press, 1968, p. 118.
14. G. Johnson, 'Chitpavan Brahmins and Politics in Western India in the Late nineteenth and Early twentieth centuries' in E. Leach and S. N. Mukherjee (eds), *Élites in South Asia*, Cambridge University Press, 1970, p. 105.
15. R. Tucker, 'The Early Setting of the non-Brahmin movement in Maharashtra', *The Indian Historical Review*, July. 1980–Jan. 1981, vol. 2, nos 1–2, p. 137.
16. R. O'Hanlon, *Caste, Conflict and Ideology Mahatma Jotirao Phule and Low Caste Protest in Nineteenth-Century Western India*, Cambridge University Press, 1985, pp. 65–6.
17. Ambedkar, who was sensitive to the fact that Ranade had drafted for the Mahars the text of the petition which they submitted in 1892 against the ending of army recruitment of their caste, argues that Ranade had 'a passion for social reform' but he had to admit that this reformism did not translate into concrete social attitudes (Dr B. R. Ambedkar, 'Ranade, Gandhi and Jinnah' in Dr Babasaheb Ambedkar, *Writings and Speeches*, vol. 1, Bombay: Govt. of Maharashtra, 1979, p. 217).
18. R. Tucker, *Ranade and the Roots of Indian Nationalism*, Bombay: Popular Prakashan, 1972.
19. R. Kumar 'The New Brahmans of Maharashtra' in D. A. Low (ed.), *Soundings in Modern South Asian History*, Berkeley, CA: University of California Press, 1968, p. 115.
20. See, for example, S. R. Mehrotra, 'The Poona Sarvajanik Sabha: The early phase (1870–1880),' *The Indian Economic and Social History Review* 6 (3), Sept. 1969, p. 293–324.
21. Dayananda Saraswati, *The Light of Truth* [*Satyarth Prakash*], transl. G. P. Upadhyaya, Allahabad, 1981, p. 113.
22. R. Thapar, 'Imagined Religious Communities? Ancient History and the Modern Search for a Hindu identity', *Modern Asian Studies*, 23 (2), 1989, p. 229.
23. The biographical details which follow are taken from D. Keer, *Mahatma Jotirao Phooley: Father of Indian Social Revolution*, Bombay: Popular Prakashan, 1974.
24. J. Phule, *Slavery: Collected Works of Mahatma Jotirao Phule*, vol. 1, Bombay: Govt. of Maharashtra, 1991, p. xxvii.
25. J. Phule, *Slavery*, op. cit., pp. 36–8.
26. Ahmednagar's American Marathi Mission noticed in 1881 that 'the main part of our Christian converts are the Mahars' (quoted in E. Zelliot, *Dr Ambedkar*, op. cit., p. 29). In 1910, the Mahars petitioned for army recruitment of members of their caste, bearing out that 'the beneficial contact with the Christian religion immediately raised the Mahars'.

    They did not hesitate also to mention that 'Such of us as have attended schools and colleges, as Christian converts, have attained a distinction in the

Indian University Examinations, and hold positions of Pleaders, Doctors, Professors, Magistrates, and Judges in this and other Presidencies.' Many Mahars also became priests according to this petition ('The Conference of the Deccan Mahar, to the Right Honorable the Earl of Crewe', Bombay, Dec., 14, 1910, pp. 4–5. Private Papers of Ambedkar, Nehru Memorial Museum and Library [hereafter NMML, New Delhi], Microfilm Section).

27. *Collected works of Mahatma Jotirao. Phule*, vol. 2, Bombay: Govt. of Maharashtra, 1991, p. 8.
28. M. S. Gore, *Non-Brahman Movement in Maharashtra*, New Delhi: Segment Books, 1989, p. 24.
29. See, for example, 'Priestcraft exposed' in J. Phule, *Collected Works of Mahatma Jotirao Phule*, vol. 2, op. cit., p. 67–8; 'A poem about the Crafty, Cunning Spurious (religious) books of the Brahmins (A Contrast between the Comfortable lives of the Brahmins and the Miserable Lives of the Shudras)' in *Slavery—Collected Works of Mahatma Jotirao Phule*, vol. 1, op. cit., p. 81.
30. R. O'Hanlon, *Caste, Conflict and Ideology*, op. cit., p. 223.
31. In 1885, Phule published a pamphlet attacking Ranade in which he criticised—without naming him—his élitism and in particular his disregard of farmers. (J. Phule, 'A warning' in *Collected Works of Mahatma Jotirao Phule*, vol. 2, op. cit., p. 48–9)
32. J. Phule, *Slavery*, op. cit., pp. 58–9.
33. J. Phule, *Collected works*, vol. 2, op. cit., p. 25.
34. Ibid., p. 99.
35. Ibid., p. 29.
36. 'We understand by the nation a society materially and morally integrated, to a stable permanent central power, with defined borders, a related moral, mental and cultural unity of the inhabitants who adhere consciously to the State and to its laws' ('La nation', *Oeuvres*, vol. 3, Paris: Minuit 1969, p. 584.)
37. 'Jotirao Govindrao Phule (1827–90)' in *Collected Works of Mahatma Jotirao Phule*, vol. 1, op. cit., p. xix.
38. For instance, he described the way in which Mahars would have, in the mythical past, attacked the 'Bhats [Brahmins] to free their Shudra brethren from their clutches' (*Slavery*, op. cit., p. 25).
39. Ibid., p. 49.
40. Ibid., p. 161.
41. G. Omvedt, *Cultural Revolt in a Colonial Society: the Non-Brahmin Movement in Western India*, Poona: Scientific Socialist Education Trust, 1976.

Chapter 2 Ambedkar, Son of a Mahar Soldier

1. M. S. A. Rao, 'Some conceptual issues in the study of Caste, Class, Ethnicity and Dominance' in F. Frankel and M. S. A. Rao (eds), *Dominance and State power in Modern India*, vol. 1, Delhi: Oxford University Press, 1989, pp. 25–7.
2. E. Zelliot, *Dr Ambedkar and the Mahar Movement*, University of Pennsylvania, PhD, 1969, p. 28.
3. J. Gokhale, *From Concessions to Confrontation*, op. cit., pp. 41–2.

4. T. Pillai-Vetschera, *Mahars*, op. cit., p. 296.
5. Ibid., pp. 288–90. The most dramatic depiction of Mahars eating dead cattle is found in N. Jadhav, *Intouchable. Une famille de parias dans l'Inde contemporaine*, Paris: Fayard, 2002, pp. 85–6.
6. However Mahars never 'fell to the lowest': they did not clean latrines, as did the Bhangis of North India—some of whom were 'imported' to carry out these tasks in Maharashtra.
7. The myth of origin of the Mahars which, as always with Untouchables, seeks to explain their decline, presents their Untouchability as resulting from consuming beef. According to this myth, Mahars descended from Mahamuni, an orphan. One day the gods asked him to watch a pot in which beef was being cooked—at that time its consumption was not prohibited. Mahamuni accidentally let a piece fall to the ground, and not wishing to put it back in the pot and make the entire amount impure, he ate it. He was nonetheless punished for his carelessness and condemned, as were his descendants, to eat dead cows—thus giving birth to the Mahar caste (R. V. Russell and Hira Lal, *The Tribes and Castes of the Central Provinces of India*, vol. 4, op. cit., p. 132). For other Mahar myths of origin see T. Pillai-Vetschera, *Mahars*, op. cit., pp. 6–7.
8. R. V. Russell and Hira Lal, *The Tribes and Castes of the Central Provinces of India*, vol. 4, op. cit., p. 143.
9. T. Pillai-Vetschura, *Mahars*, op. cit., p. 40.
10. S. Kamble and Baby Kamble, *Parole de femme intouchable*, op. cit., pp. 213–14. A similar testimony appears in N. Jadhav, *Intouchable*, op. cit., p. 35. In this life story of two Mahars who followed Ambedkar as early as the 1920s, this Mahar's 'duty' is called *yeskar*.
11. A. Robertson, *The Mahar Folk*, Calcutta: YMCA Publishing House, 1938, pp. 20–1.
12. T. Pillai-Vetschera, *Mahars*, op. cit., p. 3.
13. J. Gokhale, *From Concessions to Confrontation*, op. cit., p. 32. 'The role of messenger also allowed Mahars to weave a network of relations favourable to the setting up of a common organisation.' (R. J. Miller, '"They will not die Hindus": the Buddhist conversion of Mahar ex-Untouchables', *Asian Survey*, 2 (9), Sept. 1967, pp. 637–44).
14. D. Pawar, *Ma vie d'Intouchable, op. cit.*, p. 62.
15. 'The Conference of The Deccan Mahars to the Right Honourable The Earl of Crewe', doc. cit., p. 3.
16. S. Cohen, 'The Untouchable Soldier: Caste, Politics and The Indian Army', *Journal of Asian Studies*, 28 (3), 1969, p. 455.
17. E. Zelliot 'Learning the Use of Political Means: Mahars of Maharashtra' in R. Kothari (ed.), *Caste in Indian Politics*, New Delhi: Orient Longman, 1970, p. 30.
18. E. Zelliot, *Dr Ambedkar*, op. cit., p. 39.
19. See G. R. Pradhan, *Untouchable Workers of Bombay City*, Bombay: Karnataka Publishing House, 1938.
20. G. Omvedt, *Dalits and the Democratic Revolution: Dr Ambedkar and the Dalit movement in colonial India*, New Delhi: Sage, 1994, p. 141. In Nagpur, according to

V. Moon, 40–45 per cent of the mill workers were Mahars in the 1940s (V. Moon, *Growing up untouchable in India*, op. cit., p. 71).

21. Morris David Morris, *The Emergence of an Industrial Labor Force in India: A study of the Bombay Cotton Mills, 1854–1947*, Berkeley/Los Angeles: University of California Press, 1965, p. 74.
22. The maharwada locality of Daya Pawar's village was in fact deserted even before the 1950s. Only two widows still lived there when he returned to it after the war (D. Pawar, *Ma vie d'intouchable*, op. cit., p. 154).
23. E. Zelliot, 'Learning the Use of Political Means', op. cit., p. 63. The life story of Narendra Jadhav's father, who became a railwayman in 1924, offers an excellent illustration of social upward mobility due to the railways (N. Jadhav, *Intouchable*, op. cit., p. 41.)
24. E. Zelliot, 'Learning the Use of Political Means', op. cit., p. 64. In 1929, the Bombay Presidency had the highest rate of literacy among Untouchables: 4.1 per cent as against 1.1 per cent in Punjab and 3.5 per cent in the Madras Presidency (E. Zelliot, *Dr Ambedkar*, op. cit., p. 162).
25. Ibid., p. 7.
26. M. G. Bhagat, 'The Untouchable classes of Maharashtra', *The Journal of the University of Bombay*, 4 (1), July, 1935, p. 19. I am using here an off-print found in the private papers of Ambedkar at the Nehru Memorial Museum and Library (NMML).
27. Ibid., p. 27.
28. Ibid., p. 14.
29. Ibid., p. 15.
30. Ibid., p. 16.
31. Ibid., pp. 10–14.
32. Ibid., p. 38.
33. Ibid., p. 40.
34. Ibid., p. 41.
35. Ibid., p. 21.
36. Ibid., p. 44.
37. K. N. Kadam, *Dr. Babasaheb Ambedkar and the Significance of his Movement*, Bombay: Popular Prakashan, 1991, p. 9.
38. In 1894, Ramji Sakpal addressed a memorandum to the Government 'to reopen the doors of military service to Mahars' (cited in ibid. p. 18).
39. In 1910, the Conference of the Deccan Mahars met in Poona, under the aegis of one of its numbers, a retired serviceman named Gopalak Vitthalnak Walangkar, to request that posts till then offered to Mahars in the army and the police again be made accessible to them, through the formation of a homogeneous Mahar regiment ('The Conference of the Deccan Mahars to the Right Honourable The Earl of Crewe', op. cit., p. 1). During the First World War, two companies, the 71st and the 111th, were created on this model but dissolved soon after the conflict ended. They regrouped Mahars—essentially from the Konkan coastal regions—with Punjabi Christians (A. Robertson, *The Mahar Folk*, op. cit., p. 63). Ambedkar was later to campaign successfully for the establishment of a

Mahar regiment in the Second World War. This Mahar Machine Gun Regiment, founded in Belgaum in 1941, gave two generals to the Indian army and in the 1990s accounted for twenty battalions (*National Mail*, Oct. 1, 1991).

40. C. Vaudeville. *Au cabaret de l'amour, Kabir*, Paris: Unesco/Gallimard, 1959.
41. Ambedkar's father re-joined the army (the 25th Regiment of Infantry) after he returned to Bombay (letter from Lieutenant-Colonel Sheikh Moiuddin to C. B. Khairmonday, 23 March 1950, Ambedkar's private papers, NMML, New Delhi, section of microfilms Reel no. 2, File no. 4).
42. This princely ruler had difficulties in recruiting teachers: only Muslims and Arya Samajists agreed to teach in such schools (*Presidential speech of His Highness the Maharajah Gaekwar at the All-India Conference on the Abolition of untouchability, Bombay, 23 March 1918*, Bombay: British India Press, 1918, p. 101, Private Papers of Ambedkar NMML, Section of microfilms).
43. Vitthal Ramji Shinde, a Maratha who later became an important social reformer in Maharashtra, was supported throughout his studies at Oxford University by the Baroda Maharajah's patronage (G. M. Pawar, *Vitthal Ramji Shinde*, New Delhi: National Book Trust, 1990, p. 13).
44. For more details and an account of the first meeting of the Maharajah and Ambedkar, see F. Gaekwad, *Sayajirao of Baroda*, Bombay: Popular Prakashan, 1989, p. 307.
45. M. Malgonkar, 'Maharajah's Help to Ambedkar', *Statesman* (Delhi), July 13, 1992.
46. E. Zelliot, *From Untouchable to Dalit. Essays on the Ambedkar Movement*, Delhi: Manohar, 1992, p. 80.
47. Ibid., p. 83.
48. E. Zelliot, *Dr Ambedkar*, op. cit., p. 87.
49. This assignment was decided according to the scholarship agreement made on June 4, 1913. In January 1913 Ambedkar had joined the Baroda State Forces as a lieutenant before winning the scholarship that enabled him to go to the United States.
50. Bhagawan Das (ed.), *Thus spoke Ambedkar*, vol. 4, op. cit., p. 69.
51. The Maharajah of Kolhapur had earlier attended a meeting of Untouchables at which Ambedkar was present and had declared: 'You have found your saviour in Ambedkar', before sharing a meal with the participants, a remarkable gesture given that such a practice flouted the rules of commensalism (D. Keer, *Dr Ambedkar*, op. cit., pp. 42–3).
52. M. S. Gore, *Non-Brahman Movement in Maharashtra*, op. cit., p. 54
53. Chandra Mudaliar, *The Kolhapur Movement*, Kolhapur: Shivaji Vidhyapith [s.d.]
54. Shahu Chhatrapati's letter to Alfred Pease, of June 23, 1920 (Private Papers of Ambedkar, NMML, Section of microfilms Reel no. 1, File no. 1).
55. These pieces of information draw from two sources: the letter of E. B. Fox (Registrar of Columbia University) to C. B. Khairmoday, dated Nov. 17, 1950 and the letter of the Registrar of the LSE to C. B. Khairmoday dated Dec. 7, 1950 (Private Papers of Ambedkar, NMML Microfilm section, Reel 2, File no. 5).

Chapter 3 Analysing and Ethnicising Caste to Eradicate it More Effectively

1. O. Herrenschmidt, '"L'inégalité graduée" ou la pire des inégalités. L'analyse de la société hindoue par Ambedkar', *Archives européennes de sociologie*, 37 (1997), p. 7.
2. O. Mendelsohn and M. Vicziany recognise the striking similarities 'between Dumont's work and that of Ambedkar' without really analysing them (Mendelsohn and Vicziany, *The Untouchables*, op. cit., p. 20). Both feature an interpretation of caste as forming a *system*, whose twin pillars abide by the practice of endogamy and a hierarchical organisation based on ritual purity.
3. It was the case, for instance, of the 'Untouchables or the Children of India's Ghetto', in Dr Babasaheb Ambedkar, *Writings and Speeches*, vol. 5, Bombay: Govt. of Maharashtra, 1989.
4. B. R. Ambedkar, 'Castes in India. Their Mechanism, Genesis and Development', *Indian Antiquary*, May 1917, vol. 61, reprinted in Dr Babasaheb Ambedkar, *Writings and Speeches*, vol. 1, Bombay: Govt. of Maharashtra, 1979, p. 22.
5. Ibid., p. 21.
6. Ibid., p. 15.
7. Srinivas defined it as the imitation of the upper castes by the lower castes which adopt, for example, a vegetarian diet in order to be ascribed a higher status. (M. N. Srinivas, *Religion and Society among the Coorgs of South India*, Oxford University Press, 1965)
8. I am grateful to Ramachandra Guha for drawing my attention to the proto-history of the notion of Sanskritisation.
9. B. R. Ambedkar, 'Castes in India', op. cit., p. 8. He also writes in the same vein: 'The castes in the singular number is an unreality. Castes exist only in the plural number. There is no such thing as caste: there are always castes.' (ibid., p. 20)
10. B. R. Ambedkar, 'Castes in India', op. cit., p. 6
11. Ibid., p. 16
12. Ibid., pp. 17 and 19
13. Louis Dumont, *Homo Hierarchicus. Le système des castes et ses implications*, Paris: Gallimard, 1966.
14. Ibid., p. 61
15. *Hymnes spéculatifs du Veda*, (translated by Louis Renou), Paris: Gallimard-Unesco, 1956, p. 99 (Rig Veda, chant X, strophe 90).
16. B. R. Ambedkar, 'Who were the Shudras? How They came to be the Fourth Varna in the Indo-Aryan Society?', in Dr Babasaheb Ambedkar, *Writings and Speeches*, vol. 7, Bombay: Govt. of Maharashtra, 1990, p. 25
17. Ibid., p. 26.
18. Ibid., pp. 32–3. Metaphors of the body are never innocent, as demonstrated by J. Schlanger in *Les métaphores du corps*, Paris: Vrin, 1971. I am grateful to Olivier Herrenschmidt for drawing my attention to this book.
19. B. R. Ambedkar, 'Who were the Shudras?', op. cit., p. 26.
20. B. R. Ambedkar, 'The Buddha and his Dhamma' in Dr Babasaheb Ambedkar, *Writings and Speeches*, vol. 11, Bombay: Govt. of Maharashtra, 1992, p. 91.

21. For a discussion of exceptional subtlety of this category, see O. Herrenschmidt, 'L'inégalité graduée', art. cit., p. 16–17.
22. K. R. Narayanan, 'En souvenir d'Ambedkar', *Les Temps modernes*, in July, 1993, p. 133.
23. B. R. Ambedkar, 'Philosophy of Hinduism', in Dr Babasaheb Ambedkar, *Writings and Speeches*, vol. 3, Bombay: Govt. of Maharashtra, 1987, p. 66.
24. B. R. Ambedkar, 'Revolution', in ibid., p. 320.
25. B. R. Ambedkar, 'Untouchables or The Children of India's Ghetto' in Dr Babasaheb Ambedkar, *Writings and Speeches*, vol. 5, Bombay: Govt. of Maharashtra, 1989, pp. 101–2.
26. On this point, see J. -L. Chambard, 'Les castes dans L'Inde moderne, leur place dans la vie politique et économique', *Revue économique et sociale* (Lausanne), September, 1967.
27. O. Herrenschmidt, 'L'inégalité graduée', op. cit., p. 14.
28. B. R. Ambedkar, 'Held at Bay', in Dr Babasaheb Ambedkar, *Writings and Speeches*, vol. 5, op. cit., p. 266.
29. Dr Babasaheb Ambedkar, *Writings and Speeches*, vol. 2, Bombay: Govt. of Maharashtra, 1982, p. 489. At the same time, he took the case of Brahmins to illustrate the theory according to which 'Caste, to be real can exist only by disintegrating a group. The genius of caste is to divide and to disintegrate' (B. R. Ambedkar, 'The Curse of Caste', in Dr Babasaheb Ambedkar, *Writings and Speeches*, vol. 5, op. cit., p. 211).
30. O. Herrenschmidt, 'L'inégalité graduée', op. cit., p. 20.
31. B. R. Ambedkar, 'Who were the Shudras?', op. cit., pp. 65–85.
32. Ibid., p. 110.
33. Ibid., p. 111.
34. Ibid., p. 112.
35. Ibid., p. 114.
36. Ibid., p. 156.
37. Ibid., pp. 174–5.
38. B. R. Ambedkar, 'The Untouchables. Who were they and why they became Untouchables?' in Dr Babasaheb Ambedkar, *Writings and Speeches*, vol. 7, op. cit., pp. 290–303.
39. Ibid., p. 305.
40. Ibid., p. 275.
41. According to Russel and Lal, 'the balance of opinion seems to be that the native name of Bombay, Maharashtra, is derived from that of the [Mahar] caste.' (R. V. Russel, Hira Lal, *The Tribes and Castes of the Central Provinces of India*, vol. 4, op. cit., p. 129).
42. We can thus qualify his association though he did not wish to limit its influence to the Mahars. Indeed 'Anarya Dosh Pariharak Samaj' means 'the association for the elimination of the stigmas of untouchability'; but, in practice, Mahars were its main supporters (see R. E. Enthoven, *The Tribes and Castes of Bombay*, Bombay: 1922, and R. V. Russel and Hira Lal, *The Tribes and Castes of the Central Provinces of India*, vol. 4, op. cit., p. 129).
43. B. R. Ambedkar, 'The Untouchables', art. cit., p. 317.

44. Ibid., p. 350.
45. G. Omvedt, 'Undoing the Bondage: Dr Ambedkar's Theory of Dalit Liberation', in K. C. Yadav (ed.), *From Periphery to Centre Stage*, op. cit., p. 132.
46. Ibid., p. 134.
47. Walangkar 'used to listen Phule addressing the soldiers at Poona military camps on Sundays'—another indication of the role of the army in the Mahars' growing social awareness (Philip Constable, 'Early Dalit Literature and Culture in late nineteenth- and early twentieth-century Western India', *Modern Asian Studies*, 31 (2), 1997, p. 318).
48. Ibid., p. 322.
49. Ibid.
50. J. Gokhale, *From Concessions to Confrontation*, op. cit., pp. 68–9.
51. G. Omvedt, *Dalits and the Democratic Revolution*, op. cit., p. 109.
52. E. Zelliot, *From Untouchable to Dalit*, op. cit., p. 65.
53. *The Indian and Pakistan Year Book and Who's Who 1948*, Bombay: The Times of India, 1948, p. 1182.
54. Quoted in E. Zelliot, *Dr Ambedkar*, op. cit., p. 77.
55. J. Gokhale, *From Concessions to Confrontation*, op. cit., p. 73.
56. In 1935 Bansode broke with Ambedkar when the latter envisaged converting to another religion, thus permitting him to free himself from Hinduism's social system (ibid., p. 79).
57. In 1918, two years before his death, Tilak declared at a meeting against Untouchability that if a god tolerated this social evil he would not recognise him as a god, but he later refused to sign a petition for the abolition of Untouchability. (G. P. Bradhan and A. K. Bhagwat, *Lokamanya Tilak. A biography*, Bombay: Jaico, 1959, p. 306)
58. While he insisted that Untouchables were genuine autochthons and had inherited a superior culture, Shinde dissociated himself from the non-Brahmin movement which, he said, was 'detrimental to unity' of society. (G. M. Pawar, *Vitthal Ramji Shinde*, op. cit., p. 47)
59. G. Omvedt, *Dalits and the Democratic Revolution*, op. cit., p. 142.
60. J. Gokhale, *From Concessions to Confrontation*, op. cit., p. 75.
61. M. S. Gore, *The Social Context of an Ideology: Ambedkar's Political and Social Thought*, New Delhi: Sage, 1993, p. 77. In 1919 Ambedkar opposed Shinde who testified to the Southborough Committee that 'instead of having representatives of Untouchables from amongst themselves, their interests would be better safeguarded by caste-Hindus'. (K. N. Kadam, *Dr Babasaheb Ambedkar and the significance of his movement*, Bombay: Popular Prakashan, 1991, p. 21)
62. E. Zelliot, *Dr Ambedkar*, op. cit., p. 77.
63. G. Omvedt, *Dalits and the Democratic Revolution*, op. cit., p. 111. Ambedkar had already distanced himself from Shinde in 1917 when the latter and Chandavarkar had suggested giving him a public honour on his return to India, an offer Ambedkar refused. (ibid., p. 144)
64. Ibid., pp. 112–13.
65. Ambedkar embarked on a career in public life when living in India from 1917 to 1920. In May 1920, for example, he participated in the All India Depressed

Classes' Conference, chaired by the Maharajah of Kolhapur. He used the occasion severely to criticise Shinde (ibid., p. 147). But his public career really took off after he settled down in India in 1924.

66. Letter of D. Ramrao (sub-inspector to Mahuli) Commissioner of Police, Bombay (December, 1925), *Source Material on Dr Babasaheb Ambedkar and the Movement of Untouchables*, vol. 1, op. cit., p. 4.
67. *The Bombay Chronicle*, April 26, 1926, ibid., p. 8.
68. J. Gokhale, *From Concessions to Confrontation*, op. cit., p. 84.
69. D. Keer, *Dr Ambedkar*, op. cit., p. 62.
70. *Source Material*, op. cit., pp. 6–7. Ambedkar founded caste associations in the mid-1930s, such as the Mahar Sabha and the Mahar Panchayat, albeit in a very specific context, while he was preparing the ground for conversion to a religion other than Hinduism: according to him, such a move had to take place within the caste framework because castes had to convert *en bloc*. In 1938 Ambedkar's elder brother formed the Mahar Samaj Seva Sangha and took over the helm of the association in 1941. (A. Jurane, *Ethnic Identity and Social Mobility*, Jaipur/Delhi: Rawat, 1999, p. 39).
71. J. Gokhale, *From Concessions to Confrontation*, op. cit., p. 52.
72. Quoted in D. Keer, *Dr Ambedkar, op. cit.*, p. 55.
73. Ibid., p. 62.
74. Quoted in E. Zelliot, *Dr Ambedkar*, op. cit., p. 122.
75. *Appeal on behalf of the Depressed Classes Institute* (1931) in Private Papers of Ambedkar, NMML, Section of microfilms, Reel no. 1.
76. S. K. Bole had already been excommunicated by his fellow Bhandaris—a caste of alcohol distillers—for having participated in an 'inter-caste' meal organised by the Arya Samaj (D. Keer, *Dr Ambedkar*, op. cit., p. 52).
77. Quoted in ibid., p. 53.
78. Quoted in ibid., p. 71.
79. On the Mahad Satyagraha, see the testimony of Damodar Runjaji Jadhav (N. Jadhav, *Intouchable*, op. cit., p. 43). The author recalls that there were many Mahar ex-servicemen among the participants (ibid., p. 46).
80. Quoted in D. Keer, *Dr Ambedkar*, op. cit., p. 99.
81. Interestingly, Ambedkar then borrowed from Gandhi the notion of *satyagraha* to organise peaceful demonstrations.
82. Quoted in G. Poitevin, 'Préface' in S. Kamble and B. Kamble, *Parole de femme intouchable*, op. cit., p. 17.
83. Quoted in B. Kamble, 'Notre existence', ibid., p. 242.
84. Quoted in D. Keer, *Dr Ambedkar*, op. cit., p. 109.
85. E. Zelliot, *Dr Ambedkar*, op. cit., p. 196.
86. Ibid., p. 99.
87. On the Nasik *satyagraha* see the memoirs of D. R. Jhadav, who emphasises the personalisation of the movement—there were posters depicting Ambedkar and a temple throughout the town—and its impressive organisation by Ambedkarites (N. Jhadav, *Intouchable*, op. cit., pp. 179–80).
88. Quoted in E. Zelliot, *Dr Ambedkar*, p. 114.
89. Quoted in ibid., pp. 116–17.
90. Ibid., pp. 125 and 128.

Chapter 4 In the Political Arena, Against Gandhi

1. M. S. Gore, *The Social Context of an Ideology*, op. cit., p. 85.
2. E. Zelliot, 'Congress and the Untouchables—1917–1950' in R. Sisson and S. Wolpert (eds), *Congress and Indian Nationalism—The Pre-Independence Phase*, Delhi: Oxford University Press, 1988, pp. 183–4.
3. 'Evidence before the Southborough Committee on franchise. Examined on 27th January 1919' in: Dr Babasaheb Ambedkar, *Writings and Speeches*, vol. 1, Bombay: Govt. of Maharashtra, 1979, pp. 251–3.
4. Ibid., p. 252.
5. This ambivalence explains that according to Keer, he considered both options (*Dr Ambedkar*, op. cit., p. 40) whereas for Zelliot he prioritised 'a common electorate with reserved seats' ('Learning the Use of Political means', art. cit., p. 41).
6. 'Supplementary written statement of Mr. Bhimrao R. Ambedkar' in Dr Babasaheb *Ambedkar Writings and Speeches*, vol. 1, op. cit., p. 271.
7. 'Evidence before the Southborough Committee', art. cit., p. 265.
8. This attitude is all the more surprising given that sixteen of the eighteen Dalit organisations consulted by the Simon Commission in the Bombay Presidency favoured separate electorates. For instance, the joint testimony of the Depressed India Association and the Servants of Somavamshiya Society before the Simon Commission stipulated: 'experience has shown during the last two decades that [a separate electorate] has served as a powerful lever to raise our Muslim brethren who in consequence are making rapid headway and coming into line with more advanced sections.' (*The Servants of Somavamshiya Society, Bombay*, July 9, 1928, p. 2, in Private Papers of Ambedkar, NMML, Microfilm Section, Reel no. 2).
9. B. Ambedkar, 'Report on the Constitution of the Govt. of Bombay Presidency' in *Dr Babasaheb Ambedkar Writings and Speeches*, vol. 2, Bombay: Govt. of Maharashtra, 1982, pp. 338, 400.
10. 'Evidence of Dr Ambedkar before the Indian Statutory Commission on 23rd October 1928', ibid., p. 465. Ambedkar justified this demand for universal suffrage for the underprivileged (who would never achieve the tax quota required for voting rights) because they, above all, needed it to protect themselves against the dominant castes ('Report on the Constitution', op. cit., p. 338). He added that, notwithstanding their illiteracy, they were intelligent ('Evidence of Dr Ambedkar', op. cit., p. 473).
11. Ibid., p. 351.
12. Ibid., p. 479.
13. Ibid., p. 483.
14. The passage in which these words are found deserves to be quoted in its entirety: 'Having regard to the fact that the cancer of untouchability is before their minds every minute of their lives, and having regard to their being alive to the fact that political power is the only solvent of this difficulty, I emphatically maintain that the depressed class voter would be an intelligent voter' (ibid., p. 477).
15. Vidhu Verma, 'Colonialism and Liberation: Ambedkar's Quest for Distributive Justice', *EPW*, Sept. 25, 1999, pp. 2804–10.

16. *The Bombay Chronicle*, August 18, 1930 in *Source Material on Dr Ambedkar*, op. cit., p. 40. *Indian Round Table Conference—12th Nov., 1930–19th Jan. 1931—Proceedings*, Calcutta: Govt. of India, 1931, p. 440.
17. This conversation—whose content and date are not fully ascertained—is reproduced in part in D. Keer, *Dr Ambedkar, op. cit.*, pp. 166–7.
18. Ibid., p. 173.
19. Quoted in ibid., p. 189.
20. D. E. U. Baker, *Changing Political leadership in an Indian province—The Central Provinces and Berar*, 1919–1939, Delhi: Oxford University Press, 1979, p. 116.
21. This grandson of a soldier (like Ambedkar) had received Rao Bahadur's title in 1922 after his entry to the Madras Legislative Council as the first Untouchable representative.
22. *Indian Annual Register*, 1932, vol. 1, Calcutta, 1932, p. 333.
23. Quoted in R. Kumar, 'Gandhi, Ambedkar and The Poona Pact, 1932' in J. Masselos (ed.), *Struggling and ruling—The India National Congress, 1885–1985*, London: Oriental University Press, 1987, p. 95.
24. Rajah had been apparently convinced of the reforming good faith of the Arya Samaj (Nanak Chand papers, NMML (section on manuscripts), 'Autobiography', p. 139).
25. Moonje papers, NMML, Section of microfilms File no. 63 reel no. 9. Letter of Moonje to Raja Sahib [Narendra Nath?] of June 30, 1932.
26. *Indian Annual Register, 1932*, vol. 1, Calcutta, 1932, p. 16.
27. E. Zelliot, 'Congress and the Untouchables', art. cit., p. 186.
28. *Young India* (5 Jan. 1921, p. 2), cited in N. K. Bose (ed.), *Selections from Gandhi*, Ahmedabad: Navajivan Publishing House, 1948, p. 233.
29. See for example 'Le système des castes' in M. K. Gandhi, *La Jeune Inde*, Paris: Stock, 1948 (translated by Hélène Hart, with an intro. by Romain Rolland), pp. 152–3; 'L'intouchabilité disparaît' (April 27, 1921), ibid., pp. 222–4; 'Les Panchamas' (29 Sept. 1921), ibid., pp. 222–3.
30. 'Les classes "supprimées"', *ibid.*, p. 219.
31. E. Zelliot, 'Gandhi and Ambedkar—A study in leadership' in J. M. Mahar (ed.), *The Untouchables in Contemporary India*, Tucson, AZ: The University of Arizona Press, 1972, p. 80.
32. B. Parekh, *Colonialism, Tradition and Reform—An Analysis of Gandhi's Political Discourse*, New Delhi: Sage, 1989, p. 223.
33. Swami Shraddhananda, a highly active Arya Samajist who campaigned on behalf of the Untouchables, resigned from the sub-committee soon after its formation for that reason (J. T. F. Jordens, *Swami Shraddhananda—His life and Causes*, Delhi: Oxford University Press, 1981, p. 24).
34. 'The caste system', *Young India*, 8 Dec. 1920, *The Collected Works of Mahatma Gandhi*, vol. XIX, Ahmedabad: Navajivan Trust, 1966, pp. 83–5.
35. J. Brown, *Gandhi, Prisoner of Hope*, Delhi: Oxford University Press, 1990, p. 207.
36. Quoted in D. Dalton, 'The Gandhian View of caste, and Caste after Gandhi' in P. Mason (ed.), *India and Ceylon: Unity and Diversity*, London: Oxford University Press, 1967, p. 171.

37. R. Guha, *An Anthropologist Among the Marxists and Other Essays*, Delhi: Permanent Black, 2002, p. 94.
38. At that time, Gandhi was so unfamiliar with Ambedkar's pedigree that he thought he was a Brahmin.
39. Quoted in E. Zelliot, 'Gandhi and Ambedkar', art. cit.
40. Quoted in M. S. Gore, *The Social Context of an Ideology*, op. cit., p. 103. See also G. Omvedt, 'Gandhi and Ambedkar—Why the confrontation?' in M. L. Ranga (ed.), *B. R. Ambedkar*, op. cit., p. 84.
41. Cited in E. Zelliot, 'Gandhi and Ambedkar', art. cit., p. 83. This sub-committee included heavyweight conservatives such as Madan Mohan Malaviya, who had just revived the Hindu Mahasabha.
42. Quoted in Pyarelal, *The Epic Fast*, Ahmedabad: Mohanlal Maganlal Bhatt, 1932, pp. 114–15.
43. Quoted in E. Zelliot, 'Gandhi and Ambedkar', art. cit., p. 85.
44. U. Baxi, 'Emancipation as Justice', op. cit., p. 61. Baxi elaborates on this in a very perceptive manner: 'Gandhi knew that, all said and done, Ambedkar was a political liberal. And Gandhi knew *par excellence* how to deal with liberals. Through his experience, Gandhi had acquired the shrewd insight that the mainstream political liberals do not usually know strategies of handling or coming with non-violently manufactured crisis other than those of procrastination and compromise. Liberals, unlike revolutionaries, cannot comfortably face the opponents who undertake to die for a manifest cause.' (Ibid.)
45. R. Kumar, 'Gandhi, Ambedkar and the Poona Pact, 1932', op. cit., p. 96.
46. If for a large section of the public—including Untouchable organisations—the priority was to save Gandhi's life, many others supported Ambedkar. In the distant Punjab, for instance, the Balmiki Ad-Dharm Mandal was closer to Ambedkar. (V. Prashad, *Untouchable freedom: A Social History of a Dalit Community*, Delhi: Oxford University Press, 2000, p. 87)
47. The list of participants from the Congress side was highly significant. Besides M. M. Malaviya, one found M. R. Jayakar, B. S. Moonje, N. C. Kelkar, G. D. Birla and Rajendra Prasad, who had all previously participated in Hindu Mahasabha meetings. On their side were also found other participants from the Congress, all of them upper caste (with the exception of A. V. Thakkar): Tej Bahadur Sapru, M. S. Aney, C. Rajagopalachari, Hridayanath Kunzru and Purushottam Thakurdas. Of the Untouchables, besides Ambedkar, M. C. Rajah and P. Baloo, the cricket player, had also been invited. This list draws on names obtained from the following sources: G. Omvedt, *Dalits and the Democratic Revolution, op. cit.*, p. 173, R. Kumar, *'Gandhi, Ambedkar and the Poona Pact, 1932'*, art. cit., p. 97) and the British archives (P/Conf/81 Proceedings of the Home Department (Political) for the year 1932. India Office Library and Records (London), File no. 41–4/32).
48. Rajah was to join Ambedkar six years later, in 1938, after having been dismayed by the conservatism of the government formed by Congress in his province of Madras. He complained about it to Gandhi, who advised him to be patient and reaffirmed his confidence in the leader of the Madras government, a Brahmin, Rajagopalachari. Rajah, demoralised, thus came to regret the Poona Pact and

opposed, like Ambedkar, the Quit India Movement of 1942 (O. Mendelsohn and M. Vicziany, *The Untouchables*, op. cit., p. 110).

49. Quoted in B. R. Nanda, *In Gandhi's footsteps—The Life and Times of Jamnalal Bajaj*, Delhi: Oxford University Press, 1990, p. 198.
50. 'Gandhi had thus achieved what, as a true Satyagrahi, he always strove for: he had won his opponent's heart!' (R. Kumar, 'Gandhi, Ambedkar and the Poona Pact, on 1932', op. cit., p. 98).
51. For the complete text of the pact, see R. Kumar, 'Gandhi, Ambedkar and the Poona Pact, 1932', op. cit., pp. 153–5.
52. Cited in Appendix 1 to M. L. Ranga (ed.), *Dr. B. R. Ambedkar*, op. cit., p. 131.
53. *Indian Annual Register, 1932*, vol. 2, Calcutta, 1932, pp. 257–9.
54. The word *Harijan* was borrowed by Gandhi from a seventeenth-century Gujarati saint, Narsinh Mehta, as a delicate and honourable way of referring to Untouchables. But Ambedkar rejected it because of its condescending connotations. He preferred the term Dalit (broken, oppressed people). Ambedkar and other elected members of his party left the Bombay Legislative Assembly when Congress registered the name 'Harijan' under the Local Boards Act (J. Gokhale, *From Concessions to confrontation*, op. cit., p. 139). The word Harijan sowed doubts about the ancestry of the Untouchables as if their unbridled sexual customs were such that one no longer had any idea who was the child of whom. In fact this term was often used to designate the children of women dedicated to the gods (*devdasis*) in temples who were sometimes abused by priests and whose progeny were exiled from society.
55. B. Ray (ed.), *Gandhi' campaign against untouchability, 1933–34—An account from the Raj's secret official reports*, New Delhi: Gandhi Peace Foundation, 1996, pp. 49–50.
56. Ibid., p. 74.
57. Ibid., p. 117.
58. Ibid., pp. 157–8.
59. Ibid., p. 191.
60. Ibid., p. 234.
61. Quoted in D. Keer, *Dr Ambedkar*, p. 221.
62. Quoted in ibid., p. 222.
63. Quoted in ibid., p. 227.
64. Quoted in ibid., p. 230.
65. Ibid., p. 217.
66. O. Mendelsohn and M. Vicziany, *The Untouchables*, op. cit., p. 106.
67. D. Keer, *Dr Ambedkar*, op. cit., p. 232.
68. Cited in 'Appendix 1, Face to face: Ambedkar and Gandhi on Temple-Entry Legislation put Forward by Ranga Iyer (Two Bills, February 1933)', in M. L. Ranga (ed.), *B. R. Ambedkar* op. cit., p. 131.
69. Cited in D. Keer, *Dr Ambedkar*, op. cit., pp. 218–19.
70. Quoted in O. Mendelsohn and M. Vicziany, *The Untouchables*, op. cit., p. 107.
71. B. Parekh, *Colonialism, Tradition and Reform*, op. cit., p. 238–9.
72. Cited in B. Ray (ed.), *Gandhi's Campaign against Untouchability*, op. cit., p. 243.

73. On Rajaji's conservatism, see J. P. Waghorne, 'Rajaji, the Brahmin', in B. L. Smith (ed.), *Religion and the legitimation of power in South Asia*, Leiden: E. J. Brill, 1978, pp. 53–72.
74. Cited in S. Bandhyopadhyay, 'Transfer of Power and the Crisis of Dalit Politics', op. cit., p. 899.
75. For the province by province distribution, see B. A. V. Sharma, 'Development of Reservation Policy' in B. A. V. Sharma and K. M. Reddy (eds), *Reservation Policy in India*, New Delhi: Light and Light Publishers, 1982, p. 15–16.
76. Cited in R. Guha, *An Anthropologist among the Marxists*, op. cit., p. 98.
77. Quoted in B. R. Ambedkar, *Annihilation of Caste*, New Delhi: Arnold Publishers, 1990, p. 16.
78. Ibid., p. 21. For the Arya Samaj the Vedas were the scriptures of Hinduism *par excellence.*
79. Ibid., p. 67.
80. He refers here to the Third Round Table Conference.
81. Letter of Ambedkar to Dattoba of August 3, 1933. Private papers of Ambedkar, NMML, Microfilm section, reel no. 2, file no. 3.
82. *Times of India*, November 21, 1934 in *Source material on Dr Ambedkar and the Movement of Untouchables*, vol. 1, Bombay: Govt. of Maharashtra, 1982, p. 124.

Chapter 5 Searching for an Electoral Strategy

1. 'Independent Labour Party. Its Formation and its Aims', *The Times of India*, 15 August 1936. (A reprint is available in Ambedkar Private Papers, NMML, Microfilm section, Reel no. 2, file no. 9.)
2. J. Gokhale, *From Concessions to Confrontation*, op. cit., pp. 132–3.
3. 'Independent Labour Party—Its Formation and Its Aims', op. cit., pp. 4–5.
4. Ibid., p. 5.
5. Ibid., p. 8.
6. J. Gokhale, *From Concessions to Confrontation*, op. cit., p. 140.
7. B. R. Ambedkar, *Annihilation of Caste*, op. cit., p. 47.
8. Ibid., p. 42.
9. Ibid., p. 46.
10. E. Zelliot, *Dr Ambedkar*, op. cit., p. 249. *Janata*, the newspaper founded by Ambedkar in 1929, supported about ten of the other independent candidates from the upper castes.
11. R. I. Duncan, *Levels, the Communication of Programmes and Sectional Strategies in Indian Politics, with reference to the Bharatiya Kranti Dal and the Republican Party of India in Uttar Pradesh State and Aligarh district (UP)*, Ph.D., University of Sussex, 1979, p. 214.
12. E. Zelliot, 'Learning the Use of Political means', op. cit., p. 50.
13. In the Central Provinces and in Berar, these hereditary functions and the advantages which accompanied them had been already abolished and replaced by a monthly salary. Robertson gives evidence of the growing desire of the Mahar elite of the Bombay Presidency to emulate those of CP and Berar: 'The more enlightened among the Mahars themselves recognise that their vatandar

privileges though precious in the light of sentiment, are yet occasions of bondage as all privileges are, and that economically it would be well for them if the example set by the Central Provinces and Berar were extended to all public servants everywhere.' (A. Robertson, *The Mahar Folk*, op. cit., pp. 28–9)

14. Dr Babasaheb Ambedkar, *Writings and Speeches*, vol. 2, op. cit., p. 90.
15. Ibid., p. 96.
16. *Indian Annual Register, 1937*, vol. 2, Calcutta, 1937, p. 188.
17. Quoted in G. Omvedt, *Dalits and the Democratic Revolution*, op. cit., pp. 197–8.
18. Ibid., p. 198.
19. D. Keer, *Dr Ambedkar, op. cit.*, p. 300.
20. Ambedkar was also disappointed with the socialists who did not bring enough support to his private bill (ibid., p. 310).
21. J. Gokhale, *From Concessions to Confrontation*, op. cit., p. 136.
22. Dr Babasaheb Ambedkar, *Writings and Speeches*, vol. 2, op. cit., pp. 201–32.
23. D. Keer, *Dr Ambedkar*, op. cit., pp. 313–16 and G. Omvedt, *Dalits and the Democratic Revolution*, op. cit., pp. 199–200.
24. E. Zelliot, *Dr Ambedkar*, op. cit., p. 25.
25. D. Keer, *Dr Ambedkar*, op. cit., p. 480.
26. V. Moon, *Growing up Untouchable in India*, op. cit., p. 66.
27. G. Omvedt, *Dalit and the Democratic Revolution*, op. cit., p. 207.
28. B. R. Ambedkar, 'Objections to Cripps proposals, App. IX to What Congress and Gandhi have done to Untouchables', Dr Babasaheb Ambedkar, *Writings and Speeches*, Bombay, Govt. of Maharashtra, vol. 9, p. 339.
29. D. Keer, *Dr Ambedkar*, op. cit., 350.
30. E. Zelliot, 'Learning the Use of Political Means', *art. cit.*, pp. 52–3.
31. The impact of the propositions of the Cripps Mission on the Dalit leaders had been tremendous. This formula brought even M. C. Rajah to become still closer to Ambedkar. Like him, he regretted the absence, in this set of proposals, of a provision granting a separate electorate to Untouchables (ibid., p. 67, note 48). During his tour in the south, in 1944, Ambedkar was invited by M. C. Rajah to Madras (*Indian Express*, 26 Sept. 1944, Private Papers of Ambedkar, NMML, Microfilm Section, Reel no. 1).
32. D. Keer, *Dr Ambedkar*, op. cit., p. 63 and p. 128.
33. At the same time, just as he had been angered by the lack of consideration shown towards Untouchables by the Cripps Mission, Ambedkar protested against their being kept at a distance during the negotiations between Gandhi and Jinnah in Sept. 1944. *The Times of India*, 5 Sept. 1944.
34. 'The political demands of the Scheduled Castes—Resolutions passed by the Working Committee of the All-India Scheduled Caste Federation', App. XI to B. R. Ambedkar, *What Congress and Gandhi have done to Untouchables*, op. cit., pp. 346–7.
35. Resolution 8 considered that 'in the absence of an alternative system, the Parliamentary system of Government may have to be accepted' but the SCF demanded that Ministers representing the minorities should be inducted in the government after being designated by the minority communities themselves.

Resolution 11 demanded that the Constitution should establish a framework 'for the transplantation of the Scheduled Castes from their present habitations and form separate Scheduled Castes villages away and independent of Hindu villages'—a formula already used by Ambedkar in 1942. (Ibid., p. 353)

36. Cited in B. Nicholas, '"Below the Bottom Rung": a British Estimate of Dr Ambedkar, 1944' in K. C. Yadav, *From Periphery to Centre Stage*, op. cit., p. 47.
37. *The Times of India*, 24 Sept. 1944.
38. Cited in *The Hindu* (Madras), 26 Sept. 1944.
39. Cited in *The Liberator*, 26 Sept. 1944.
40. Ibid., 24 Sept. 1944.
41. P. D. Reeves, B. D. Graham and J. M. Goodman, *Elections in UP, 1920–51*, New Delhi: Manohar, 1975, pp. 315–19.
42. *Jai Bheem* (Madras) Dec. 25, 1946. Typescript among the Private Papers of Ambedkar, NMML, Microfilm Section, Reel no. 1. In a note from July 1947 he considered that Untouchable candidates, co-opted and elected by Congress in the constituencies where the high castes were in a majority, did not constitute anything else but 'an instrument of the Hindus'. (*Jai Bheem*, 16 July 1947)
43. E. Zelliot, 'Learning the Use of political means', op. cit., p. 53.
44. S. Bandyopadhyay, 'Transfer of power and the crisis of Dalit politics in India, 1945–47', *Modern Indian Studies*, 34 (4), 2000, p. 913.
45. E. Zelliot, Dr Ambedkar, op. cit., p. 265.
46. V. Moon, *Growing up Untouchable in India*, op. cit., p. 102. Moon also points out that 'the newspapers systematically [were] spreading the emotional propaganda that Ambedkar's party opposed independence.' (ibid., p. 96)
47. 'The Scheduled Castes' Federation Manifesto', in S. P. Singh Sud and Ajit Singh Sud (eds), *Indian Elections and Legislators*, Ludhiana: All India Publications, 1953, pp. 39–40.
48. Ibid., p. 39.
49. It is probably why the Election Manifesto of the SCF mentions not only Untouchables but also Other Backward Classes and—very probably for the first time with such an emphasis—Tribals. In fact, Ambedkar began to suspect that a solution to his political indecisiveness was to be found in a political strategy focussed on status groups which would advocate the cause of all the victims of discrimination based on birth.
50. Ibid., p. 39. On this question the manifesto says that the SCF 'regards the growing rate in the increase of population in the country so grave an evil that it would not hesitate to advocate more drastic methods of controlling it' (ibid., p. 40.)
51. Ibid., p. 40.
52. J. Duncan, *Levels, the Communication of Programmes and Sectional Strategies in Indian politics*, op. cit., p. 236.
53. Ibid., p. 226–7.
54. J. Gokhale, *From Concessions to Confrontation*, op. cit., p. 216. At that time his hostility towards communism was fostered by his awareness of the situation prevailing in the Soviet bloc. There, said Ambedkar, Communists 'establish by means of violence what they call the dictatorship of the proletariat. They

deprive all people who have property of political rights. They cannot have representation in the legislation; they cannot have right to vote, they must remain what they call second grade subjects of the State, the ruled not sharing authority or power.' (Cited in 'Appendix 5; Essentials of Dr Ambedkar's Thinking: Buddhism and Communism', in M. L. Ranga (ed.), *B. R. Ambedkar* op. cit., p. 146)

55. J. Gokhale, *From Concessions to Confrontation*, op. cit., p. 217.
56. *Election Manifesto of the Scheduled Castes Federation*, SCF, 1957, p. 14 (Ambedkar papers, NMML, Section of microfilms, Reel no. 2.)
57. J. Duncan, *Levels* op. cit., p. 236.
58. As G. Omvedt points out, 'Ambedkar's political career was devoted to finding forms through which Dalits could exert themselves in an autonomous fashion and at the same time build an enduring alliance with non-Brahmans, Shudras, workers and peasants.' (G. Omvedt, 'Undoing the bondage', op. cit., pp. 139–40)
59. J. Gokhale, *From Concessions to Confrontation*, op. cit., p. 115.
60. S. Bandyopadhyay, 'Transfer of Power and the Crisis of Dalit Politics in India, 1945–47', op. cit., p. 898.
61. Ambedkar was then provisionally allocated the Labour portfolio in the new Executive Council which never saw light because Jinnah eventually refused to cooperate.
62. Ibid., pp. 920 and 924.

Chapter 6 Opposition or collaboration? Ambedkar's Pragmatism and Resilience

1. 'The Conference of the Deccan Mahars to the Right Honourable The Earl of Crewe', op. cit., p. 5.
2. Ibid., p. 2.
3. *The Servants of Somavamshiya Society*, op. cit.
4. B. R. Ambedkar, *Appeal on behalf of the Depressed Classes Institute.* This document is found in the Ambedkar Private Papers (NMML, Microfilm section Reel no. 2).
5. V. Verma, 'Colonialism and Liberation', art. cit., p. 2807.
6. *Proceedings, Indian Round Table Conference—12th November, 1930–19th January, 1931*, Calcutta: Government of India, 1931, p. 123.
7. *The Bombay Chronicle*, August 18, 1930, in *Source material on Dr Babasaheb Ambedkar*, vol. 1, op. cit., p. 38.
8. *Indian Round Table Conference—12th November*, op. cit., p. 124.
9. Ibid., p. 125.
10. K. M. Munshi, a traditionalist Hindu, was the Home Minister of the Bombay Government at that time. For more details about Munshi, who was to be a key figure in the Drafting Committee of the Indian Constitution, see C. Jaffrelot, *The Hindu Nationalist Movement*, London: Hurst, 1996, pp. 84–5.
11. G. Omvedt, *Dalits and the Democratic Revolution*, op. cit., p. 199.
12. *The Times of India*, 27 Dec. 1939. Cited in *Source Material*, vol. 1, op. cit., p. 206. Ambedkar had earlier protested against the refusal of the Congress government

to introduce universal suffrage in local elections, whereas it had promised to do so. (*Bombay Sentinel*, 31 Jan. 1938, Ibid., p. 164)

13. To Gandhi, who objected that whatever he might say to the contrary, Ambedkar remained a patriot, he replied: 'You say I have a homeland, but I repeat that I am without it. How can I call this land my own homeland and this religion my own wherein we are treated worse than cats and dogs, wherein we cannot get water to drink? I do not feel sorry for being branded as a traitor; for the responsibilities of our actions lie with the land that dubs me a traitor.' (Quoted in D. Keer, *Dr Ambedkar*, op. cit., p. 166)
14. Dr Babasaheb Ambedkar, *Writings and Speeches*, vol. 2, op. cit., p. 258.
15. Quoted in M. S. Gore, *The Social Context of an Ideology*, op. cit., p. 187.
16. Dr Babasaheb Ambedkar, *Writings and Speeches*, vol. 10, Bombay Govt. of Maharashtra, 1991, pp. 110–11.
17. Ibid., vol. 2, op. cit., pp. 256–7.
18. When, in October 1939, B. G. Kher, the Chief Minister of the Bombay Presidency, denounced the Dalit separatism of Ambedkar in the name of the nationalist cause embodied by Congress, his dialogue with Ambedkar contained several significant sociological notions. B. G. Kher said: '... The part can never be greater than the whole. The whole must contain the part'. B. R. Ambedkar replied: 'I am not a part of the whole at all; I am a part apart.' (Ibid., p. 261)
19. *The Bombay Chronicle*, 24 Oct. 1939, in *Source Material*, vol. 1, op. cit., p. 201.
20. *The Bombay Chronicle*, 23 July 1942, ibid., pp. 255–6.
21. *The Times of India*, 6 Feb. 1940 and Ambedkar's letter to *The Times of India*, in June 18, 1941, quoted in the *Source material*, vol. 1, *op. cit.*, p. 210 and pp. 227–8.
22. Lelah Dushkin, 'Special Treatment Policy' in *The Economic Weekly*, vol. XIII, nos 43–6 and E. Zelliot, *Dr Ambedkar*, op. cit., p. 265. In 1946, the quota of 8.33 per cent was increased to 12.5 per cent so as to be more proportional to the population of Untouchables.
23. *The Liberator* (Madras), 24 Sept. 1944.
24. 'Dr Ambedkar as a Member of the Governor-General Executive Council, 1942–46', in Dr Babasaheb Ambedkar, *Writings and Speeches*, vol. 10, Bombay, Govt. of Maharashtra, 1991.
25. Ibid., p. 257 and p. 320.
26. Ibid., p. 323.
27. B. R. Ambedkar, 'Grievances of the Scheduled Castes' in Dr Babasaheb Ambedkar, *Writings and Speeches*, op. cit., pp. 416–17.
28. *The Hindu*, September 26, 1944, and *Jai Bheem*, March 12, 1946.
29. 'Dr Ambedkar and Mr Rajah to Sir S. Cripps' in Dr Babasaheb Ambedkar, *Writings and Speeches*, vol. 10, op. cit., p. 447.
30. S. Bandyopadhyay, 'Transfer of Power and the Crisis of Dalit Politics', op. cit., p. 925.
31. V. Moon, *Growing up Untouchable in India*, op. cit., p. 102.
32. S. Bandyopadhyay, 'Transfer of Power and the Crisis of Dalit Politics', op. cit., p. 928.
33. *The Bombay Chronicle*, April 27, 1942, in *Source material*, vol. 1, op. cit., p. 247.

34. *Constituent Assembly Debates* [hereafter *CAD*], New Delhi: Lok Sabha, 1989, vol. 1, pp. 100–1. Ambedkar was also loudly applauded when he said, about the form of the state to be built: 'I like a strong united Centre.' (ibid., p. 102)
35. D. Keer, *Dr Ambedkar,* op. cit., p. 382.
36. G. Austin, *The Indian Constitution—Cornerstone of a Nation*, Bombay: Oxford University Press, 1972, p. 13 (fn) and H. S. Verma and N. Verma, 'Dr Ambedkar and the framing of the Indian Constitution', paper presented to the colloquium 'Contribution of Dr B. R. Ambedkar to Law and Constitution of India', Lucknow, April 15, 1997.
37. A veteran of the Constituent Assembly, R. M. Nalawade, emphasised that Nehru and Patel were lukewarm about allocating ministerial office to Ambedkar but that Gandhi insisted that he be included in the project of national construction (S. M. Gaikwad, 'Ambedkar and Indian nationalism', *EPW,* March 7, 1998, p. 518). This hypothesis is accredited by a conversation of 1946 between the Mahatma and two foreign visitors—Muriel Lester, an English Quaker, and Miss Descher, an American missionary—during which he expressed the wish that Ambedkar should become a part of the first government of independent India. (M. S. Gore, *The Social Context of an Ideology,* op. cit., p. 180)
38. Quoted in G. Austin, *The Indian Constitution*, op. cit., p. 19–20.
39. On Ambedkar's views regarding economic policies and planning, see S. K. Thorat, 'Ambedkar's Thought on Economic Development and Planning', in Shyam Lal and K. S. Saxena (eds), *Ambedkar and Nation-Building,* Jaipur: Rawat, 1998, pp. 76–98.
40. Cited in U. Baxi, 'Emancipation and Justice: Legacy and Vision of Dr Ambedkar' in K. C. Yadav (ed.), *From Periphery to Centre Stage*, op. cit., p. 55.
41. Some of Ambedkar's followers were appalled by his joining hands with the Congress. SCF leaders seceded to join the Socialists and the UPSCF 'desintegrated' (S. Pai, *Dalit Assertion and the Unfinished Democratic Revolution*, New Delhi: Sage, 2002, p. 63).
42. 'Ambedkar's Memorandum and Draft Articles on the Rights of States and Minorities' in B. Shiva Rao (ed.), *The Framing of India's Constitution*, vol. 2, New Delhi: Indian Institute of Public Administration, 1967, pp. 93–4.
43. Ibid., p. 95.
44. Ibid., p. 109.
45. The book appeared in the form of a series of questions aiming to delimit the terms of the debate but Ambedkar ended it in a clear-cut manner: 'Once it becomes certain that the Muslims want Pakistan there can be no doubt that the wise course would be to concede the principle of it' ('Reprint of Pakistan or the Partition of India', in Dr Babasaheb Ambedkar, *Writings and Speeches*, vol. 8, Bombay: Govt. of Maharashtra, 1990, p. 368).
46. 'Ambedkar Memorandum', op. cit., p. 112.
47. 'Scheduled Castes' Federation Manifesto', art. cit., p. 40.
48. R. K. Kshirsagar, *Dalit Movement in India and its leaders,* New Delhi: MD Publications, 1994, pp. 247–8.
49. B. Shiva Rao (ed.), *The Framing of India's Constitution*, vol. 2, op. cit., p. 327.

50. Ibid., p. 331.
51. 'Reports on minority rights—August on 1947', in ibid., p. 412.
52. Ibid., p. 415.
53. *CAD*, vol. 5, p. 259.
54. Ibid., p. 260.
55. Ibid., p. 265.
56. Ibid., p. 272.
57. Ibid., p. 270.
58. Ibid., vol. 7, p. 39.
59. S. Bandyopadhyay, 'Transfer of Power and the Crisis of Dalit Politics', op. cit., p. 893.
60. Cited in ibid.

Chapter 7 Shaping the Indian Constitution

1. G. M. Tartakov, 'Ambedkar Statues', *Dalit International Newsletter*, vol. 3, no. 2, June, 1998, p. 1. This Westernised appearance was a source of pride to Dalit supporters of Ambedkar, as is testified by the memoirs of Baby Kamble: 'a big and sturdy stature, the brightness of youth, the skin fair, the wide forehead, a voice sweet as nectar, *a suit and shoes as white sahibs*'. (B. Kamble, 'Notre existence', op. cit., p. 242, emphasis added)
2. A. Shourie, *Worshipping False Gods, Ambedkar and the Facts which have been Erased*, New Delhi: ASA, 1997, p. 586.
3. This is what one deduces from the interview of the biographer of Nehru, Brecher (Michael Brecher, *Nehru: A Political Biography*, London: Oxford University Press, 1959, p. 423).
4. H. S. Verma and N. Verma, 'Dr Ambedkar and Framing of the Indian Constitution: a Contemporary re-assessment', op. cit.
5. Ambedkar was a member of the two sub-committees of the Advisory Committee (the one on fundamental rights, the other one on rights of the minorities) and of the Union of the Powers Committee.
6. *CAD*, vol. 7, p. 231. Rajendra Prasad, the President of the Constituent Assembly, gave a similar assessment: 'Sitting in the Chair, and watching the proceedings from day to day, I have realised, as nobody else could have, with what zeal and devotion the members of the Drafting Committee, and especially its Chairman, Dr Ambedkar, in spite of his indifferent health have worked. We could never make a decision which was or could be ever so right as when we put him on the Drafting Committee, and made him its Chairman. He has not only justified his selection but has added lustre to the work which he has done.' (cited in K. N. Kadam, *Dr Babasaheb Ambedkar*, op. cit., p. 51)
7. *CAD*, vol. 7, op. cit., p. 402.
8. Ibid., p. 494.
9. Ibid., p. 518.
10. Ibid., p. 582.
11. Ibid., p. 589.
12. Ibid., p. 952.

13. Ibid., p. 1139.
14. Ibid., p. 31.
15. Ibid., p. 38–9.
16. A mantra, in Hinduism, is a ritual formula. Here, it refers to the constitutional project to which Gandhi had given his blessing shortly before his death.
17. *CAD*, vol. 7, op. cit., pp. 218–19.
18. Ibid., p. 256.
19. Ibid., p. 316.
20. Ibid., p. 426.
21. Ibid., p. 426.
22. Ibid., p. 520.
23. Ibid., p. 523.
24. Ibid., p. 524.
25. Ibid., p. 525.
26. Ibid., p. 41.
27. Ibid., p. 532. Ambedkar generously replied: '… Sir, as there is a considerable amount of feeling that the Directive Principles should make some reference to cottage industries, I am agreeable in principle to introduce in article 34 some words to give effect to the wishes of the Members of this House.' (Ibid., p. 535)
28. Ibid., p. 499.
29. Ibid., p. 566.
30. Ibid., p. 223.
31. Ibid., p. 568.
32. Ibid.
33. Quoted in D. Keer, *Dr Ambedkar*, op. cit., p. 415.
34. *CAD*, vol. 7, op. cit., p. 781, speech of December 2, 1948.
35. Ibid., vol. 5, speech of April 9, 1948.
36. M. Yasin, 'Hindu Code Bill and Dr Ambedkar', *Towards Secular India*, 2 (1), Jan.–March 1996, p. 24.
37. Reba Som, 'Jawaharlal Nehru and the Hindu Code: A victory of Symbol over Substance?' *Modern Asian Studies*, 28 (1), 1994, p. 171.
38. Quoted in D. Das (ed.), *Sardar Patel Correspondence, 1945–1950*, Ahmedabad: Navajiyan, 1947, vol. vi, p. 40a.
39. D. Keer, *Dr Ambedkar*, op. cit., p. 426.
40. R. Som, 'Jawaharlal Nehru and the Hindu Code', art. cit., p. 185–7.
41. D. Keer, *Dr Ambedkar*, op. cit., pp. 435–6.
42. Quoted in R. Som, 'Jawaharlal Nehru and the Hindu Code', art. cit., p. 184.
43. Eventually, the various elements of the Hindu Code Bill were adopted between 1955 and 1961:

    — the Hindu Marriage Act was voted in May, 1955. It prohibited polygamy,— and reinforced the legal status of inter-castes marriages and divorces.

    — the Hindu Succession Act was voted in May, 1956. It raised girls to the rank of the legal heir, in the same way as widows or sons.

    — the Hindu Adoptions and Maintenance Act was voted in December, 1956. It legalised the adoption of girls, till then little practised as foster parents invariably tried to adopt a son.

— Finally, the Dowry Prohibition Act was voted in July, 1961 to forbid the practice of Dowry—but it was hardly followed by any positive effects.

Chapter 8 The 'Solution' of Conversion

1. J. Gokhale, *From Concessions to Confrontation*, op. cit., pp. 159–60.
2. Quoted in M. S. Gore, *The Social Context of an Ideology*, op. cit., p. 91.
3. D. Keer, *Dr Ambedkar*, op. cit., pp. 130–2. A little later, Untouchables in a village near Nasik made known to Ambedkar their willingness to convert to Islam, but he recommended patience instead (ibid., p. 252). In May, 1932, the General Secretary of the Buddha Mahasabha called upon Untouchables to become Buddhists, albeit without much effect (ibid., p. 200).
4. Ibid., p. 240.
5. Ibid., p. 252. On November 9, 1935, a committee called the *Hindu Dharma Tyag* (renouncement of Hinduism) prepared a list of Untouchables willing to leave Hinduism (E. Zelliot, *Dr Ambedkar*, op. cit., p. 206).
6. This decision was also over determined by the horrific massacres of Dalits in the Gujarat village of Kavitha in 1935.
7. Cited in Bhagawan Das, *Thus spoke Ambedkar*, vol. 4, op. cit., p. 108.
8. Ibid., p. 47.
9. Ibid., p. 51.
10. See *Indian Annual Register, 1936*, vol. 1, Calcutta, 1936, p. 277.
11. Ibid., p. 278.
12. J. Gokhale, *From Concessions to Confrontation*, op. cit., p. 189. That Ambedkar qualified conversion to Islam and to Christianity as 'denationalisation' is not insignificant given that it was also a term—and interpretation—to which the Hindu nationalists have had recourse (see C. Jaffrelot, 'Militant Hindus and the Conversion Issue (1885–1990): From Shuddhi to Dharm Parivartan. The Politisation and the Diffusion of an 'Invention of Tradition', in J. Assayag (ed.), *The Resources of History: Tradition, Narration and Nation in South Asia*, Paris/Pondichéry: EFEO/IFP, 1999, pp. 127–52).
13. *Indian Annual Register, 1936*, vol. 1, Calcutta, 1936, p. 278.
14. *Indian Annual Register, 1935*, vol. 2, Calcutta, 1935, p. 32.
15. Ibid., pp. 232–3.
16. Ibid., p. 132, and D. Keer, *Dr Ambedkar*, op. cit., p. 254.
17. E. Zelliot, *Dr Ambedkar*, op. cit., p. 218.
18. Cited in D. Keer, *Dr Ambedkar*, op. cit., p. 254.
19. E. Zelliot, *Dr Ambedkar*, op. cit., p. 221.
20. Ibid., p. 220.
21. Bhagwan Das, *Thus spoke Ambedkar*, vol. 4, op. cit., p. 140.
22. Ibid., p. 117.
23. D. Keer, *Dr Ambedkar*, op. cit., p. 255.
24. Ibid., p. 265.
25. K. Meadowcroft, 'Trading in Religio-Political Identities? The 1936 Moonje-Ambedkar Pact', in H. Johnston, R. Chowdhari-Tremblay and John R. Wood

(eds), *South Asia between turmoil and hope*, South Asia Council of Canadian Asia Studies Association and Shastri Indo-Canadian Institute, 2000, p. 115.

26. *India Annual Register 1935*, vol. 2, p. 30.
27. Ibid., p. 305.
28. For a biography of Baloo, see Ramchandra Guha, *A Corner of a Foreign Field: The Indian History of a British Sport*, London: Picador, 2002, pp. 81–186.
29. K. Meadowcroft, 'Trading in Religio-Political Identities', p. 104.
30. *The Times of India*, April 14, 1936.
31. C. Jaffrelot, *The Hindu Nationalist Movement*, op. cit., chapter 1.
32. *The Times of India*, April 14, 1936.
33. Cited in V. Moon, *Growing up Untouchable in India*, op. cit., p. 40.
34. Ibid.
35. Private Papers of Moonje, Nehru Memorial Museum and Library (New Delhi) (Section of microfilms) reel no. 11 (Letter of Moonje to Kelkar of June 18, 1936).
36. Moonje was certainly unwilling further to integrate Dalits in Hindu society. Meadowcroft points out that he even compared them to snakes (K. Meadowcroft, 'Trading in Religio-Political identities', op. cit., p. 105).
37. *The Times of India*, April 14, 1936.
38. J. Lütt, 'The Shankaracharya of Puri' in A. Eschmann (ed.), *The Cult of Jagannath and the Regional Tradition of Orissa*, New Delhi: Manohar, 1978, p. 416; I. Prakash, *A Review of the History and Work of the Hindu Mahasabha and the Hindu Sangathan Movement*, New Delhi: Akhil Charatiya Hindu Mahasabha, 1938, p. 344.
39. Quoted in Bhagwan Das (ed.), *Thus spoke Ambedkar*, vol. 4, op. cit., p. 208.
40. Private Papers of Moonje, NMML (Section of Microfilms), Reel no. 11 (Moonje's letter to the Maharajah of Patiala, June 20, 1936).
41. *Indian Annual Register*, 1936, vol. 1, Calcutta, 1936, p. 278.
42. Private Papers of Moonje, NMML (Section of microfilms), Reel no. 11 (Moonje's letters to the Maharajah of Patiala, June 28 and July 8, 1936).
43. Ibid., Letter of Moonje to Malaviya, August 23, 1936.
44. K. Meadowcroft, 'Trading in Religio-Political Identities?', op. cit., p. 95.
45. Bhagwan Das (ed.), *Thus Spoke Ambedkar*, vol. 4, op. cit., p. 110.
46. Quoted in ibid., p. 310.
47. Quoted in ibid., p. 148–9.
48. *Indian Annual Register, 1936*, vol. 1, op. cit., p. 279.
49. Ibid. Gandhi, unsurprisingly, approved of Rajah's stand. In a letter he sent him on July 26 he said: 'I do not understand Dr Moonje's or Dr Ambedkar's position. For me removal of Untouchability stands on a footing all (sic) its own. It is to me a deeply religious question.' (Ibid.)
50. Bhagawan Das (ed.), *Thus spoke Ambedkar*, op. cit., p. 155. Rajbhoj, a Chambhar from Poona as mentioned above, joined the Hindu Mahasabha, which offered him a prestigious platform. He supported thus Malaviya's initiative concerning the Mantra Diksha. However, he was to join Ambedkar's Scheduled Castes' Federation in 1942 and to convert to Buddhism in 1956, before opting

definitively for the Congress after Ambedkar's death in 1956 (M. Gautam, *Bapusaheb Rajbhoj*, Aligarh: Siddhartha Gautam Sikshan and Sanskriti Samiti, 1995).

51. Bhagawan Das, *Thus spoke Ambedkar*, vol. 4, op. cit., p. 161.
52. Ibid., p. 230.
53. E. Zelliot, *Dr Ambedkar…* op. cit., p. 214–15. The organisers convened a new meeting in Poona on 10 April 1937. Jagjivan Ram criticised the gathering's main architect, Baldev Prasad Jaiswar, for being a stooge of the Christian missions, and the day before the session began, Jagjivan Ram's associates took control of the meeting, which declared against conversions.
54. Quoted in Bhagwan Das (ed.), *Thus spoke Ambedkar*, op. cit., p. 307.
55. Exceeding their mission, they were converted before returning to Bombay where Ambedkar received them without much warmth (D. Keer, *Dr Ambedkar*, op. cit., p. 284).
56. E. Zelliot, *Dr Ambedkar*, op. cit., p. 225.
57. D. C. Ahir, *Dr Ambedkar and Punjab*, Delhi: B. R. Publishing, 1992, p. 12.
58. H. K. Puri, 'Scheduled Castes in Sikh Community', *EPW*, 28 June 2003, p. 2698.
59. Private Papers of Moonje, NMML (Section of microfilms), Reel n° 11. Letter of Moonje to Malaviya, June 10, 1936.
60. V. Moon, *Growing up Untouchable in India*, op. cit., p. 44.
61. Ibid., p. 131.
62. Ibid., p. 133.
63. On May 24, 1956, during a meeting organised in honour of the anniversary of Buddha, he declared: 'At the very young age of fourteen, Mr. Dadasaheb Keluskar had in a meeting presented me with a biography of Bhagwan Buddha. Since then my mind has always been under the influence of Buddhism.' (Dr Babasaheb Ambedkar, 'Buddhism and Hinduism are not the same thing', a talk given on May 24, 1956 (Marathi), Private Papers of Ambedkar, NMML (Section of microfilms), Reel no. 2).
64. In 1951, he named the second college he created the 'Milind College', after the name of the Greek king who had converted to Buddhism.
65. *CAD*, vol. 3, p. 501.
66. D. Keer, *Dr Ambedkar*, op. cit., p. 481. These symbols received the general approval of secularists such as Nehru because they allowed India to root the new Republic in a nationalist past, being quite neutral on a religious plane, as distinct from the most numerous and politically aware communities—the Hindus, Muslims, Sikhs and Christians.
67. Interviews of May 5, 1950 and of May 25, 1950 cited in D. Keer, *Dr Ambedkar*, op. cit., p. 421.
68. Ibid., pp. 423–4.
69. V. Rodrigues, 'Making a Tradition Critical: Ambedkar's Reading of Buddhism' in P. Robb (ed.), *Dalit Movements and the Meanings of Labour in India*, Delhi: OUP, 1993, p. 307.
70. Ibid., op. cit., p. 311.
71. Ibid., p. 326.

72. Ibid., p. 327.
73. Cited in ibid., p. 327.
74. For example, Hinduism took over Lord Buddha by making him Vishnu's seventh incarnation.
75. Quoted in K. N. Kadam (ed.), *Dr B. R. Ambedkar: The Emancipator of the Oppressed*, Bombay: Popular Prakashan, 1993, p. 1.
76. On this notion see, R. Kothari, 'Tradition and Modernity Revisited', *Government and Opposition*, summer 1968, p. 273–93.
77. O. Lynch, 'Dr B. R. Ambedkar—Myth and Charisma' in J. M. Mahar (ed.), *Untouchables in Contemporary India*, op. cit., p. 97.
78. Dr Babasaheb Ambedkar, 'Buddhism and Hinduism are not the same', *art. cit.*
79. Quoted in D. Keer, *Dr Ambedkar*, op. cit., p. 500.
80. Cited in G. S. Lokhande, *Bhimrao Ramji Ambedkar*, New Delhi: Intellectual Publishing House, 1977 (1982), pp. 255–6.
81. According to Ambedkar, 380,000 people took part in this unprecedented mass-conversion (V. Rodrigues, 'Making a Tradition Critical', op. cit., p. 299).
82. E. Zelliot, *Dr Ambedkar*, op. cit., p. 236. The wife of D. R. Jadhav, who took part in this ceremony gives a fascinating account in N. Jadhav, *Intouchable*, op. cit., p. 260.
83. E. Zelliot, *Dr Ambedkar*, op. cit., p. 239.
84. E. Zelliot, *From Untouchable to Dalit*, op. cit., pp. 138–9.
85. D. Keer, *Dr Ambedkar*, op. cit., p. 521.
86. Cited in ibid., p. 503.
87. Quoted in ibid., p. 498.
88. A converted Mahar whose autobiography we have already quoted, Baby Kamble, cites in this respect two poems of her composition where one finds the lyric of *bhakti*. One of them begins by establishing a link between Ambedkar and a saint of Maharashtra ('Chokhoba we have prepared for Indra's heavenly court a pure nectar. But it is my Bhim which brought it to us on earth and distributed it in our huts and our shanties'). The other one deserves to be quoted in its entirety:

    Bhim, what I have, I make you the offering of it
    At your feet my flower,
    Of misfortune I broke the silence.
    One by one all the glow of misfortune.
    Given flower,
    Tears fallen from my eyes, Bhim,
    I bathe your feet.
    From bottom of the soul fire burns, its light burns
    In this all embracing light, here is Buddha Bhim.
    (Baby Kamble, 'Notre existence', art. cit., p. 159)

89. O. Lynch, '*Dr B. R. Ambedkar*', op. cit., p. 106.
90. B. Kamble, 'Notre Existence', art. cit., p. 257.
91. Cited in N. Jadhav, *Untouchable*, op. cit., p. 263.
92. Cited in J. Gokhale, *From Concessions to Confrontation*, op. cit., p. 182.

93. A. C. Pranjpi, 'The "Becoming" of Dr Ambedkar: A Socio-psychological Study', in M. L. Ranga (ed.), *B. R. Ambedkar: Life, work and relevance*, Delhi: Manohar, 2000, p. 38.
94. A. Kurane, *Ethnic Identity and Social Mobility*, Jaipur: Rawat, 1999, p. 107.
95. Ibid., p. 148.
96. Ibid., pp. 165–71. However, inter-caste marriages are very few and spatial segregation in well identified neighbourhood remains the rule.
97. S. Pai, *Dalit Assertion*, op. cit., p. 55.
98. O. Lynch, 'Dr B. R. Ambedkar—Myth and Charisma', op. cit., p. 105.
99. For more details see C. Jaffrelot, *India's Silent Revolution: The Rise of the Lower Castes in North India*, London: Hurst, 2003, p. 208.
100. G. Omvedt, 'Undoing the bondage', op. cit., p. 136.
101. Cited in N. Jadhav, *Intouchable*, op. cit., p. 247.
102. Cited in G. Poitevin, *The Voice and the Will*, op. cit., p. 179.
103. E. Zelliot, *From Untouchable to Dalit*, op. cit., p. 219.
104. Ibid., p. 220.
105. Ibid.
106. Ibid., p. 195.
107. Ibid., p. 209.
108. Ibid., p. 139.
109. B. Kamble, 'Notre existence', op. cit., p. 245.
110. D. Pawar, *Ma vie d'intouchable*, op. cit., p. 94.

Chapter 9 The Impact and Relevance of Ambedkar Today

1. Mark Jürgensmeyer, *Religious Rebels in the Punjab: The Social Vision of Untouchables*, Delhi: Ajanta Publications, 1988, p. 163.
2. O. Lynch, *Politics of Untouchability*, op. cit., pp. 86–7.
3. O. Mendelsohn and M. Vicziany, *The Untouchables*, p. 73.
4. Sukumar Muralidharan, 'New writing on Ambedkar', *Seminar* 425, Jan. 1995, p. 76.
5. *The Times of India*, Sept. 10, 1992. The first volume of Ambedkar's collected works had been published in 1979 and the second in 1982 but the project had been suspended at that point, hence the third appeared only in 1987.
6. D. R. Nagaraj, *The Flaming Feet: A Study of the Dalit Movement*, Bangalore: South Forum Press, 1993, p. 57.
7. Ibid., p. 56.
8. *Harijan*, 17 September 1934.
9. S. Palshikar, 'Gandhi-Ambedkar Interface… When shall the Twain Meet'?, *EPW*, 3 Aug. 1996, p. 202.
10. Anupama Rao, 'Arguing against Inclusion', *EPW*, Feb. 22, 1997, pp. 427–8. See also Palshikar's answer, 'Gandhi and Ambedkar', *EPW*, in July 26, 1997, pp. 1918–19.
11. A. Shourie, *Worshipping False Gods: Ambedkar and the Facts which have been Erased*, New Delhi: ASA, 1997, p. 82.
12. Ibid., p. 229.

13. Ibid., p. 41.
14. Ibid., p. 70.
15. S. M. Gaikwad, 'Ambedkar and Indian Nationalism', *EPW*, March 7, 1998, p. 517.
16. Ibid.
17. Ibid.
18. A. Shourie, *Worshipping False Gods*, op. cit., p. 374.
19. Ibid., p. 43.
20. Ibid., pp. 380–1.
21. Moreover, Shourie quotes one of the ideologues of the Sangh Parivar, P. Parmeswaran, the author of Narayan Guru's biography (P. Parmeswaran, *Narayan Guru, The Prophet of Renaissance*, New Delhi: Suruchi Sahitya, 1979).
22. A. Shourie, *Worshipping False Gods*, op. cit., p. 329.
23. Ibid., p. 371.
24. Ibid., p. 364.
25. J. Gokhale, *From Concessions to Confrontation*, op. cit., p. 2.
26. I. Duncan, *Levels, the Communication of Programmes and Sectional Strategies in Indian Politics*, op. cit., p. 245.
27. Ibid., p. 251.
28. J. Gokhale, *From Concessions to Confrontation*, op. cit., p. 220.
29. M. Gautam, *Bapusaheb Rajbhoj*, Aligarh: Siddhartha Gautam Sikshan and Sanskriti Samiti, 1995.
30. Interview with B. P. Maurya, Nov. 15, 1997, New Delhi.
31. *The Hindustan Times*, 27 July 1999.
32. Interview with Kanshi Ram, November 12, 1996 Delhi.
33. S. Pai, *Dalit Assertion*, op. cit., p. 123.
34. R. Ramaseshan, 'Dalit Politics in U.P.', *Seminar*, Jan. 1995, p. 73.
35. C. Jaffrelot, 'The Bahujan Samaj Party in North India: No longer just a Dalit party?' *Comparative Studies of South Asia, Africa and the Middle East*, 18 (1) 1998, pp. 35–51.
36. S. Pai, *Dalit Assertion*, op. cit., p. 1990. In 1980 Kanshi Ram toured North India with a pictorial display of Ambedkar's life and views. Called 'Ambedkar on wheels' it visited thirty-four destinations in nine states (Mendelsohn and Vicziany, *The Untouchables*, op. cit., p. 222).
37. Kanshi Ram, *Bahujan Samaj ke lye asha ki kiran*, New Delhi: Bahujan Publications, 1992, p. 58 (Hindi).
38. *Bahujan Sangathak*, Nov. 11, 1996 (Hindi).
39. P. Kumar, 'Dalits and the BSP in Uttar Pradesh—issues and challenges', *EPW*, April 3, 1999, p. 826.
40. P. Brass, 'General Elections, 1996 in Uttar Pradesh: Divisive Struggles Influence Outcome', *EPW*, Sept. 20, 1997, p. 2410.
41. P. K. Kumar, 'Dalits and the BSP in Uttar Pradesh', op. cit., p. 822.
42. S. Pai, *Dalit Assertion*, op. cit., p. 71.
43. Ibid., pp. 101–2.
44. Narayanan—from the Paravan fishermen's caste of Kerala—started his career like Ambedkar since it was due to the a philanthropic organisation, later to the

Tata firm and a reference letter of Nehru to Harold Laski that he was able to pursue his studies at LSE. But he opted then for the Indian Foreign Service (an elite corps of the Indian administration which took him to the post of India's ambassador to the United States) and to politics: the year of his retirement in 1992, he was elected as a MP on the Congress ticket. (I am grateful to Eleanor Zelliot for this piece of information. See also R. Krishnakumar, 'A long Journey: From Ushavoor to Rashtrapati Bhavan', *Frontline*, July 11, 1997, pp. 12–161.)

45. K. R. Narayanan, 'En Souvenir d'Ambedkar', art. cit., pp. 116–24.

Conclusion

1. Cf. Arjun Dangle (ed.), *Poisoned Bread-Translations from Marathi Dalit Literature*, Hyderabad: Orient Longman, 1992; one can also read in French the biography of one such Dalit poet, Daya Pawar, *Ma vie d'intouchable*, op. cit., and Guy Poitevin's chapter, 'La Littérature Dalit' in C. Jaffrelot (ed.), *L'Inde Contemporaine de 1950 à nos jours*, Paris: Fayard, 1997.
2. Prahlad Gangaram Jogodand, *Dalit Movement in Maharashtra*, New Delhi: Kanak, 1991, pp. 70–86.
3. *The Hindustan Times*, Aug. 21, 1999.
4. *The Hindu*, Aug. 2, 1997.
5. See G. M. Tartakov, 'Ambedkar's statues', *Dalit International Newsletter*, 3 (2), June 1998, p. 1.
6. P. Kumar, 'Dalit and the BSP in Uttar Pradesh', op. cit., p. 824.
7. In Delhi, two statues of S. C. Bose and of Bhagat Singh, two figures of the independence movement known for their hostility to Gandhian non-violence, were installed overnight on plinths reserved for two statues of Ambedkar and Chhotu Ram, a peasant leader (*The Hindu*, 2 Oct. 1999).
8. J. V. Deshpande, 'Behind Dalit Anger', *EPW*, Aug. 16, 1997, p. 2090.
9. For a detailed analysis of this violence see *Broken People. Caste violence against India's Untouchables*, New York: Human Rights Watches, 1999, p. 127–38.

Select Bibliography

A. WORKS BY DR AMBEDKAR

Dr Babasaheb Ambedkar, *Writings and Speeches*, vol. 1, Bombay: Govt. of Maharashtra, 1979.

Dr Babasaheb Ambedkar, *Writings and Speeches*, vol. 2, Bombay: Govt. of Maharashtra, 1982.

Dr Babasaheb Ambedkar, *Writings and Speeches*, vol. 3, Bombay: Govt. of Maharashtra, 1987.

Dr Babasaheb Ambedkar, *Writings and Speeches*, vol. 5, Bombay: Govt. of Maharashtra, 1989.

Dr Babasaheb Ambedkar, *Writings and Speeches*, vol. 7, Bombay: Govt. of Maharashtra, 1990.

Dr Babasaheb Ambedkar, *Writings and Speeches*, vol. 8, Bombay: Govt. of Maharashtra, 1990.

Dr Babasaheb Ambedkar, *Writings and Speeches*, vol. 9, Bombay: Govt. of Maharashtra, 1990.

Dr Babasaheb Ambedkar, *Writings and Speeches*, vol. 10, Bombay: Govt. of Maharashtra, 1991.

Dr Babasaheb Ambedkar, *Writings and Speeches*, vol. 11, Bombay: Govt. of Maharashtra, 1992.

B. R. Ambedkar, *Annihilation of Caste*, New Delhi: Arnold Publishers, 1990.

Source material on Dr Ambedkar and the Movement of Untouchables, vol. 1, Bombay: Govt. of Maharashtra, 1982.

Bhagawan Das (ed.), *Thus spoke Ambedkar*, vol. 4, Bangalore: Ambedkar Sahithya Prakashana, n.d..

V. Rodrigues (ed.), *The Essential Writings of of B. R. Ambedkar*, Delhi: Oxford University Press, 2002.

B. BOOKS

G. Austin, *The Indian Constitution—Cornerstone of a Nation*, Bombay: Oxford University Press, 1972.

D. E. U. Baker, *Changing Political Leadership in an Indian Province—The Central Provinces and Berar, 1919–1939*, Delhi: Oxford University Press, 1979.

Arjun Dangle (ed.), *Poisoned Bread: Translations from Marathi Dalit Literature*, Hyderabad: Orient Longman, 1992.

F. Frankel and M. S. A. Rao (eds), *Dominance and State Power in Modern India—Decline of a Social Order*, vols 1 and 2, Delhi: Oxford University Press, 1989 and 1990.

F. Gaekwad, *Sayajirao of Baroda*, Bombay: Popular Prakashan, 1989.

M. Gautam, *Bapusaheb Rajbhoj*, Aligarh: Siddhartha Gautam Sikshan and Sanskriti Samiti, 1995.

V. Geetha and S. V. Rajadurai, *Towards a Non-Brahmin Millenium—From Iyothee Thass to Periyar*, Calcutta: Samya, 1998.

J. Gokhale, *From Concessions to Confrontation: The Politics of an Indian Untouchable Community*, Bombay: Popular Prakashan, 1993.

M. S. Gore, *Non-Brahmin Movement in Maharashtra*, New Delhi: Segment Books, 1989.

M. S. Gore, *The Social Context of an Ideology: Ambedkar's Political and Social Thought*, New Delhi: Sage, 1993.

R. Guha, *An Anthropologist among the Marxists and Other Essays*, Delhi: Permanent Black, 2002.

C. Jaffrelot, *The Hindu Nationalist Movement and Indian Politics*, London: Hurst, 1996.

———, *India's Silent Revolution: The Rise of the Lower Castes in North India*, London: Hurst, 2003.

M. R. Jayakar, *The story of my life*, Bombay: Asian Publishing House, 1958, vol. 1.

Jogodand, Prahlad Gangaram, *Dalit Movement in Maharashtra*, New Delhi: Kanak, 1991.

Mark Jürgensmeyer, *Religious Rebels in the Punjab: The Social Vision of Untouchables*, Delhi: Ajanta Publications, 1988.

K. N. Kadam, *Dr Babasaheb Ambedkar and the significance of his movement*, Bombay: Popular Prakashan, 1991.

——— (ed.), *Dr B. R. Ambedkar—Emancipator of the Oppressed*, Bombay: Popular Prakashan, 1993.

Shantabai Kamble and Baby Kamble, *Parole de femme intouchable*, Paris: Côté-femmes éditions, 1991.

D. Keer, *Mahatma Jotirao Phooley—Father of Indian Social Revolution*, Bombay: Popular Prakashan, 1974.

R. Kothari (ed.), *Caste in Indian Politics*, New Delhi: Orient Longman, 1970.

R. K. Kshirsagar, *Dalit Movement in India and its leaders*, New Delhi: MD Publications, 1994.

W. N. Kuber, *B. R. Ambedkar,* New Delhi: Govt. of India, 1978.

———, *The Life of Dr Ambedkar,* Hyderabad: Babasaheb Dr Ambedkar Memorial Society, 1979.

Shyam Lal and K. S. Saxena (eds), *Ambedkar and Nation-Building,* Jaipur: Rawat, 1998.

J. M. Mahar (ed.), *The Untouchables in Contemporary India,* Tucson, AZ: University of Arizona Press, 1972.

David Morris, *The Emergence of an Industrial Labor Force in India: A study of the Bombay Cotton Mills, 1854–1947,* Berkeley/Los Angeles: University of California Press, 1965.

D. R. Nagaraj, *The Flaming Feet, A Study of the Dalit Movement,* Bangalore: South Forum Press, 1993.

R. O'Hanlon, *Caste, Conflict and Ideology: Mahatma Jotirao Phule and Low Caste Protest in Nineteenth-Century Western India,* Cambridge University Press, 1985.

G. Omvedt, *Cultural Revolt in a Colonial Society: the Non-Brahmin Movement in Western India,* Poona: Scientific Socialist Education Trust, 1976.

———, *Dalits and the Democratic Revolution—Dr Ambedkar and the Dalit movement in Colonial India,* New Delhi: Sage, 1994.

P. Parmeswaran, *Narayan Guru, The Prophet of Renaissance,* New Delhi: Suruchi Sahitya, 1979.

G. M. Pawar, *Vitthal Ramji Shinde,* New Delhi: National Book Trust, 1990.

J. Phule, *Slavery: Collected works of Mahatma Jotirao Phule,* vol. 1, Bombay: Govt. of Maharashtra, 1991.

———, *Collected works of Mahatma Jotirao Phule,* vol. 2, Bombay: Govt. of Maharashtra, 1991.

T. Pillai-Vetschera, *The Mahars,* New Delhi: Intercultural Publications, 1994.

G. Poitevin, *The Voice and the Will: Subaltern Agency: Forums and Motives,* New Delhi: Manohar/CSH, 2002.

G. R. Pradhan, *Untouchable Workers of Bombay City,* Bombay: Karnataka Publishing House, 1938.

Pyarelal, *The Epic Fast,* Ahmedabad: Mohanlal Maganlal Bhatt, 1932.

Kanshi Ram, *Bahujan Samaj ke lye asha ki kiran,* New Delhi: Bahujan Publications, 1992 (Hindi).

B. Shiva Rao (ed.), *The Framing of India's Constitution,* vol. 2, New Delhi: Indian Institute of Public Administration, 1967.

B. Ray (ed.), *Gandhi's Campaign against Untouchability, 1933–34—An account from the Raj's secret official reports,* New Delhi: Gandhi Peace Foundation, 1996.

A. Robertson, *The Mahar Folk,* Calcutta: YMCA Publishing House, 1938.

B. A. V. Sharma and K. M. Reddy (eds), *Reservation Policy in India*, New Delhi: Light and Light Publishers, 1982.

Shikare, *Dr Ambedkar*, Poona: Jayant and Co, 1963.

A. Shourie, *Worshipping False Gods: Ambedkar and the Facts which have been Erased*, New Delhi: ASA, 1997.

K. C. Yadav, (ed.), *From Periphery to Centre Stage. Ambedkar, Ambedkarism and Dalit Future*, Delhi: Manohar, 2000.

E. Zelliot, *From Untouchable to Dalit. Essays on the Ambedkar Movement*, Delhi: Manohar, 1992.

C. ARTICLES AND CHAPTERS IN BOOKS

S. Bandyopadhyay, 'Transfer of power and the crisis of Dalit politics in India, 1945–47', *Modern Asian Studies*, 34 (4), 2000.

M. G. Bhagat, 'The Untouchable classes of Maharashtra', *Journal of the University of Bombay*, 4 (1), July 1935.

S. Cohen, 'The Untouchable Soldier: Caste, Politics and the Indian Army', *Journal of Asian Studies*, 28 (3), 1969.

P. Constable, 'Early Dalit Literature and Culture in late nineteenth—and early twentieth—century Western India', *Modern Asian Studies*, 31 (2), 1997.

J. V. Deshpande, 'Behind Dalit Anger', *Economic and Political Weekly*, Aug. 16, 1997.

S. M. Gaikwad, 'Ambedkar and Indian nationalism', *Economic and Political Weekly*, March 7, 1998.

O. Herrenschmidt, '"L'inégalité graduée" ou la pire des inégalités. L'analyse de la société hindoue par Ambedkar', *Archives européennes de sociologie*, 37 (1997).

C. Jaffrelot, 'The Bahujan Samaj Party in North India, No longer just a Dalit party?', *Comparative Studies of South Asia, Africa and the Middle East*, 18 (1) 1998.

P. Kumar, 'Dalits and the BSP in Uttar Pradesh—issues and challenges', *Economic and Political Weekly*, April 3, 1999.

R. J. Miller, '"They will not die Hindus": the Buddhist conversion of Mahar ex-untouchables', *Asian Survey*, 2 (9), Sept. 1967.

Sukumar Muralidharan, 'New writings on Ambedkar', *Seminar*, 425, Jan. 1995.

K. R. Narayanan, 'En souvenir d'Ambedkar', *Les Temps modernes*, July 1993.

G. Omvedt, 'Development of the Maharashtrian Class structures, 1818 to 1931', *EPW*, Special Number, Aug. 1973.

S. Palshikar, 'Gandhi-Ambedkar Interface… When shall the Twain Meet?', *EPW*, 3 August 1996.

——— 'Gandhi and Ambedkar', *EPW,* July 26, 1997.

A. C. Pranjpi, 'The "Becoming" of Dr Ambedkar: A Socio-psychological Study', in M. L. Ranga (ed.), *B. R. Ambedkar: Life, Work and Relevance*, Delhi: Manohar, 2000.

Anupama Rao, 'Arguing against Inclusion', *EPW,* Feb. 22, 1997.

V. Rodrigues, 'Making a Tradition Critical: Ambedkar's Reading of Buddhism' in P. Robb (ed.), *Dalit Movements and the Meanings of Labour in India*, Delhi: Oxford University Press, 1993.

G. M. Tartakov, 'Ambedkar Statues', *Dalit International Newsletter,* vol. 3, no. 2, June 1998.

R. Tucker, 'The Early Setting of the non—Brahmin movement in Maharashtra', *Indian Historical Review,* July. 1980–Jan. 1981, vol. 2, nos 1–2.

Vidhu Verma, 'Colonialism and Liberation: Ambedkar's Quest for Distributive Justice', *EPW,* Sept. 25, 1999.

M. Yasin, 'Hindu Code Bill and Dr Ambedkar', *Towards Secular India*, 2 (1), Jan–March 1996.

D. UNPUBLISHED SOURCES

B. R. Ambedkar private papers, Nehru Memorial and Museum Library, New Delhi (section of microfilms)

E. Zelliot, 'Dr Ambedkar and the Mahar Movement', unpubl. PhD thesis, University of Pennsylvania, 1969.

H. S. Verma and N. Verma, 'Dr Ambedkar and the framing of the Indian Constitution', paper presented to the colloquium 'Contribution of Dr B. R. Ambedkar to Law and Constitution of India', Lucknow, April 15, 1997.

R. I. Duncan, '"Levels": the Communication of Programmes and Sectional Strategies in Indian Politics, with reference to the Bharatiya Kranti Dal and the Republican Party of India in Uttar Pradesh State and Aligarh district (UP)', unpubl. PhD thesis, University of Sussex, 1979.

Index